SHIFTING GEO-ECONOMIC POWER OF THE GULF

The International Political Economy of New Regionalisms Series

The *International Political Economy of New Regionalisms* series presents innovative analyses of a range of novel regional relations and institutions. Going beyond established, formal, interstate economic organizations, this essential series provides informed interdisciplinary and international research and debate about myriad heterogeneous intermediate level interactions.

Reflective of its cosmopolitan and creative orientation, this series is developed by an international editorial team of established and emerging scholars in both the South and North. It reinforces ongoing networks of analysts in both academia and think-tanks as well as international agencies concerned with micro-, meso- and macro-level regionalisms.

Shifting Geo-Economic Power of the Gulf
Oil, Finance and Institutions

Edited by

MATTEO LEGRENZI
University of Ottawa, Canada

BESSMA MOMANI
University of Waterloo, Canada

Routledge
Taylor & Francis Group

LONDON AND NEW YORK

First published 2011 by Ashgate Publishing

2 Park Square, Milton Park, Abingdon, Oxon OX14 4RN
711 Third Avenue, New York, NY 10017, USA

Routledge is an imprint of the Taylor & Francis Group, an informa business

First issued in paperback 2016

British Library Cataloguing in Publication Data
Shifting geo-economic power of the Gulf : oil, finance and
    institutions. -- (The international political economy of
    new regionalisms series)
    1. Persian Gulf States--Economic conditions. 2. Persian
    Gulf States--Economic policy. 3. Persian Gulf States--
    Foreign economic relations. 4. Sovereign wealth funds--
    Persian Gulf States. 5. Investments, Persian Gulf States.
    I. Series II. Legrenzi, Matteo. III. Momani, Bessma.
    338.9'536-dc22

Library of Congress Cataloging-in-Publication Data
Legrenzi, Matteo.
    Shifting geo-economic power of the Gulf : oil, finance, and institutions / by Matteo
Legrenzi and Bessma Momani.
        p. cm. -- (International political economy of new regionalisms series)
    Includes index.
    ISBN 978-1-4094-2670-7 (hardback)
    1. Persian Gulf States--Commerce. 2. Finance--Persian Gulf States. 3. Petroleum industry
and trade--Persian Gulf States. 4. Geopolitics--Persian Gulf States. 5. Persian Gulf States--
Economic conditions--21st century. I Momani, Bessma. II Title.
    HF3762.Z5L44 2011
    330.9536--dc22

                                                                                    2011003886

ISBN 978-1-4094-2670-7 (hbk)
ISBN 978-1-138-26135-8 (pbk)

Contents

PART II GULF ARAB INVESTMENTS AND TRADE

List of Figures

List of Tables

Notes on Contributors

Samer N. Abboud is Assistant Professor of International Studies at Arcadia University. Abboud's research interests focus on the political economy of the Middle East, with a particular interest in the impacts of privatization. He has published two monographs called *Syrian Trade Policy and Syria and the Transitions Paradigm*, in addition to two forthcoming book chapters concerned with economic diffusion and economic policy in Syria. In addition to his work on Syria, he has published articles on reconstruction in Lebanon and post-occupation economic policy in Iraq. He is currently completing a monograph entitled *Neoliberalism, Privatization, and Political Change in the Arab World*.

Andrew Baker is Senior Lecturer at Queen's University in Belfast, in the field of International Political Economy. His research has examined how global financial orders are created and sustained, and the patterns of politics and political conditions required to change and transform those orders. He is also one of the deputy editors of the *British Journal of Politics and International Relations* and a co-editor of the Warwick Studies in Globalization book series, published by Routledge. Major publications include a research monograph *The Group of Seven: Financial Ministries, Central Banks and Global Financial Governance* and an edited volume *Governing Financial Globalization*, both published by Routledge in 2006 and 2005 respectively.

Sara Bazoobandi is a PhD candidate at the Institute for Arab and Islamic Studies, University of Exeter. Her research interests focus on the Gulf Arab Sovereign Wealth Funds (SWFs), and two major aspects on the funds activities: the issue of transparency; and the Arab-Asian economic relationship, in particular the flow of investment from the Gulf states to Asia.

Sven Behrendt is Managing Director at Geoeconomica, a political risk management consulting firm. He specializes in corporate strategy and political risk management and most recently has focused on the interdependencies amongst global financial markets and geopolitics. He held various analyst and management positions at the Bertelsmann Group on Policy Research, the World Economic Forum and the Carnegie Endowment for International Peace. He holds a Masters degree in Public Administration and Policy and a PhD in International Relations from the University of Konstanz/Germany.

Christopher M. Davidson is a Senior Lecturer at the School of Government and International Affairs, University of Durham. He is co-editor of the book series 'Power and Politics in the Gulf' published simultaneously by Columbia University Press (in the US) and Hurst & Co (in the UK). He is a United Nations (Alliance of Civilizations) and Middle East Policy Council expert on the Gulf monarchies, notably the United Arab Emirates, with a secondary interest in Lebanese politics.

Paul Doherty is Director of the Centre for Business, Entrepreneurship and Technology (CBET) at the University of Waterloo. He currently teaches Entrepreneurial Applications of Business Technology for the Master of Business, Entrepreneurship and Technology (MBET) program which has been specifically designed to address Canada's pressing need for more innovators. His areas of specialization include; business ethics and strategy, environmental science, energy and energy management and innovation and entrepreneurship. Dr Doherty holds a Masters degree in Corrosion Science and Engineering and a PhD from the University of Manchester as well as an MBA from Wilfrid Laurier University.

Crystal A. Ennis is a PhD candidate at the Balsillie School of International Affairs, University of Waterloo and a Balsillie Fellow at the Centre for International Governance and Innovation in Waterloo, Canada. She has formerly worked on education program development with the ministry of manpower in Oman. Her research interests include development policy and patterns in the Gulf states as well as changing demographics and labour market reform.

Steffen Hertog is a lecturer in political economy at the London School of Economics and Political Science. He was previously Kuwait Professor at the Chaire Moyen Orient at Sciences Po/Paris. His research interests include Gulf politics, Middle East political economy, political violence and radicalization. He has published in journals such as World Politics, Review of International Political Economy, Comparative Studies in Society and History, Business History, Archives Européennes de Sociologie, and International Journal of Middle East Studies. His book about Saudi state-building, *Princes, Brokers and Bureaucrats: Oil and State in Saudi Arabia* was published by Cornell University Press in 2010.

Martin Hvidt is an Associate Professor at the Center for Contemporary Middle East Studies, University of Southern Denmark, Denmark. The focus of his research revolves around the issue of development, including the economic, political, institutional and social developments in the Middle Eastern countries. Recently he has published articles concerned with developments in Dubai. His currently engaged in a research project titled 'Gulf Rising? Developmental Patterns in the Resource Rich Economies of the Arab Gulf Region' which strives to document and analyze variations in developmental strategies, developmental patterns and developmental outcomes found among the six GCC countries.

Fred Lawson is Vice Professor of Government at Mills College, California, USA. Between 1992–93 he was a Fulbright lecturer in International Relations at the University of Aleppo, Syria. He is the author of *Constructing International Relations in the Arab World* (Stanford University Press) and *Why Syria Goes to War* (Cornell University Press), among many numerous journal articles and book chapters.

Matteo Legrenzi is Assistant Professor at the Graduate School of Public and International Affairs of the University of Ottawa. He has published articles on the GCC and on the international relations of the Gulf. He is co-editor of *Beyond Regionalism? Regional Cooperation, Regionalism and Regionalization in the Middle East*, editor of *Security in the Gulf: Historical Legacies and Future Prospects*, and the author of the forthcoming *The GCC and the International Relations of the Gulf: Diplomacy, Security and Economy Co-ordination in a Changing Middle East.*

Giacomo Luciani is Senior Advisor at the Gulf Research Center and Director of the Gulf Research Center Foundation in Geneva. Professor Luciani's research interests include Political economy of the Middle East and North Africa and Geopolitics of energy. His name is primarily associated with work on the rentier state in the Arab world. Since 1997, he has been Professorial Lecturer of Middle Eastern Studies at the Johns Hopkins University Bologna Centre. From 2000–06, he was Professor of Political Economy and co-director of the Mediterranean Programme of the Robert Schuman Centre for Advanced Studies at the European University Institute.

Anton Malkin is a PhD candidate at the Balsillie School of International Affairs and a former Balsillie Fellow at the Centre for International Governance and Innovation in Waterloo, Canada.

Bessma Momani is Associate Professor at the University of Waterloo and a Senior Fellow at the Centre for International Governance and Innovation. Dr Momani examines economic liberalization in the Middle East and has written on the US Middle East Free Trade Area, Euro-Mediterranean trade initiatives, economic integration of the Gulf Cooperation Council, the future of petrodollars, and liberalization in Egypt. She is the author and editor of several books and over 20 scholarly journal articles and book chapters.

Timothy Niblock is Emeritus Professor of Middle East Politics, University of Exeter. His research interests focus on the politics, economics and international relations of the Arab and Islamic worlds, including: the political economy of the states of the Arab world; the international relations of the Middle Eastern region; Islam and the state; and issues relating to civil society and democratization in Arab and Islamic states.

Mary Ann Tétreault is the Distinguished Professor of International Affairs Political Science at Trinity University, San Antonio Texas. Her areas of expertise include: democratization, energy and oil; the Gulf; Kuwait; human rights; political economy; and US-Arab Relations. She has written and edited more than a dozen books on social movements, energy, Gulf politics, international political economy, and international relations theory. She is presently doing research on repression and dissent in five Middle Eastern countries.

Rachel Ziemba is an analyst for Roubini Global Economics, a New York-based online economic and financial research service. Her work focuses on economic developments in China and Oil Exporting economies, with a particular interest in the sovereign wealth funds. Prior to joining RGE, Rachel worked for the Canadian International Development Agency in Cairo, Egypt, and the International Development Research Centre in Ottawa, Canada. She is the author of *Scenarios for Risk Management and Global Investment Strategies* (with William T. Ziemba), published by Wiley in January 2008. Rachel has served as an expert commentator for numerous media outlets.

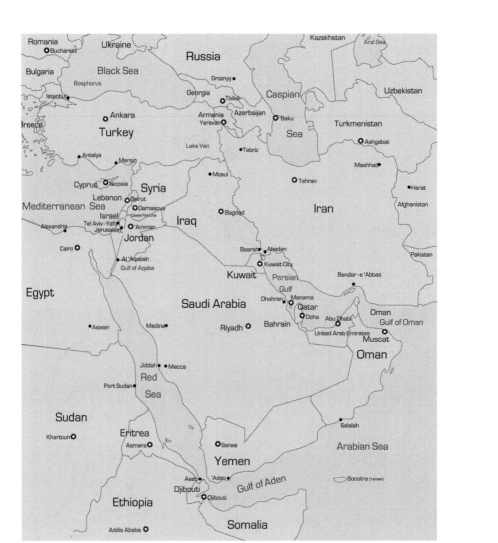

Introduction:
The Geo-Economic Power of the Gulf

Bessma Momani and Matteo Legrenzi

Bringing much needed academic rigor to a topic that is on many decision-makers' minds and populates a number of policy discussions, this volume aims to investigate the influence of some of the new regional 'power brokers' in the multi-polar world economy: the oil-exporting states of the Gulf. The Gulf Cooperation Council's (GCC) members – Bahrain, Kuwait, Oman, Qatar, the United Arab Emirates, and Saudi Arabia – collectively have the largest proven oil reserves in the world and are among the world's largest oil-exporting states. The GCC today is also flexing its new regional muscles in this multi-polar world economy. This represents a new international political development with potential geopolitical ramifications and it is in line with the rise of 'new regionalism' in response to globalization and neoliberalism. The rise of confident emerging market economies that were once viewed as subservient actors in the global political economy is a notable subject of academic analysis today. A political and economic transformation of a global scale is underway and while significant academic attention has been given to the rise of the BRICs (Brazil, Russia, India and China), there remains a dearth of academic studies on the oil-exporting Gulf states as an actor in this shift toward multi-polarity in the global economy and more importantly the result this has had on Gulf Arab states' internal and international dynamics.

Gulf Arab states have this new added confidence thanks to the astonishing rise of oil prices from 2003 to 2008 that resulted in Gulf states amassing significant capital surpluses. Moreover, oil companies in the Gulf are state-owned and Gulf Arab governments directly manage much of the oil wealth being accrued. The good health of the Gulf Arab states' economies was directly benefiting the states' coffers. Mindful of previous policy mistakes of the 1970s, the Gulf Arab states are investing a significant amount of this oil wealth into domestic infrastructure. At the same time, Gulf states are competing amongst themselves to become service hubs for financial markets; for example, Dubai has been threatening to assume the traditional primacy of Bahrain in this field. However, Gulf states' local economies are still too nascent to absorb all the surplus capital that they accrue. The necessity of turning to the global economy for investment opportunities is particularly acute for the Gulf states. However, the key difference is that Gulf states are now *actively* pursuing diverse foreign investments to absorb this liquidity as opposed to simply buying vast quantities of, mostly American, government bonds. Some of these investments are being managed by Sovereign Wealth Funds, government investment corporations, and government-controlled companies. Gulf states are also purchasing American and European companies at an unprecedented pace. At the same time, the Gulf Arab states are less hesitant about investing in the neighboring Middle East and Asia. This new, differentiated approach arguably makes more sense from a financial point of view but it naturally poses new geo-economic questions that beg for answers.

Yet, while this renewed geo-economic involvement has received a lot of media attention there has been a dearth of academic study on what this shift in global economic power means for the international economic system. The book brings together distinguished Gulf experts to analyze this renewed geo-economic prominence of the Gulf states. The contributors anchor their scholarship to traditional academic disciplines such as economics and political science. This stands in marked contrast with what has been published so far, which falls overwhelmingly in the ambiguous 'policy' category. Therefore, readers and students who are piqued by media and policy-makers' attention devoted to the GCC states can find here a scholarly treatise on the subject that further builds on the works of our colleagues: John Nugée and Paola Subacchi's *The Gulf Region: A New Hub of Global Financial Power* (2008) and Eckart Woertz' *Gulf Geo-Economics* (2007).

As we conceived this volume we had two distinct audiences in mind: academics who need to assign readings on the Gulf states to their political economy or Middle East studies classes but do not find much scholarly material and policy-makers who we hope will appreciate the different depth of this volume in scholarly terms compared to policy reports and think tank material.

The book is divided in two parts. The first part of the book analyzes the evolution of the rentier character of the GCC states. As a consequence of some policy decisions and even more of a number of semi-automatic political economy processes the political economy of Gulf Arab rentier states is changing inexorably. Steffen Hertog, one of the most astute analysts of Saudi Arabia, has chronicled the emergence of 'islands of efficiency' and the authors in this section explore this and other aspects of the changing nature of GCC economic behavior.

Mary Ann Tétreault focuses on the new strategies that GCC states employ to achieve their long term development objectives and ease the transition to a very distant future in which direct hydrocarbon revenues will be less salient to their well being. She notes, and this will be a recurrent theme throughout the book, how more diversified, less blunt investment policies on the part of the GCC states generate some nervousness amongst government leaders, if not business leaders, throughout the rest of the world. Therefore, unlike individual investors, for whom a more diverse, nimbler investment strategy is an unambiguous blessing, the sovereign governments of Gulf Arab states have to contend with national security interests and responsibilities towards other international actors and the global economy. These additional burdens make an analysis of their investment behavior a more challenging but altogether necessary task. Tétreault concludes that more active investment strategies offer risks as well as rewards for Gulf Arab governments and she helps to clarify both the challenges and opportunities involved.

Giacomo Luciani provides a fascinating overview of the evolution of the monetary systems of the Gulf Arab states as he focuses on the symbolic as well as the policy consequences of retaining individual national currencies. This analysis is particularly precious in light of the proposed GCC monetary union that has been on the drawing room for years now but whose symbolic consequences have been less explored than the policy implications. Finally, Luciani reminds us of how the peg against the dollar has served the GCC countries well in the past and of how this is very unlikely to change in spite of all the speculation surrounding this hypothesis in the Gulf and around the world. This is particularly true in light of his examination of the domestic political consequences of alternative exchange rate regimes.

Martin Hvidt tackles another topic that has been the subject of much speculation but scarcely of serious analysis: economic diversification in the Gulf Arab states. His chapter focuses on what is *the* issue when discussing economic diversification, the gap between stated objectives and actual implementation. Whereas economic diversification has been the avowed aim of all GCC countries for at least three decades the results have been mixed. Hvidt is fairly optimistic on this score arguing that GCC states have finally initiated a shift from 'allocation states' to 'production states'. However, he cautions that the jury is still out and that changes could be reversed. In particular, Gulf Arab states display significant variance in their efforts to make it easier to do business and to foster foreign direct investment. As Hvidt notes it is not an easy task to roll back thirty to fifty years of rentierism even if some of the changes are perhaps inevitable.

Steffen Hertog demonstrates how rentier states are dynamic systems and the relationship between the increasingly globalized business sector and the state is constantly evolving. In particular, during the 2003–08 oil boom the private sector contributed a larger share of GDP to national income growth. So if to be sure the GCC monarchies are still rentier economies there is less of a direct rentier relationship between government and private business. Hertog concludes that in the long term this may have political consequences leading to a renegotiation of the rentier bargain between government, population and the business class.

Andrew Baker exposes a fascinating case study of interaction between states and International Organizations during an international policy process. The case under review is the attempt to establish an International Islamic Financial Policy Forum. By charting the obstacles and the negotiations underpinning this particular process Baker sheds much light on the decision-making and bureaucratic behavior of the GCC states. By doing so Baker draws some general conclusions that actually advance the theoretical understanding of the subject while drawing inferences from the behavior of a group of states whose majority is Gulf Arab. This is a welcome departure from much of the Gulf studies literature that tends to portray Gulf Arab states as 'unique' actors in the international system.

In the last chapter of the first part of the book Samer Abboud discusses a particular aspect of the growth in the importance of the private sector in GCC economies: the increasing salience of the financial and services sector. He elaborates on the relationship between the growth of the financial sector in GCC states and the long term goal of diversification of these economies. He concludes that the growth of the financial sector is the result of deliberate government policies and that the growth of the financial industry is one of the major planks in the diversification of the GCC economies.

The second part of the book zooms in on the changing nature of the GCC states' investment and trade patterns and their financial standing in the world. This has been the subject of much speculation in the press as well as amongst analysts and the aim of the second part of the book is to subject these trends to closer scrutiny. In particular, three chapters focus on the role of Sovereign Wealth Funds, financial institutions that are intermittently feared and sought after around the world following the ups and downs of the business cycle.

The following three chapters look at some of the most debated actors in financial circles during the second oil boom: Sovereign Wealth Funds (SWF). These chapters do an excellent job in demystifying these institutions approaching them from different angles. Rachel Ziemba and Anton Malkin instead focus on the significance of SWFs for the global political economy with the aim of assessing their true impact. They conclude that far from being part of a shift away from a US-centered global financial system SWFs are part of a wider reassertion of the state in global financial markets. The appetite for diversification of investment abroad on the part of Gulf Arab states represents a wiser long term strategy and cannot be constructed as a threat or a challenge to global financial architecture.

Sara Bazoobandi and Tim Niblock trace the recent history of SWFs and discuss the issue of transparency that is often highlighted as one of the crucial issues in public policy debates. They contend that there has been no evidence of errant behavior and that SWFs could easily adopt a more transparent model similar to the Norwegian SWFs that is often hailed as a benchmark in the financial industry. Intriguingly, though, they argue that this could augment the level of domestic criticism as Gulf Arab publics increasingly question why so much money is being invested abroad. Public opinion could also question investment in particular fields or companies much as it is done during the numerous 'divestment' campaigns conducted in the name of various causes around the world.

Sven Behrendt highlights the growing importance of SWFs as an investor class and how over time this could marginally impact the ownership structure in established industrial economies. He then provides an extensive analysis of the 'Santiago Principles', outlining governance, accountability and transparency commitments. While these principles have been signed up to by all the major SWFs, Gulf Arab SWFs have displayed a low compliance and Berhendt attempts to provide some plausible explanations to why this may be the case.

In the first chapter following the section on SWFs, Bessma Momani chronicles the closer economic integration between the GCC states and the Mashreq Arab states: Egypt, Lebanon and Jordan. These increased linkages are closely connected to the growing diversification of Gulf Arab overseas investments, a recurring theme throughout the book. As GCC states partially move away from American bonds and equities, some of their investments are actively managed in the Mashreq region. As Egypt and Jordan liberalize their economies and Lebanon regains political stability, this intraregional investment process is made easier. Momani identifies the factors behind this trend and concludes that given the convergence of political and economic motives on the part of Gulf Arab investors it is likely to continue and to give birth to a new form of bottom up regionalization.

Christopher Davidson points us in what is a new and exciting direction for Gulf studies: the growing linkages between the GCC states and Asia Pacific. This is arguably one of the most interesting sub-fields in Gulf studies and Davidson provides us with an overview of this multi-dimensional, long-term mutual commitment between the two regions of the world. Davidson is careful to not overstate the strategic implications of this burgeoning trade relationship but he rightly directs our attention to the diplomatic and geo-economic implications of this increased interdependency.

Finally, Fred Lawson brings to the fore the security implications of the new raft of bilateral free trade agreements sealed in by Gulf Arab states underlining the strategic consequences that are too often neglected in the political economy literature. This sobering reading reminds us of the possible conflicts of interest both between Gulf Arab states as they forge ahead with these new agreements and between GCC states and outside actors. Lawson concludes that bilateral free trade agreements with the United States have deleterious strategic consequences for the GCC as an organization. And certainly even those who may not share such a severe assessment recognize that the bilateral free trade agreements threw a wrench in the workings of the staff of the GCC General Secretariat trying to conclude the long sought free trade agreement with the European Union. The entrepreneurial spirit displayed by smaller Gulf Arab states such as Bahrain from the economic point of view and Qatar on the diplomatic front points to a newly found confidence of these smaller actors on the global stage.

In conclusion, Crystal Ennis and Paul Doherty blend the lessons learned throughout this volume in the final chapter, and seek to draw some overarching conclusions regarding the shifting geo-economic power of the Gulf. They highlight three factors which have facilitated the endurance of the Gulf states as rentiers; specifically vast oil wealth allowing for rapid commodity-driven development, the experience of many economic successes in diversification attempts away from oil and the responsiveness of Gulf governments to changing environmental situations. They also draw attention to several issues confronting Gulf states in the twenty-first century. These include the challenge of transparency and accountability, the question of authority in the global system, the difficulty in achieving regional consensus and the burgeoning problem of unemployment. Overall, they suggest that the means of development in the GCC are gradually transforming to account for their changing global and domestic environments.

Due to record high oil prices, the GCC states have experienced impressive economic growth and have consequently flexed their international economic muscle. There has been renewed attention to the geo-economic power of the Gulf Arab states because of their new sense of boldness in the world economic arena. In line with a global shift of economic power to emerging market economies, the Gulf Arab states are playing more active and overt roles in global finance and trade. Overall the contributors to this volume help us to gain a better understanding of the economic and political implications of these new protagonists on the world economic scene. In doing so they provide with wider insights on the new important role that small states can play in today's interdependent world. From a different point of view they rescue the sub-field of Gulf studies from the margins of Middle East studies and its purported 'exceptionalism'. Alongside more theoretically sophisticated work on the Gulf as a security sub-complex, they raise the bar of Gulf studies to a new level.

PART I
Economic Diversification and Rentier Politics in the Gulf Arab States

Chapter 1

Gulf Arab States' Investment of Oil Revenues

Mary Ann Tétreault

Introduction

Gulf Arab oil-exporting countries have an especially fragile relationship with the world economy. Their rapid transition from small tribal societies engaged in subsistence agriculture, fishing, and regional maritime trade to owners of vast quantities of hydrocarbons have earned them huge incomes from oil exports. At the same time, oil exports have locked these countries firmly into global capitalist networks with an international division of labor and production that has consequently made them increasingly dependent on overseas markets (Tétreault 1980). The oil revolution of the 1970s was partly explained by the international financial instability at the time, which helped transfer economic power to oil exporters, enabling them to increase crude prices. In spite of what looked like oil-exporter victories, however, the rapid accumulation of income resulted in new costs to oil exporters, including enhanced welfare expectations among their citizens and the necessity of making structural adjustments to national budgets to accommodate them (Tétreault 1985). Although oil exporters expected oil prices to remain high – even continue to rise – the onset of global hyper-inflation insured that many products imported by Gulf Arab countries would become financially and politically burdensome to acquire.

Illusions about continued rising wealth might have made oil exporters less careful than they should have been with regard to how to recycle their windfall incomes. In spite of concerns that 'petrodollars' might cause a depression if oil exporters proved unable to spend enough to keep the world economy afloat (Cleveland and Brittain 1975), spending *per se* was not a problem. How to spend wisely, however, was, and remains a problem, one that requires constant consideration and adjustment especially with regard to how to invest for the future.

The situation is aggravated by oil price instability, a normal feature of commodity markets that has been exacerbated by changes in global finance – see below. This translates directly into unstable state revenues and national budgets, and sometimes, into volatile national politics in hydrocarbon-dependent states. With now far larger, better educated, multi-national, and politically volatile populations, 'petrostates' have sought other sources of externally generated income to supplement the volatile income derived from oil exports. Oil affects Gulf Arab state investment policies quite broadly, including with regard to investments undertaken to develop local economies so as to reduce their dependence on income from exported oil and gas (Aissaoui 2009). Gulf Arab policy-makers must consider complex trends in global trade and financial markets (including their effects on oil prices) and examine ways to use hydrocarbon windfalls to generate supplementary income streams. This chapter examines how Gulf Arab oil exporters have adjusted to their new role as participants in international trade and finance. In particular, the question of how to generate investments with the aim of securing the future prosperity of Gulf Arab citizens will be addressed.

Gulf Arab petrostates employ multiple strategies to achieve development objectives and prepare a cushion to soften their eventual landing in a world without oil. Their task was complicated by a plethora of internal and external demands as to how oil earnings should be spent. This push-and-pull has only increased over time. As power shifted from the Western oil companies to the petrostates following the oil revolution, pressures on Gulf Arab governments increased. How the Gulf Arab states would navigate the rough waters of oil production and world markets while meeting the needs of local populations, pursuing national security interests, and maintaining balance in the global economy promised to be an especially risky adventure.

Historical Review of Managing Oil Price Instability

Prior to the 1970s oil revolution, the global oil regime was managed by a small number of large international companies (IOCs) supported by the US and UK governments (Blair 1976/1978; Sampson 1974). This 'petroleum cartel'[1] worked to further Western interests at numerous points in modern history. The oil regime coordinated production and delivery of compensatory supplies to consumer markets during the oil supply disruptions triggered by Arab–Israeli conflicts in 1956 and 1967 (Sankari 1976). Earlier, the government of Iran under Mohammed Mossadeq, faced a decisive and eventually violent response when it challenged the authority of the global oil regime managers. After Iran nationalized its industry in 1953, the managers imposed and enforced a boycott on Iranian oil. The loss in world oil supplies was made up through additional production elsewhere and the crisis ended when the US government sponsored a regime-changing coup to restore the political *status quo ante*. Post-crisis reconstruction also effected a partial redistribution of ownership of Iranian oil from British to US oil companies, confirming Britain's decline from the status of equal partner to a subordinate role

---

1   This is what researchers at the Federal Trade Commission called it. See United States Congress, Senate, Select Committee on Small Business, Subcommittee on Monopoly, *The International Petroleum Cartel: Staff Report to the Federal Trade Commission*, Washington: US Government Printing Office, 1952. The director of research for this project brought the analysis forward in a later volume (Blair 1976/1978). 'Cartel' is a pejorative word; in this chapter, I use the term 'manager' for the functions it describes.

in oil regime management (Foran 1993; Gasiorowski 1987; Sampson 1974). As the cartel in its post-World War II form began to unravel, the IOCs imposed two large cuts in posted prices across the board: about 8 percent in 1959, and another 6 percent in 1960 (Mikdashi 1972, 31–32). The cuts redistributed some of the adjustment costs resulting from the greater competition the IOCs were experiencing in their global operations to the oil-exporting countries. In reaction, Venezuela, Iraq, Iran, Saudi Arabia, and Kuwait created OPEC in 1960. OPEC was designed to bargain with the IOCs to restore posted prices, thereby transferring the full effect of rising costs of doing business back to the IOCs. This goal took ten years to achieve.

The international financial regime was already under stress when oil-exporting countries shocked the world's major powers by mounting a successful 'oil revolution' in the 1970s (Tétreault 1985). The oil revolution caused crude oil prices to quadruple over the span of one year and initiated a transfer of equity from the IOCs to oil-exporting governments largely regarded in the West as corrupt or incompetent (and sometimes both). Oil exporters were disdained as *nouveaux riches* and urged to recycle their windfalls in the importers' economies for the sake of global economic balance and stability. This was recognized by analysts from the Middle East as little more than a campaign to pressure oil exporters to manage their oil and their money in line with Western conceptions of the common good. Western economists sought to bolster these arguments by asserting the existence of a direct link between oil prices and worldwide macroeconomic performance, charging that changes in oil prices, especially large price increases, were responsible for global financial disarray. Following the oil shock of 1979–80, these economists felt confident in their basic assumption that rapid increases in oil prices explained both the stagflation of the 1970s, a situation that combines price inflation with economic stagnation or contraction, and the deep recession of the early 1980s. Decades of research have failed to support this hypothesis, however. Although some studies found that oil prices influence macroeconomic variables, others show no connection at all. In fact, a few studies found inverse effects between oil prices and overall economic performance – i.e., they found that macroeconomic instability leads to sharp movements in oil prices (these studies are reviewed in Barsky and Kilian 2004).

The proposition that macroeconomic pressures drove the 1970–74 oil revolution has been argued and supported in previous publications of the author (e.g., Tétreault 1985). From this perspective, the poor economic performance of the 1970s, like the oil revolution itself, was the result of globalization. Globalization was not yet a familiar concept to academics, but the outlines of this new phenomenon were described in the interdependence literature by scholars struck by the vulnerability of world markets to events in small countries. The connection between oil prices and global finance – perhaps a relationship that is better conceived of as co-dependency or covariation than as interdependence (Tétreault 1980) – remains deep and complex. Both developing and developed countries need to manage this fragile relationship skillfully to minimize unfavorable impacts on national economies.

As oil-exporting countries accumulated entitlements to crude, they sold un-contracted-for supplies of 'spot' oil – i.e., cargo by cargo.[2] Beginning in 1978–79, when panic sparked by fears of shortages from revolutionary Iran caused prices to shoot up, spot markets for crude and oil products became prominent arenas for adjustment. Exporters cancelled crude sales contracts and made new, usually shorter-term agreements at higher and higher prices. The delight of exporters at these developments did not last, however: the linkage between crude spot and contract prices soon proved also to work in reverse. First, rising spot prices pulled contract prices up during the shock period; then, after panic subsided, spot prices declined and pulled prices (eventually even official OPEC prices) down (Tétreault 1985, 247–53). In 1978, futures markets opened in Britain and the United States. Spot traders used futures prices as references for their murkier transactions because futures prices, which are published, were transparent (Tétreault 1985, 91–92). Futures prices became a reference for contract pricing when the OPEC-mediated market collapsed in 1985–86 (Pearce 1983). Dependence on derivatives for pricing, along with shorter-term contracts and the market's brief venture into highly non-transparent netback pricing in 1985–86 added to price volatility, revealing that OPEC price-mediation was more illusion than reality (Mabro 1987).

People who live in the real world of 'wet barrels' initially welcomed futures markets. They promised to increase both transparency and liquidity, and offered an avenue for hedging against unfavorable price movements (Newman 2005). As derivatives markets deepened and spread in the wake of the radical financial deregulation of the 1990s, however, commodity derivatives such as oil futures attracted speculators, few of whom knew or cared about the physical markets underlying the paper assets they traded. Pension-fund managers, for example, used them as counter-cyclical investments to balance holdings in bonds and equities (Cho 2008; Mabro 2000; Verleger 2007). Despite OPEC's several attempts to counter it through supply management, oil price volatility became a fact of life.

Acute macroeconomic instability in commodity markets is just one result of financial deregulation. As had happened in the early 1970s, financial deregulation was accompanied by another oil price shock. Controls on derivatives trading, which had specified who was authorized to trade commodity derivatives, under what limitations, and in what volumes, were attenuated or ended entirely in the late 1990s (Clark 2005). Expectations that oil production would not be able to keep up with rising demand from India and China, damaging storms in offshore production regions such as hurricanes Katrina and Rita, and a low level of excess production capacity pulled oil prices, already rising since the beginning of the US military operations in Iraq in March 2003, even higher (Fattouh 2008). Bank traders and hedge fund managers moved so decisively into oil derivatives that oil futures became a virtual species of currency (Cho 2008; Soros 2008). The futures bubble that buoyed oil prices to unprecedented heights in the summer of 2008

---

2 Spot sales of products and occasional cargoes of crude were routine during the IOC-managed regime (Mabro 1987).

quickly deflated, however, as consumer demand fell in response first to high prices and then to the contraction of the global economy. Within a few months oil prices were less than half of their July 2008 high.

The contemporary global economy continues to be highly unstable. Optimistic reports that the 'Great Recession' is over are greeted with scepticism and matched by concern with the slow regulatory responses to the global financial collapse. Failure to clear the US private debt overhang, coupled with huge public debts contracted by governments in developed countries to counter the recession, continue to cast a shadow over global economic recovery. At the same time, the irrationality of modern oil markets leaves oil prices and exporting-country incomes subject to wild swings that carry little information to policy-makers devising short, medium, and long-term investment strategies. Windfall profits generate popular demands for redistribution in oil-exporting countries. These in turn generate structural maladjustments such as subsidies, higher salary scales, and other forms of economic and/or social protection that impose fiscal costs and create powerful vested interests (Chaudhry 1997) throughout national economies, in ruling families and in state bureaucracies (Hertog 2010a).

Another issue, one related to the recycling proposals of Western governments following the oil revolution, is the prominence of dollar-denominated assets in the portfolios of Gulf Arab states and the role of the US dollar as the unit of exchange for most oil transactions (see Momani 2008). Oil markets experience macroeconomic instabilities not only from oil and derivatives prices but also from changes in currency values, especially the value of the dollar. In addition, Gulf Arab oil exporters use dollars and holdings in US government securities as another kind of investment: security guarantees from the US government (*Kuwait Times* 2009; Katzman 2009; Woertz 2009). How should Gulf Arab investment policies deal with these issues?

Gulf Arab Investment Dilemmas in an Unstable World

Gulf Arab oil exporters make investment decisions under interacting layers of uncertainty and risk. On the one hand, oil income has become more variable because of acute price instability. Some price variation is normal and minor adjustment has always been a fact of life. Increasingly however, price swings are not normal because they have become unmoored from *oil* market conditions:

> The information available to economic agents – oil companies, traders, oil-exporting countries etc. – about the key parameters – production, exports, demand and stocks – is so poor that the responses to this information which are important determinants of price formation in futures exchanges and elsewhere do not always relate to actual economic conditions. (Mabro 2000, 2)

Economist Walter J. Levy (1978/79) called oil-exporters' responses to 1970s windfalls 'the years that the locust hath eaten'. While it is true that this first explosion of oil revenues was spent with abandon, the locust did not eat everything. Although new money went to purchases of infrastructure, weapons, and consumer goods – some of dubious value – solid investments were also made in health, education, consumer-price subsidies, and other services that improved the living conditions of citizens. With the exception of Kuwait and Bahrain, whose oil-financed general welfare programs began earlier, GCC countries did not invest much in mass education and health before 1973. By 2007, however, male and female youth literacy rates (15–24 year olds) ranged from 84.4 percent in Oman to 94.5 percent in Kuwait. Life expectancy ranged from 72.7 years in Saudi Arabia to 77.5 years in Kuwait (UN Development Programme 2009). The distributive policies of oil-dependent states are frequently criticized, most famously by the *rentier state* school of analysts. However, for those interested in social justice, it is noteworthy that three Gulf Arab states (Kuwait, Qatar, and the UAE) appear in the 'very high human development' category established by the United Nations, and that the only other major oil exporter on that list is Brunei (UN Development Programme 2009).

In 1976, Kuwait established the Reserve Fund for Future Generations (RFFG) in order to prepare for the country's post-oil future. By law, the Fund receives 10 percent of the state's oil revenues. Most RFFG funds have been invested in North America and Western Europe. Other oil exporting states also have set up so-called Sovereign Wealth Funds (SWFs) to serve as repositories for investment assets. These SWFs are less well regulated compared to the RFFG – although even the RFFG leaves much to be desired in terms of regulation (Tétreault 2000, 187; Truman 2007a). Virtually all of the SWFs today have shifted from being passive accumulators of securities issued by Western governments to aggressive direct investors and portfolio investors in a wide range of assets. And, as the size of SWFs has ballooned in recent years so has external criticism (see below).

A second strand of non-locust behavior in productive expenditures is foreign aid. OPEC states were the first developing countries to finance large foreign-aid projects. They expanded this financing in response to the first oil shock's devastating effects on developing countries. Between November 1973 and November 1974, four new multi-lateral and two new bilateral funds and development banks were established. In 1976 the OPEC Fund for International Development (OFID) was created (Tétreault 1985, 212–18; Hallwood and Sinclair 1981; Shihata and Mabro 1982). Much of the aid from these organizations went to Arab and/or Islamic countries, a reflection of the identities of most of the donor states. In contrast, over 80 percent of disbursements went to non-Arab developing countries during the first five years of the more broadly representative OFID.

Oil investments abroad appeared after the second oil shock as a third strand of long-term investment strategies. The Kuwait Foreign Petroleum Exploration Company (KUFPEC) was established in 1981 to engage in upstream operations in developing countries (Tétreault 1995, 30). Kuwait pioneered in foreign direct investment (FDI) downstream with its 1983 purchases of refining, storage, and marketing assets in Europe. Saudi Arabia and Venezuela also invested in foreign downstream assets (Marcel 2006). Upstream investments by Kuwait in the United States and in Britain proved to be less well-received, however, provoking US government opposition to the acquisition of US production rights with its purchase of Santa Fe International. This conflict culminated in a lawsuit and an eventual divestiture (Tétreault 1995, 35). Kuwait's subsequent purchase of shares of BP triggered British pressure for divestiture, an irony that is not likely to be lost on today's managers of Gulf Arab state SWFs contemplating acquiring shares of a post-Deepwater Horizon BP at distressed prices.

The history of mixed signals indicates structural obstacles to Gulf Arab state FDI. Like foreign aid, FDI gives each partner a stake in the economic health and longevity of the other. Yet FDI also draws criticism and complaints. An example of political constraints placed on GCC states by the United States is the eruption of outrage following news of the possible acquisition of a British company which operated six US ports by the widely respected firm Dubai Ports World (DP World). It should be noted however, that other potential partners welcomed DP World, in part because of its graceful handling of the US outburst.

The purchase of military goods from abroad is an example of more ambiguous investments of GCC windfalls. From Table 1.1 we can see that GCC arms purchases are volatile and appear to track oil revenues to some extent. Kuwait's post-liberation purchases appear anomalous, but should be seen as 'payback' to coalition states for participation in the rollback of Iraq's invasion of Kuwait. What is missing from this table is evidence of the recent upsurge in interest in arms deals and negotiations for nuclear power facilities, especially in the UAE. Both have burgeoned as a result of Iranian efforts to develop an independent nuclear industry with the capacity to produce materials for nuclear weapons (Slackman 2009), and with the threatening responses of the United States and European countries to this development.

Military purchases from abroad are of questionable utility for improving regional security. The GCC countries are small and defence efforts remain primarily national, concentrated on policing. Their varying sources of military equipment translate into multiple systems that portend nightmares for those managing spare parts. Weapons and weapons systems from the United States are restricted by Congressional rules on technology transfer. Yet despite these and other drawbacks, an argument can be made that arms purchases from abroad are useful security measures. One example is the Silkworm missile purchase from China by Saudi Arabia in the late 1980s, intended to deter and defend against attacks during the bitter Iran-Iraq war, and perhaps also to put the United States on notice that Saudis had ample access to sources of military transfers not limited by the US Congress. Bahrain's 2009 request to purchase air-to-air missiles from the United States may also have deterrence as its aim (*Gulf News* 2009). In addition, the Gulf Arab states are vulnerable to terrorist attacks given their proximity to theatres of ongoing conflict and their prominence as locations for US military

**Table 1.1 Trends in values of arms imports to GCC states
(at constant 1990 prices in $US million)**

Year(s)	Bahrain	Kuwait	Oman	Qatar	Saudi Arabia	UAE
1973–1980	36 (4.5)	1592 (199.0)	852 (106.5)	206 (25.8)	5378 (672.3)	1314 (164.3)
1981–1984	242 (60.5)	1141 (285.3)	719 (179.8)	775 (193.8)	6357 (1589.3)	1058 (264.3)
1985–1990	972 (16.2)	1218 (243.6)	350 (70.0)	280 (50.0)	11,463 (1910.5)	1704 (284.0)
1991–2000	718 (71.8)	4870 (487.0)	1104 (110.4)	1905 (190.5)	1476 (147.6)	4715 (471.5)
2001	31	64	34	11	59	185
2002	58	23	35	11	555	212
2003	6	45	31	11	159	693
2004	10	1	41	0	941	1262
2005	63	19	164	0	148	2176
2006	63	0	281	0	185	2014
2007	26	276	4	0	68	982
2008	2	n/a	66	0	56	671

Note: Inclusive values for ranges indicated (calculated); (annual averages) for the period in period (calculated).
Source: SIPRI, Trend Indicator Values in constant $US (1990 prices); at http://armstrade. sipri.org/arms_trade/values.php.

bases (Gulf Research Center 2007). The purchase of fighter planes and nuclear materials shores up relations with the West although they are not directly useful in the kind of policing such threats require.

GCC investment strategies must be multi-focal, capitalizing on the region's advantages to satisfy current needs and anticipate the needs of the future. As Table 1.1 implies, the pattern of GCC-member arms purchases abroad reflects their peculiar security dilemma. Their main potential enemies are Iran and Iraq. None of the small GCC states could sustain more than a blocking action, for a few days at best, if either were to launch an attack. It is also unlikely that a functional joint GCC defence would be able to rescue any member without extra-regional assistance (Legrenzi 2011). Yet despite a guarantee from France which, under President Nicolas Sarkozy, has been marketing itself aggressively to GCC states as a partner, a military response from Europe to counter such an attack is unlikely. But US policy, from president Carter's 1979 pledge to protect US access to the region's petroleum, to the July 2009 assurances by US Secretary of State Hillary Clinton that a nuclear Iran would be met by a US security umbrella over the GCC, is a gift analogous to the institution of NATO as protection for western Europe. Indeed, US interests in the Gulf allow the GCC to portray itself as an organization that is serious about regional defence without demanding that member states devote significant resources to achieving this goal (Legrenzi 2011). Consequently, in spite of a renewed interest in arms transfers, most GCC investment policy concentrates on economic decision-making, albeit with strategic dimensions.

Strategies for the Future

The economic positions of GCC states improved following the 2003 US invasion of Iraq thanks to higher oil prices. Significant accumulation in their SWFs is shifting the economic power balance between them and the G-7/G-8 countries. Globalization's open-investment regime brings the cash-rich GCC states into direct competition with developed countries. SWFs are defined by the US Treasury as 'government investment vehicles funded by foreign exchange assets that are managed separately from official reserves' (USGAO 2008, 46). Unlike official reserves, which are relatively liquid and must be available on demand, SWFs are focused on the longer term and on assets likely to earn high rates of return. Not surprisingly, SWFs are criticized as potential sources of macroeconomic instability and political pressure (see Biberovic 2008; USGAO 2008). As noted earlier, fearful reactions to Gulf Arab oil-exporters' portfolio and direct investments occurred in Britain as well as the United States.

GCC states perceive their investments to be vulnerable to the policies of host/ recipient countries. Host countries frequently impose constraints on sovereign investors; in contrast, hedge funds and other pools of concentrated capital such as investment banks rarely if ever have to deal with such political pressure. Although many countries have rules regarding the proportion of a domestic asset that can be owned by a government or private investor (Biberovic 2008; USGAO 2008, 28–32), lax regulation of private-sector investors involved in risky ventures continues, especially with regard to derivatives markets. The primary concerns of GCC sovereign wealth portfolio investors include being able to maintain, and preferably increase, the value of their capital; to maintain the security of those investments in the face of political or economic pressures; to be entitled to take an active role in companies in which they have stakes (Biberovic 2008, 6); and to be granted the same advantages as others in making acquisitions under favorable investment conditions (USGAO 2008, 32–34). Growing competition for SWF investments by recipient countries brings GCC investors closer to these goals. Indeed, the United States and European countries cite the rising amounts invested there as a kind of financial *bona fide* to elicit even more investment (Biberovic 2008; USGAO 2008). Macroeconomic instability appears to be the motivation for this recent enthusiasm. For instance, US Treasury secretary Timothy Geithner traveled to the Gulf (and China) in July 2009 to argue for dollar-supporting policies, even though new investment in US government securities may be neither advantageous nor especially wise from the investors' perspective (Woertz 2009).

Ambiguity characterizes some GCC investment in agricultural land abroad. International leasing and purchases of farmland by Gulf Arab state and private interests expanded after the fall of the Soviet Union. Some say 'food is the new oil' (Knaup and Mittelstaedt 2009); others call these land deals 'a new approach to oil for food' (see Janardhan 2009). From the perspective of GCC countries, direct investments in fertile agricultural land abroad is more practical, not to mention politically less burdensome, than food-security policies that support local attempts to grow crops unsustainable under desert conditions (AFP 2008; Chaudhry 1997, 172–85; von Braun and Meinzen-Dick 2009, 1). The land rush itself, however, adds further to macroeconomic destabilization in host countries. Soaring grain prices, especially for rice, spurred further interest in foreign land leases and purchases, both as a profitable land investment and as a source for securing food supplies. There is little transparency in these land transactions, however, while bidding up land prices cuts small farmers off from land-holdings under customary tenure arrangements and sparks fears about food insecurity in host countries (von Braun and Meinzen-Dick 2009). Critics focus on both the lack of transparency and the absence of explicit arrangements for mitigating these social and economic dislocations. Critics further question whether Gulf Arab buyers are complying with national and international trade regulations and policies, and meeting requirements for sustainability (von Braun and Meinzen-Dick 2009; Smaller and Mann 2009). Some go as far to argue that investment in foreign lands is just neocolonialism in another guise (*The Economist* 2009, 4).

Gulf Arab states must also decide how much to invest at home, and how such investments should be distributed between the hydrocarbon industry and other domestic sectors. How much hydrocarbon income should go to domestic production capacity expansion given the acute hydrocarbon dependency that already bedevils their economies? Panic over the potential consequences of peak oil and the anticipation of rapid economic growth in emerging-market countries like China and India had made capacity expansion an attractive option for some countries. However, since the autumn of 2008, global economic instability has underpinned a drop in global demand for oil. Several GCC states have been considering shifting some state investments from hydrocarbon development to other energy sources such as solar and wind, and wondering what effect this might have on oil and gas markets.

While the question of how to allocate state spending in the national economy is important, equally critical is how to increase efficiency in the domestic oil industry. Some studies see politics as one of the most difficult hurdles a national oil company faces in the GCC states. A 1995 study of the Kuwait Petroleum Corporation (KPC), for example, found competent engineers and technicians serving side-by-side with people whose jobs were conferred and/or saved by appeals to members of the ruling family. KPC also served as an arena in which one ruling family member sought to demonstrate his superiority over better-situated peers (Tétreault 1995). Can national oil companies carry the burden of orchestrating national energy investments or should GCC governments heed the clamour from transnational corporations and banks and privatize their hydrocarbon industries to maximize their value? There are no easy answers to this dilemma and a case could be made for both policy options.

On the one hand, many Gulf Arab NOCs are embodiments of the desire for autonomy and global prestige: on the home front, most NOCs command significant domestic support. These national champions are channels for international and domestic technology transfer and are developers of local skills that prepare nationals for jobs within and outside of the oil sector. Valerie Marcel describes how national oil companies are vital to national welfare, particularly in promoting local education and social development, and despite pressures to internationalize their operations through more liberal and market-friendly policies. Marcel argues that many national oil companies are innovative and can respond to structural demands for change (Marcel 2006). This is further confirmed in the study of the Kuwait Petroleum Corporation, where a subsidiary routinely employed international benchmarks to assess its efficiency (1995, 105). KPC's problems went beyond the procedural to include political conflicts arising from porous boundaries between the state and the national oil company and an absence of arms-length standards for relationships between subsidiaries (Marcel 2006, 233; Tétreault 1995, 99).

On the other hand, one could argue for joint ventures with non-national actors and international firms. The advantages of a partnership with an international firm include the removal of company decisions out of most national quarrels; enhanced market access if the joint venture includes a product user; downstream projects abroad that avoid arguments over equity transfers; and accountability to shareholders that ensures transparency of profit and loss statements (Tétreault 1995, 88–98).

Foreign investors in oil companies prefer outright privatization but this would increase the GCC states' vulnerability to macroeconomic instability. Gulf Arab states have historically enjoyed a financial buffer from hydrocarbon sales even during global economic turbulence. Indeed, the purpose of sovereign wealth funds is to mitigate the potential decline of income when oil revenues are weakest. Privatization of national oil companies would also erode Gulf Arab countries' autonomy over production decisions. The state's long-term policy horizon of stretching out oil revenues would be contracted toward an investor's short-run profit imperatives.

Cost-motivated environmental damage is another issue to consider in the debate over the advantages of national and private oil companies. Prior to the nationalization of Kuwait's oil companies, for example, private owners had flared natural gas because it was cheaper than building infrastructure to use it. One of the key arguments for nationalization in the Kuwaiti parliament was the NOC's future ability to end flaring (Naibari 1990). In Africa, Latin America, Alaska, and the Gulf of Mexico, large IOCs have repeatedly put cost considerations above environmental protection. Of course, there is the matter of direct income losses to the state from payments to the foreign owner. It is extremely doubtful that state rents would actually rise under privatization, because private oil interests historically have catered to short-term imperatives and shifted the burden of environmental and human costs to the state. While some national and regional investment should go to develop infrastructure such as power grids and rail links, and the debate over national versus private oil company ownership continues, a domestic priority in the GCC states should be regulatory reform in the wider economy. The current downturn has exposed deficiencies in GCC regulation of banking and investment. While there would undoubtedly be popular reactions against regulation, GCC states could offer compensatory benefits, like insurance on investments. Requiring insurance could reduce plausible demands for bailouts while clear rules and effective oversight would make bailouts less necessary, adding to macroeconomic stability. By improving the overall business climate in the Gulf Arab countries, the oil companies will both prosper and better compete globally.

Conclusion

Globalization has opened new places and spaces to a wide array of investments in the global economy, yet transparency remains limited and regulation remains primitive. In the past, Gulf Arab investors have had little choice other than to take the advice of the Red Queen who told Alice she would have to run as fast as she could just to stay in the same place. GCC states today, however, are faster runners than Alice. They have gained experience, expertise, and resources that allow them to leave passive investments behind and assume the risks and rewards of active agency on their own behalf. Like everyone else, however, they are vulnerable to the deficiencies of the global macroeconomy in which they are embedded. Intelligent investment decisions offer some hope of mitigating the negative effects that sharp oil-price movements can have on their populations, but nothing is guaranteed.

Profits accumulated from several years of relatively high oil prices have enlarged the menu of investment choices available to GCC states. At the same time, as the 2009 economic collapse demonstrates, globalization denies a reliably safe haven to any investor. Portfolio investments carry the risks of capital losses from insufficient regulation and oversight, even of what were considered 'blue-chip' corporations in developed countries – think of Enron. Government securities, including those issued by developed Western countries, are vulnerable to exchange rate risks possibly amplified by multi-focal political intervention. Foreign direct investment offers more hands-on control but has its own vulnerabilities in terms of sunk capital costs of infrastructure vulnerable to expropriation, the possibility of political unrest, and multiple, highly varied sources of constraints on investor autonomy. Concentrating investment in the region or at home limits economies of scale and profits, and risks introducing or reinforcing structural patterns of dependency and waste. The greatest irony is that the source of the money that provides the enviable dilemma of how to invest most productively carries dilemmas of its own. Oil prices, for all practical purposes, have become impervious to the intentional actions of producers since the onset of extreme deregulation. Even so, the strong financial position that allows GCC states to diversify their investments so broadly offers some protection against adverse movements in any particular market in which they participate.

Chapter 2

The Political Economy of Monetary Integration and Exchange Rate Regime in the GCC

Giacomo Luciani

Introduction

The provision of money is a key component of modern nation-state sovereignty. Money has not only served economic interests throughout history, but has also played an important role in achieving the 'political objectives of nation and state building' (Helleiner 2009, 11). In history, coinage and the very characteristics of money were always reserved for the sovereign, and hence the economic benefit of the process is aptly called seigniorage. This was the case even in the past, when money was defined by its metal content and coinage was meant to be only a way to guarantee that content. It is even more so in our contemporary times, when money is fiduciary, i.e. based on enforcement on the part of the state as legal tender, and on acceptance on the part of the people. Coins and bills frequently carry the image of the sovereign or ruler, and/or other symbols of national identity. As it sits in the pockets of practically every citizen, and is used on a daily basis, money is effectively more important as a symbol of sovereignty than the piece of cloth called the national flag or the music composition called the national anthem.

The nature and governance of the monetary system is therefore a key indicator of the nature of the regime, its economic and social bases, and its objective function. Is the currency freely convertible? Is its purchasing power stable or eroded by inflation? Is the central bank autonomous? Is the national currency the only currency actually in circulation? These are all key questions that one should ask to understand the nature of any political regime and sovereign power structure. Money, in this context, is as important as the fiscal system, which provides the state with the tools to extract revenue from society and pursue its objectives. Indeed, money can to some extent be a substitute for taxes, as the printing press is a way to pay for expenses in the absence of sufficient revenue, and the resulting inflation is a form of taxation.

The Gulf Arab states today have many important policy questions about the future of their currency. The region has historically been strongly tied to international economic trade and has therefore adopted currencies that facilitated its openness. The Gulf Arab rentier development model is predicated on a 'pact' with its citizens; its currency policy choices have often reflected this grand bargain and the interests of key stakeholders like national business, imported labour, and geopolitical interests. It has made good political sense for Gulf countries to peg to the dollar, albeit unofficial for many years, as it insulated potential adjustment costs of currency volatility onto the state as opposed to its citizens. This chapter examines these political economy rationales of Gulf Arab currency policies and argues against de-pegging against the dollar.

A Short History of Gulf Arab Currencies

An important indicator of the nascent nature of the modern Gulf Arab states is that they started issuing money only after independence, i.e. in most cases quite recently. In the past, the region had used 'foreign' money – specifically, currency issued from other governments and acquired through exports of goods and services. Indeed, some forms of money, e.g. Maria Theresa's Thaler, stayed in circulation in the region well beyond their demise in their country of origin (the Thaler ceased being legal tender in Austria in 1858) (see Tschoegl 2001).

After the decline of the Thaler, the Indian silver rupee and the Gold sovereign (United Kingdom) were the most common currencies in circulation in the region. The Indian rupee continued to be in use throughout the region except in Saudi Arabia until 1959, when the Government of India launched a separate currency, the Gulf Rupee. This remained in circulation in Kuwait until 1961, in Bahrain until 1965, in Qatar and the other Trucial States (not yet the UAE) until 1966, and in Oman until 1970.

Saudi Arabia first issued 'Pilgrim Receipts' in 1955. The first issue of Saudi Riyals proper came in 1961 (see Figure 2.1). Kuwait also issued its first banknotes in 1961. Bahrain did so in 1965. Qatar and the Trucial States abandoned the Gulf rupee in 1966 but did not yet issue their own currencies: Abu Dhabi adopted the Bahraini Dinar while the other emirates adopted the Saudi Riyal. Qatar and the UAE only issued their first banknotes in 1973. Oman abandoned the Gulf rupee and issued its own banknotes in 1970 (www.islamicbanknotes.com).

Currency Reputation in Open Economies

Monetary history is not the main focus of this chapter, but it is necessary to clearly keep in mind the fact that this region has been accustomed to using currencies 'imported' from the rest of the world. This has been possible because of the intensity of trade ties with other regions and the high degree of openness of the Gulf Arab economies, which pre-existed the advent of the oil era. Indeed, the Gulf Arab countries have recently been studied from the perspective of transnational merchant studies (Onley 2007). We have learned a great deal about the economic and social

Figure 2.1 The Saudi 1 riyal 'Pilgrim Receipt' of 1955

history of the region through these excellent historiographies and studies of the Gulf's transnational merchant class (see Onley 2005; Risso 1989; Fatah 1997).

Thus when the Gulf Arab countries finally decided to issue their own currencies, the modalities had to be coherent with a high degree of openness. The abandonment of the Gulf rupee was precipitated by the announcement that the Indian rupee – to which the Gulf rupee was tied – would be devalued. This indicates that the objective of issuing national currencies has been to preserve the value and purchasing power of the same from the start. In the context of the wide open Gulf Arab economies, quickly increasing oil revenue and intense economic relations between the merchants and the rest of the world, the new national currencies had to establish and maintain a strong reputation – which could only be achieved through strong reserve coverage and a rigid link to well established international currencies.

At the time the Gulf currencies were first launched, almost all other Arab countries were experiencing non-convertibility, significant inflation and in some cases significant dollarization of their economies (i.e. extensive use of the dollar for domestic transactions because of loss of confidence in the national currency). Exceptions were Lebanon and Jordan – in both cases influenced by the peculiar characteristic of their respective economies. The choice of a rigid dollar peg – a form of official dollarization which is meant to pre-empt the danger of a loss of confidence in the national currency – was then quite logical (see Owen and Pamuk 1998).

The credibility and reputation of monetary instruments is a key component of the relationship between the citizen and the state. If citizens lose confidence in the national currency, they will look for alternatives and governments may have a hard time preventing this. For example, the original decision of the Indian Government to create a special issue of rupees for the Gulf was due to the fact that regular rupees were used to buy gold in the Gulf, and gold was used as an alternative store of value to the fiduciary currency domestically. According to Symes (n.d.)

> Gold has long been a medium of exchange in India and it was estimated in 1959 that the total amount of gold in private hands in India was about $US1.75 to 2 billion – roughly two thirds of the value of paper money in circulation. While it was legal to own and to trade in gold within India, it was illegal to import or export gold.

The external circulation of the rupee was instrumental in circumventing the latter prohibition.

Limits to convertibility are a limitation on the freedom of using one's financial resources which inevitably undermine the confidence in the national economy and the state. Incentives are created to bypass whatever limits or black markets arise, and multiple exchange rates coexist in parallel and create opportunities for rent seeking for the privileged few who have access to preferential rates – all the way to the shops 'for hard currency only' that were a familiar sight in communist countries. Depending on the ability/willingness of the national government to enforce prohibitions, this may lead to parallel currency circulation in the economy. The experience of Israel in this respect has been especially well documented in the literature, but is certainly not isolated. Parallel circulation of a strong foreign currency and a weak national currency leads to fundamental distortions in the functioning of the economy (see Agénor 1992).

The Importance of Currency Reputation for the Gulf Arab Development Model

For the Gulf Arab countries, the quality of money has been a key component of the 'pact' between the rentier state and the population, especially the business community. It has also been a crucially important component of the Gulf Arab development model: the high level of dependence on imported labour power and expertise, and the crucial role of import agencies as a tool to nurture and strengthen the national bourgeoisie could only be compatible with a freely convertible currency.

In addition, the Gulf countries have enjoyed positive balance of payments and normally strong reserve positions, thanks to the inflow of oil money. It is however noticeable that not all oil exporting countries have always succeeded in maintaining strong currencies. Algeria and Iran, just to mention two notable examples, have known extensive limitations to convertibility and multiple exchange rates, which have further weakened the already feeble trust that their respective people have in the state. When then we consider the Gulf's historical background and customary reliance on money provided from abroad; the high degree of openness of the economies; and the choice of a development model based on private enterprise and the national bourgeoisie, it is clear that full convertibility has been a mandatory policy for the Gulf countries.

In most Gulf Arab countries, guaranteeing a close tie to the dollar has served as the tool of choice to establish reputation and gain the trust of the business community. Exchange rate changes have been minimal, and mostly the Gulf Arab countries have stuck to a rigid dollar peg: for most of them, the official peg was to the International Monetary Fund's Special Drawing Right unit (SDR) until the early years of the current decade, but in practice a dollar peg was enforced (the dollar is in any case a major component of the SDR) (see Abed, Erbas and Guerami 2003). Thereafter the peg to the dollar was made official, as a prelude to the creation of a common Gulf currency.

In the early 1980s, Saudi Arabia devalued the Saudi Riyal relative to the dollar, allowing it to fall from 3.5 to the dollar in 1983 to 3.75 in 1986 (a 7 percent devaluation), but has since maintained this parity. The Bahraini Dinar has not deviated from the 0.376 exchange rate against the US dollar since 1980. The Qatari Riyal has been pegged against the US dollar at a rate of QR 3.64 per USD since it was first introduced. The UAE Dirham has been pegged to the 1 US dollar = 3.6725 Dirhams since November 1997. The Omani Rial has been pegged to the US dollar since 1973; in January 1986 there was a devaluation of about 10 percent, from $2.8952 per Omani Rial to $2.6008 per Omani Rial, and since then the parity has remained unaltered.

The exception in this picture has been Kuwait, whose Dinar has registered wider fluctuations against the dollar. The Dinar was officially pegged to a basket of currencies until 2003, then to the dollar until June 2007, when the peg was switched back to a basket of currencies whose composition has not been made public – allowing the Kuwaiti Central Bank to, in essence, manage the currency as it pleases. The Dinar recorded its lowest value against the dollar in 1999, and has since appreciated. From 2003 to 2007, when the peg was to the dollar, the appreciation was 4.6 percent; between 2007 and 2008 the appreciation accelerated, but the trend has reversed since, and the Dinar is back close to its average dollar value in 2003.

The experience of Kuwait might be used as a reference case to argue that attempting to manage the exchange rate or shift from one peg to another is essentially useless in an oil economy, and may have a cost in terms of the currency reputation which is not compensated by any substantial benefit in macro policy formulation.

The Cost of the Rigid Peg

The stability of the link of the Gulf currencies to the dollar stands out as an exception in internationally. Other countries that have experienced hyperinflation and extensive dollarization have resorted to pledging a fixed exchange rate to the dollar as a way to reverse expectations and establish the reputation of new national currencies, launched in the context of monetary reform. In 2000, Ecuador has even reached to the point of purely and simply adopting the US dollar as the national currency, the first and, until 2010, sole case of a country adopting the national currency of another country as legal tender without the approval of the issuing country. Generally speaking, such policies run the risk of not being tenable in the long run, as domestic inflation does not disappear overnight and a fixed exchange rate leads to real over-valuation and loss of competitiveness for national exports (see Baliño, Bennet and Borensztein 1999).

In the GCC countries, the link to the dollar has been maintained even if Gulf Arab economies have generally experienced cycles in opposition with cyclical behavior in the United States. Until the 2008 international financial crisis, the Gulf Arab economies had prospered at times when the price of oil has been high, while the US economy has tended to perform badly under these conditions. Periods of high growth or excessive spending in the United States have favoured increased oil prices, and opened the door to periods of slow growth just when the Gulf Arab economies were booming. Conversely, low oil prices have facilitated sustained growth in the industrial economies, and led to recession in the Gulf.

The rigid link to the dollar has therefore meant that the Gulf Arab countries have followed a cyclical rather than countercyclical exchange rate policy. When oil prices have been high and domestic spending created significant inflation, the dollar has tended to be weak relative to most other currencies, just when the Gulf Arab countries should have considered some revaluation. Conversely, when the oil price has been low and the Gulf Arab economies have been experiencing recession, the dollar has appreciated relative to other currencies just when the Gulf Arab economies would have preferred a weaker currency. The 2008 international financial crisis has broken this pattern, because the decoupling theory has been proven wrong, and the Gulf Arab countries are to a large extent experiencing a downturn as much as the industrial countries – still however growing.

Periodically, calls are heard to use the exchange rate tool counter cyclically, either devalue to sustain domestic growth and protect from cheap foreign imports in case of a recession, or revalue at times of high inflation and growth (IMF 2006; *The Economist* 2007). These calls have so far fallen on deaf ears in decision-making circles: instead, the main thrust of monetary policy in the region has been to aim at currency integration with the establishment of a common Gulf currency – although one thing which is not clear about the new currency is which exchange rate regime it will follow. Obviously, if all that is implied by launching a common currency is transitioning from a rigid dollar peg for each individual currency, to a rigid dollar peg for the common currency, it will not amount to much of a change. Thus one suspects that establishing a common currency may be a prelude to some greater flexibility in exchange rate management, although this is not said and may in fact not follow.

The Need for a Political Economy Approach

The effort at establishing a common currency and the rigid dollar peg have been criticized and ridiculed by analysts for an approach that is purely economic and void of political considerations. The main thrust of my argument is that the behavior of the Gulf Arab monetary authorities can only be understood if one takes into account the political economy significance of the exchange regime.

There are two sets of political justifications for the Gulf Arab countries' attachment to the dollar peg: the first is related to international relations, the second to domestic dynamics.

International Considerations

On the first aspect, it would be difficult to disentangle the peg to the dollar from the close political relationship that the Gulf Arab countries have maintained with the United States in the context of the latter's global economic and security dominance (also see Momani 2008). It is to be noted that the different elements of this overall relationship came in place at different times: if the strategic Saudi-US relationship dates back to the historic meeting between King Abdulaziz and President Roosevelt, and was preceded by Standard Oil of California's first oil discovery, the other Gulf Arab countries remained in the British sphere of influence much longer. If the adoption of a pegged exchange rate was, as argued, an inevitable policy choice, the peg was originally the SDR than to the dollar. It is only much more recently that a de facto dollar peg was made official, and at least in the case of Kuwait, the new policy did not last long. Thus, on the one hand it would be difficult to deny the political undertone of the dollar peg, but on the other it would probably be a mistake to exaggerate the connection. The close political and strategic relationship with the United States does not necessitate the dollar peg – the latter would have been abandoned if the Gulf Arab countries had found that doing so would serve their interests better.

Rather than being an absolute political necessity, the dollar peg is a matter of expediency. It is tied to the fact that crude oil is traded in dollars, that the bulk of Gulf Arab international investment – public and private – is in the United States (perhaps increasingly diversified in recent years, but still predominantly in the

US, or in dollar-denominated assets; see IIF 2007), and available alternatives like the euro are not very convincing. True, the bulk of Gulf Arab oil exports do not go to the US, but they are priced and paid in dollars nevertheless; similarly, the bulk of Gulf Arab imports do not originate from the US, and mostly are priced in currencies different from the dollar, but this does not seem to be reason enough to switch to the euro or the yen (see Essayad and Algahtani 2005; Noreng 2004; Essayad and Marx 2001). Therefore, politically speaking 'abandoning the dollar' is a step that may create a lot of attention but has little practical purposes.

Domestic (Distributional) Considerations

In contrast, domestic political considerations are crucially important. The key point is that in an oil exporting economy the distributional effect of a change in the exchange rate are much more important than the effect on the competitiveness of domestically produced goods and services, or on aggregate demand. And the distributional effects are not so much between different groups of producers or income earners within the private sector, as they are between the government and the people.

Exchange rate changes always have an impact on income distribution. In a diversified economy, devaluation will increase the earnings of exporters and producers of import-competing goods and services, and damage the purchasing power of producers or consumers depending on imports. A revaluation obviously does the opposite. Indeed, these distributional effects are needed in order to incentivize a shift of means of production from the non-tradables sector to the export or import-competing sectors, and improve the country's balance of trade. Distributional effects are normally deemed to be small, because it is assumed that factors of production can migrate easily from one sector to another, and the average wage may not change at all (if international wage equalization is assumed, the average wage changes in parallel with the exchange rate; but this is not the standard assumption).

In reality, distributional effects always have some importance, because factors of production do not in fact easily migrate between sectors. Nevertheless, for diversified economies these effects are always considered less important than the impact on competitiveness or aggregate demand (which includes exports minus imports, and therefore tends to be larger after devaluation, and smaller after a revaluation). However, in an oil exporting economy the pecking order of exchange rate changes effects is completely different. As oil is priced in dollars and the price is tied to that of internationally traded benchmark crude oils, a change in the exchange rate neither improves nor damages the competitiveness of the country's main export item. As the economy normally includes only a few import-competing activities, there also is limited scope for import substitution.

Rather, a change in the exchange rate will directly change the value of exports as expressed in the national currency. As a very large share of export proceeds constitute a rent, which accrues directly to the state, the immediate effect of a change in the exchange rate will be felt on government oil revenue as expressed in the national currency. At the same time, all whose income is fixed in the national currency will experience a decline or improvement of purchasing power, as the price of imported goods is likely to quickly reflect the change in the exchange rate. Thus, the exchange rate has an immediate distributional impact and very limited impact on the competitiveness of the economy. Devaluation is exactly equivalent to a cut in wages and all other payments in the national currency. In economies in which the bulk of the national workforce is employed by the government, devaluation benefits the government budget at the expense of the real wage of employed nationals.

Furthermore, as expatriates presumably have an income and savings target in the currency of their country of origin or in one international currency, devaluation will eventually lead to an increase in the cost of expatriates. While existing contracts may not be invalidated, some expatriates will find that local employment is no longer attractive and leave, and new hires will require higher wages. This is likely to be more pronounced at the level of skilled professionals who are normally better paid than nationals, thus widening an existing gap that is politically touchy at times. At lower skill levels the effect is likely to be slower, and may be positive, because foreigners normally accept wages much lower than nationals, and this is one cause for nationals' unemployment: this gap will be reduced.

As foreigners are primarily employed by the private sector, devaluation is more likely to increase the costs of the private sector than of the government. Also, as the private sector is primarily engaged in imports, and only marginally in import competing activities, devaluation will be viewed as a threat, and probably translate into rapid transfer of higher import prices to the final consumer. In short, the real economy effects of devaluation are likely to be minimal, and the main effect will be an immediate improvement of the government budget balance as expressed in the national currency (which is how it is normally expressed) to the detriment of various private sector interests, especially national.

A revaluation will have the opposite effect: an immediate deterioration in the government budget balance, and increased purchasing power of all incomes that are fixed in the national currency. This will allow employers of foreigners to bid their wages down, reduce the cost of imported merchandise, and improve market conditions generally. Producers of import competing goods may suffer to some extent, but exporters are unlikely to be seriously affected, because so much of their cost base is in fact priced in international currency (whether it is inputs of crude oil or gas, or imported labor). From the point of view of the government a revaluation simply means that the expected budget surplus will be reduced, and the government will enjoy more limited latitude in its decision-making over destination of the oil revenue. A revaluation is a way to distribute the benefit of increased oil revenue in a non-selective, non-targeted fashion. Politically speaking, this is not a very interesting proposition. Conversely, the government will certainly be tempted to solve its budget problems by simply devaluing, but this will be very unpopular, and likely to have a high cost in terms of legitimacy.

Alternative Exchange Rate Regimes

It may be useful to explore some alternative exchange rate regimes, primarily in view of gaining a better understanding of the political implications of each solution. The reference solution is a pegged exchange rate – which can be modified from time to time, but requires a policy decision for this to happen. I have already argued that this decision is likely to be politically unpalatable – indeed this has been the experience of all countries, including diversified advanced economies for as long as they operated under a peg.

Whether the peg is to the dollar or to another monetary sign does not matter much. As mentioned, for a long time the Gulf Arab currencies' peg was officially to the SDR, and the link to the dollar was de facto. The point is that SDRs are not commonly used in business transactions, and the dollar is a major component of the SDR: therefore, using SDRs rather than the dollar increases uncertainty and transaction costs while yielding a very similar result to just using the dollar. In actual practice, a peg to the dollar ends up being used as an approximation to the officially preferred peg to the SDR.

A peg to a currency different from the dollar – the most commonly quoted alternatives are the euro or the yen – would not have any obvious advantages. There have been significant oscillations in the bilateral exchange rates of these currencies, so one cannot say that a peg to the euro or the yen would make no difference with respect to a peg to the dollar. However, there is no convincing a priori justification for preferring one to the other, and in the end the dollar remains the most widely used currency internationally. Thus, unless one may think of a regime based on a shifting peg, moving frequently from one reference currency to another depending on the evolution of their bilateral exchange rates and the requirement of the Gulf Arab economies, the alternative cannot be a different peg. Similarly, arguing in favor of a 'floating' or flexible peg regime means simply invoking the superior wisdom of 'the market', but tells us nothing about how the Gulf Arab exchange rates may actually evolve. It may very well be that in the end the best solution is adding some flexibility to whatever rule is used, but flexibility is not a rule per se.

If an alternative to a peg is followed, then there are two main rules that deserve to be explored – not because they may be realistically implemented, but in order to understand the implications of deviating from the peg. The first rule we may call the 'balanced budget' rule, and would consist in simply opting for the exchange rate which will balance the budget once revenue and expenditure are independently determined.[1] In this approach, the government steers away from both accumulating surpluses and deficits, and relies on the exchange rate to balance the budget. If there is no fiscal discipline, this may be the perfect solution

---

1   If x is the exchange rate, R_N is revenue in the national currency, R_X is revenue in the foreign currency, E_N is expenditure in the national currency, and E_X is expenditure in the foreign currency, we have the following: $x = (E_N - R_N)/ (R_X - E_X)$.

for fiscal irresponsibility: you run expenses as large as 'needed', and simply devalue as much as necessary to balance the budget. This would not be very much different from funding government expenditure through the printing machine, but would 'look' much better. Conversely, a conservative government that does not well know how to spend all the money that it is receiving (e.g. Abu Dhabi) may be spared the embarrassment of deciding how to invest the surplus by simply revaluing systematically and running a balanced budget.

Neither solution is realistic, but consideration of such an exotic exchange rate regime shows that an oil exporting country enjoys considerable room for manipulation of accounting and monetary rules. This is well understood by the citizens, who are accordingly very suspicious of any instance of use of this added degree of freedom. An external anchor is therefore all the more needed, just because it would be so easy for the authorities to package irresponsibility in a wrap of fiscal orthodoxy.

The second, more interesting rule is linking the external value of the currency to the price of oil. In its simplest formulation, this may be viewed as an oil peg – moving the dollar exchange rate in parallel with dollar price of oil. This implies that the price of oil in the national currency remains constant – which does not mean that oil has to be traded in the national currency. But, if in fact oil is sold in the national currency, one easy way to implement this rule is to fix the price of oil in the national currency, and let the dollar exchange rate fluctuate. This rule has already been proposed and discussed in the literature. In a 2003 article, Jeffrey Frankel proposed that small commodity-exporting countries should adopt what he calls PEP (for peg the export price). Interestingly, Frankel's article does not consider any of the Gulf Arab countries, because, he argues, they have not suffered significant deficits and have not incurred international debt (Frankel, 2003).[2] More recently, Brad Setser (2007) has argued in favor of adopting this rule in the Gulf Arab countries, but has shun away from its extreme implications by proposing either a 50 percent link or a 30 percent link – i.e. taking into account only a fraction of the volatility in oil prices. Now, it so happens that the interesting part of the story is exactly the volatility and what this rule means for managing it.

As long as revenue exceeds expenditure in foreign currency, and expenditure exceeds revenue in national currency there will be a positive value of the exchange rate that achieves a balanced budget.

2   Frankel considers the following: Nigeria, Venezuela, Ecuador, Indonesia, Mexico and Russia. Of these, Indonesia is the only country that has succeeded in significantly diversifying its economy. The main thrust of Frankel's argument is that, had they pegged their currency to the oil price, these economies would have avoided some of the disasters they experienced. His discussion is purely economic: a consideration of distributional factors would have shown that incompetent governments in oil exporting countries can shift the burden of their mistakes on their people through manipulation of the exchange rate. But clearly the solution is not making the people pay, the solution is getting rid of incompetent government. The Gulf countries do not serve as good examples to Frankel's argument because by and large their governments have been quite competent.

An oil exporting state pegging its currency to the value of oil may appear at first sight perfectly reasonable and justifiable. After all, oil is the key component of national wealth, and issuing money which represents this tangible wealth, and is in a sense freely convertible into it (you can buy the oil with that money at a fixed price; one can view bills in circulation as oil certificates), is the most sensible rule one can think of. But *oil prices in dollars are volatile*. A government pegging its currency to the price of oil would make itself immune to fluctuations in the dollar price of oil. Its oil revenue as expressed in the national currency would be purely a function of exported volumes, and totally independent of the export price in foreign currency. Who would be affected by the volatility then? Simply, all earners of fixed incomes in the national currency. Their purchasing power would be volatile and follow fluctuations in the dollar price of oil. The meaning of a fixed currency peg then becomes clear: it means that the government takes upon itself the entire risk of fluctuating oil prices. If the peg is to the dollar, all the volatility is absorbed by the government budget. Earners of incomes in the national currency are made immune from exposure to oil price volatility. In this case, the national economy is only affected by changes in the price of oil to the extent that government expenditure in the purchase of goods and services from the national economy is increased or decreased. But if the government manages to ride through the waves managing a fiscal reserve or stabilization fund so well that expenditure is kept on a steady path, the national economy is completely sheltered from the storm.

It is, I submit, a crucial component of the rentier state model to be the institutional intermediary between the oil rent and the national economy. The role of the rentier state is to receive the oil rent and inject it into the national economy through expenditure. Smoothing the fluctuations in oil revenue is part and parcel of the brief of a successful rentier state. A rentier state that gives up on this task and simply passes the risk on to its people has no raison d'être. A straight oil peg would be exactly equivalent to redistributing the oil rent in accordance with some automatic rule, e.g. an equal sum to each citizen at the end of the year – a large check in good years, a small one in bad. This is a state that gives up on politics, as the essence of power is the ability to redirect resources according to whatever are your political priorities. In practice, rentier states may not be terribly good at smoothing expenditure and isolating their economies from oil price fluctuations. Indeed, all the countries discussed by Frankel have been especially bad at that, supported by the incompetence of international banks and financial markets: at times of high oil prices they borrowed internationally, in the expectations that tomorrow will be even brighter than today; and eventually ran into insolvency. The Gulf Arab states have performed better at this game, but still far from being able to stabilize expenditure in the face of wildly swinging revenue.

The problem is that running an effective stabilization scheme requires some knowledge of future prices and revenue. With time, volatility has increased to the point that future oil prices are anybody's guess. Biblical Joseph enjoyed unfair advantage, because good God told him that he should expect seven fat years followed by seven lean years. But if no good God is passing the info to you – it is very difficult to guess right. It is then quite normal and to be expected that expenditure will be tied to revenue and some fluctuation will remain, albeit reduced. And it is then very understandable that the temptation may arise to compensate for that with at least partial adoption of an oil peg. An exchange rate regime reflecting some fraction of the volatility in oil prices, as proposed by Setser, would not entirely negate the role of the rentier state, but would equally, to some extent, represent an acknowledgement of weakness, a limitation of the state's responsibility – which would be reflected in a loss of legitimacy.

Regional Monetary Integration and the Future of the Dollar Peg

The Gulf Arab currencies are all pegged to the dollar, and consequently their bilateral exchange rates have barely changed in decades. This is true even for the Kuwaiti dinar, as fluctuations in the dinar/dollar exchange rate have in practice been very limited. Therefore, monetary integration already is a fact: substituting national currencies with a common currency in circulation may facilitate trade and cross investment, but is unlikely to have any dramatic effect. Also, there has been significant debate on whether the Gulf Arab states constitute an 'optimal currency area' (see Mundell 1961; Fasano and Iqbal 2002), but these studies have failed to note that even in successful monetary unions like the EU, the rationale was political as opposed to economic (see Cohen 1998, ch. 4). Surely, the rationale for a GCC regional currency is not that the GCC is an optimal currency area: it is very easy to demonstrate that the GCC is not an optimal currency area – trade within the area is a fraction of trade with the rest of the world, the countries mostly export the same products and are not complementary, their economic structures are different and they do not react in parallel to external shocks (in contrast, see Fasano and Iqbal 2002).

Thus, it would appear that the creation of a regional currency may amount to little more than window dressing and a continuation of the dollar peg – and indeed this is the official position of at least three out of four countries involved (Kuwait's position is more nuanced). If the dollar continues to be in demand as the international medium of exchange and reserve asset, then it is quite possible that nothing much will change. In fact, if the position of the dollar as the international currency were not in question, the GCC countries would be very happy continuing the dollar peg indefinitely, notwithstanding the costs involved. However, the position of the dollar has been questioned from several sides, including within the United States, where the question is being asked whether it is indeed in the best interest of the US that their currency serves as the international medium of exchange (see Helleiner and Kirshner 2009; Bowles 2009; Katada 2009, Momani 2008).

Greater reliance on the SDR has been proposed as a strategy to progressively reduce the role of the dollar as international currency, and an evolution towards a multiple currency system has been advocated (Ocampo 2009). If indeed the system evolves towards multiple international currencies, the close peg to the dollar may come to be questioned. In fact, the United States is not the main trading partner of the GCC, whose trade is increasingly directed towards the rest of Asia (see Davidson in this volume). This divergent trend is expected to continue in the coming years, potentially exposing the GCC private sectors to growing volatility in the exchange rates of the Asian countries relative to the dollar. If the Asian currencies – the Chinese renminbi first and foremost – become more easily convertible and are included in the basket of currencies which defines the SDR, the argument in favor of shifting from a simple dollar peg to an SDR peg is likely to gain traction.

The use of the dollar as the numeraire for expressing the price of oil may also come to be questioned. Since 2004 the price of oil has increasingly been influenced by expectations concerning the dollar's strength or weakness. Variations in market sentiment on the stability of the dollar have become a further cause of instability in oil prices, which is not in the best interest of oil exporters and importers alike. Oil is traded in dollars because use of the currency facilitates international price comparisons. Furthermore, the price of crude oils exported by the GCC countries is indexed to prices discovered by trading on the Nymex or ICE futures markets, where trading takes place in dollars. These are structural factors which are unlikely to change easily or any time soon, yet the extreme volatility of prices determined on the futures markets is an obvious problem for the oil producers (see Momani 2008).

In the context of a redefinition of the way in which oil is traded and prices are arrived at, it is possible that pricing of oil in a numeraire more stable than the dollar may be sought. In a multiple currency world in which the SDR plays a growing role, trading in SDRs may be considered. But SDRs are mostly reserve instruments rather than mediums of exchange, and the lack of SDRs in circulation may make it impossible to envisage payment of oil exports in SDRs. However, if the Gulf currency is pegged to the SDR, in practice trading may take place in the Gulf currency. Note that it would be difficult to have a free float of the Gulf currency if this is used to pay for oil exports, because the GCC countries run a structural balance of payments surplus, and the currency would tend systematically to appreciate, unless the Central Bank intervened to sell the currency and add foreign currencies to reserves, in which case this would no longer be a free float.

The proposed common currency then serves the purpose of creating conditions for overcoming the straightjacket of the rigid dollar peg, in a context in which the role of the dollar as international currency is declining. If the dollar no longer is a stable anchor, an alternative must be found. A regional currency collectively controlled by a group of central banks is more likely to maintain its reputation than a purely national currency that has lost its anchor. But simply substituting the national currencies will not be sufficient to eliminate the need for an anchor, and a new one eventually will have to be found.

Conclusion

The history of the Gulf Arab region is one where merchants were intimately linked to the global economy. In some ways, things have not changed in the Gulf Arab states where they are inextricably linked to the global economy through oil, investments, and trade. The Gulf Arab states' currency policy choices have often been judged by analysts and pundits through a myopic economic lens of currency theories. As this chapter argues, these may not be useful paradigms, however, for a region with a distinct development model predicated on rentier politics.

When the Gulf Arab states are understood through a political economy lens, we get a better appreciation and justification of their respective currency choices. Gulf Arab states have maintained close ties to the dollar in order to establish a positive reputation in the global economy for adopting the US' stable monetary policy. This policy has not always been easy to maintain; indeed, prior to the 2008 international financial crisis there were many domestic calls for a revaluation of the Gulf currencies and a de-pegging from the dollar. To better understand Gulf Arab currency choices, we need to use a political economy lens to assess the matter. By maintaining the dollar peg, the Gulf Arab countries have fostered better political and security relations with the United States. Currency revaluation in these rentier states will negatively affect national budgets, and local labour markets. Other exchange rate regimes have been debated – such as pegging to SDRs, euro or yen – but these are not politically viable and do not offer the monetary reputation and the regional security of the greenback. It appears that the future of the dollar peg in the Gulf Arab states will remain intact barring larger changes in the global economy and in the grand bargain between GCC governments and its citizens.

Chapter 3

Economic Diversification in the Gulf Arab States: Lip Service or Actual Implementation of a New Development Model?

Martin Hvidt

Introduction

Judging from official statements, development projects under implementation and the significant investment in economic assets currently undertaken by the GCC states, these Gulf Arab states seem to be in the process of adopting a more liberal, globalized and pro-business development model. This chapter analyzes the claim that throughout the Gulf Arab states, a production-oriented model is displacing the rentier-state development model that has – and is – dominating throughout the region. Using Luciani's (1990) classic distinction between 'allocation states' and 'production states', this chapter finds that the region is in a process of adjusting its underlying economic structures to make way for a more production-oriented economic model.[1]

Construction has visibly exploded throughout the GCC during the oil boom from 2002 to 2008. Each emirate or sultanate seems to strive to establish a skyline in glass, artificial islands with luxury homes, marinas, golf courses and themed shopping malls. In addition, significant investments are being made to attract foreign firms and individual investors in new areas of economic activity: financial institutions, office facilities, free zones, aviation, airports, harbours and, more than anything, tourism. Due to high levels of government spending, moreover, construction continues throughout the GCC, albeit at a slower pace after the 2008 international financial crisis (IMF 2009b, 5).

According to the *Institute of International Finance* (IIF), the combined export earnings of GCC states were $1.5 trillion during 2002 to 2006 which doubled national incomes compared to the preceding period (IIF 2007, 1). Using IMF data, the IIF estimates that approximately $1 trillion was spent on imports in the region, and that the remaining $500 billion was saved. As such, the estimated total foreign assets owned by the GCC states rose to $1.6 trillion by 2006 year-end (IIF 2007,

1   I would like to thank the Danish Social Science Research Council for funding this research, and not least the Gulf Research Center in Dubai for hosting me during several periods of field work.

2). In addition to these public funds, significant private funds are present in the region (IIF 2008a).

The medium and long-term effects of the 2008 international financial crisis are still unclear, however, the IIF reports that the GCC states are 'relatively well positioned to withstand the effects of the current global credit crisis with little enduring damage' (IIF 2008b, 13).[2] It furthermore states that

> Overall the risks are containable give the ample resources of the region and strong macroeconomic fundamentals. An ambitious investment program is currently under way to expand capacity in real estate, tourism, transportation, manufacturing, and hydrocarbon sectors. These investments exceed $1 trillion [1000 billion] for the next five years (about the combined size of the GCC economies) even after assuming that half of the planned projects will be cancelled or postponed due to the current global credit crunch. (IIF 2008b, 13)

Immediately after the onset of the 2008 international financial crisis, oil prices plummeted but then reverted in early 2009 and by mid 2009 the price of oil returned to a level around $70 a barrel. So despite the international financial crisis, the GCC states can still be considered to be in a financial boom period, albeit a more modest one than the 2003–08 period. Furthermore, construction prices have decreased drastically in comparison with the boom years. Engineering, procurement and construction costs are reported to have dropped 45 percent in late 2009 from a peak of the market in July 2008, which provides the GCC states with considerable incentive to carry on their investment programs (Mirza 2009).

In comparison with previous oil-booms, the recent one has taken a different form. In the 1970s, the small and relatively underdeveloped economies of the Gulf Arab states had limited ability to incorporate and utilize substantial capital in a productive manner and consequently decided to place a significant amount of its 'petrodollars' passively into international banks and international financial institutions like the IMF and World Bank (Todaro and Smith 2009, 677). One of the characteristics of the second oil boom is the fact that the region is increasingly incorporating substantial investments into the domestic economies. As energy analyst Fareed Mohammed notes in the *Middle East Economic Digest* (*MEED*), the region showed:

> Excellent macroeconomic policies, strong technocratic capacity, a vastly improved regulatory environment, a private sector willing to both invest and innovate, and strong global links in services. (Molavi 2007, 18)

There is indeed a renewed and strengthened attempt of Gulf Arab states to invest oil money in a manner that creates real economic assets. Current projects within industry, education and service provision indicate that the GCC states are utilizing

---

2   IMF expresses the same understanding of the situation (IMF 2009a).

income to promote real economic diversification. Thus, 'development', has once again captured the Gulf Arab countries' political agendas.

Official statements and development plans from the other GCC states further supports the observation that economic diversification has taken political priority in the GCC. All GCC states have launched development plans, stating that the overall goal of reforming their economies is to become less reliant on oil and gas income. In other words, economic diversification has become their key economic and political aim, and the means to achieve this is a combination of state investments, a (re)vitalization of the private sector and extensive foreign investments (GSDP 2008; Hancock 2008; Martin 2009; Niblock and Malik 2007, 173ff; Nield 2009; Redfern 2008a; Redfern 2008b). These development plans further suggest that time has come to displace the rentier-state development model which has dominated these states' economies since the advent of oil and gas, and to replace it with a model which to a greater extent is market-driven and private sector-focused.

Allocation vs. Production in the Gulf Arab States

Allocation- states, also referred to as distribution or rentier-states, are characterized by a unique circumstance that allows the state to be largely dislocated from the national economy. The allocation- state functions because of the state's own procurement of a sizeable income from resource extraction (e.g. exports of oil or gas or other 'rents'), which allows it to avoid levying direct taxes on the local economy and its citizens to finance its activities. Furthermore such an economy depends on the creation of wealth within a small fraction of the society (Beblawi 1990, 87). Thus, the allocation-state is relieved from the societal pressures to develop an efficient economic basis. Instead, the state takes on the task of distributing the money that flows into the country to meet its societal needs. In the production-state the situation is reversed. Here, it is essential that the production-state foster a solid economic base for its society through promoting economic growth and collecting taxation to strengthen its national and international capacities. In this way economic growth becomes the main political, as well as economic, aim of all production-states (Luciani 1990, 71 and 75).[3] The difference between allocation and production states must be understood as extremes on a continuum, and as such most states will lie somewhere between the two models. Luciani defined an allocation- state as one that attains the greatest share of its national revenue, at least 40 percent, from oil or from external revenue and where state expenses constitute a significant fraction of domestic income (Luciani 1990, 72). Using this definition, Luciani (1990, 72) finds the Arab oil-producing states are typical examples of allocation states.

---

3   For a detailed discussion of whether Dubai is a production or allocation state see (Hvidt 2007, 562).

As pointed out by Beblawi (1990, 86), it is important to note that there is a considerable difference between income 'earned' through productive activities and income attained passively. Beblawi argues that a rentier-economy gives rise to a certain societal frame of mind called the *rentier-mentality*. Here, the normal link between work effort and payoff is disconnected. Payoff – be it income or fortune – is not the result of productive work, but rather a coincidence. In other words, in a rentier-mentality wealth may best be compared to lottery winnings. This is, of course, in direct contrast to the case of production-oriented economies, where a person is rewarded for the work-effort or for having performed well in a risky investment. Here the payoff is the result of a process, which may be the result of many years' education or hard work.

Emphasizing Beblawi's argument about the rentier-mentality, Kurbursi (1999, 311) claims that the plentiful and easily earned oil-income has destroyed the economic structures in the oil rich states. He thus points to dependency on oil as the most fundamental problem for the Arab economies:

> Dependency on the rent from oil has reduced Arab incentives to diversify their economies, develop alternative manufacturing capacities, promote export-oriented industries, encourage domestic savings, and anchor income on solid productivity grounds.

It follows from the definition of the allocation-state that rentier systems do not require an efficient economic basis for its society, and consequently governments have very little incentive to foster production, private sector development and jobs in the productive sectors. This is part of the explanation for why there has been a call for significant economic reforms of many Middle Eastern economies including the Gulf Arab states since the beginning of the 1990s, when the neoliberal doctrine embodied in the Washington Consensus became the dominant economic paradigm (see Hvidt 2002; 2003). Furthermore it could be argued that the inward oriented, rentier based Gulf Arab economies would be unable to produce sufficient wealth and particularly jobs to sustain the needs of the allocation-state; analysts argued that the cost of remaining outside the globalized economy was simply growing too large (ibid.). Gulf Arab states are indeed reflections of what Luciani defined as an allocation state. Note that between 62 and 80 percent of state income originates from oil and gas in the Gulf Arab states. While timeseries data is unavailable, 2007/8 data figures paint the following picture (see Table 3.1).

Thus, the GCC states can still be classified as allocation states, since 40 percent or more of their income stems from sources originating from outside their own economies. The gross domestic income figures further indicate that despite the central role of oil in these economies, other production and service activities are indeed taking place. In addition to oil and gas incomes, energy income supports and leverages other contributions to the national budgets, especially through foreign investments returns such as sovereign wealth funds. For example, Kuwait places 10 percent of its annual income into its *Reserve Fund for Future Generations,*

Table 3.1 Oil as a percentage of export earnings, state income, GDI, and estimated total foreign assets ($US billion, end-2006)

Country	Oil as % of export earnings	Oil as % of state income	Oil as % of GDI	Total foreign assets (est.) ($US billion, end-2006)
Bahrain	>60	>70	11	20
Kuwait	95	80	App. 50	400
Oman	n/a	62	45	10
Qatar	85	70	>60	70
Saudi Arabia	90	75	45	450
UAE	n/a	n/a	35	600
Total				1550

Source: (IIF 2007, 3); All values relating to Oil earnings are from (Europa Publications 2007, see the respective country sections) or (CIA 2008). The figures concerning Oman are from (Global Investment House 2008). It has not been possible to attain time series of these data.

where foreign assets peaked at $100 billion in 1990–91 and the fund's return on investments is estimated to be comparable to the entire annual Kuwaiti income from oil and gas (Europa Publications 2007, 689). As Table 3.1 notes, the size of those funds in the GCC-states is quite significant.[4]

Note that even at a modest 5 percent interest earnings on these investments will secure the Gulf Arab states an additional $77 Billion of annual income.

The current drive toward economic diversification, as further expressed in the GCC states' development plans, might be viewed as a manifestation of a new political understanding among the leaders in the Gulf Arab states. This chapter further explicates this argument.

The Emergence of a New Development Model in the Gulf Arab States

Because economic reforms are both time consuming and politically difficult to implement, such reforms are only implemented if a government has compelling reasons to do so. Often governments are pressured to undertake economic reforms by lending agencies such as the IMF or the World Bank or by poor economic performance that threatens to shake the stability of the incumbent regime. Alternatively, economic liberalization could arise from

---

4   As a result of the 2008 international financial crises, it is estimated that assets prices have fallen sharply (by approximately 40 percent) which has decreased the value of the Sovereign Wealth Funds. Their relative size and influence in the global market will however remain large (IMF 2009b, 11).

strong felt wishes, visions or beliefs of the decision-makers, business groups, and distributional coalitions within a country. In a liberalization and economic reform process there are winners and losers. It is expected that those who stand to lose by economic liberalization and reforms – for example persons who so far have benefitted from advantages and privileges provided by the ruling-bargain – will vigorously try to oppose such reforms in order to defend the status quo (Richards and Waterbury 2008, 3). As such economic liberalization is often met with significant criticism from various societal sectors and thus are most likely to be implemented in states which have strong governments which posses autonomy from powerful societal groups and thus can avoid 'state capture' (Evans 1989, 563). In an allocation-state, the promotion of economic liberalization policies are particularly problematic as it can upset the political status quo of the rentier states. It is plausible that the promotion of economic liberalization in the Gulf Arab states is explained by decision-makers' reasoning that the rentier state is as finite as the oil resource it depends on and therefore these politically tough policies are an acknowledgement of the need to shift towards a more production oriented development model.

Among the policies implemented to liberalize an economy are transparent procedures and decision-making structures, reliance on a free market, the easing of customs and other factors that facilitate cross-border trade, and many other policies. Governments promote and enact these politically difficult economic liberalization policies in order to create an efficient environment for private sector operations and investments – and when there is an explicit aim to stimulate the growth of the productive sectors of the economy (private as well as public). Furthermore a package of liberal policies are enacted if a government attempts to attract foreign investments.

In this chapter, economic reforms such as privatization and deregulation of the Gulf Arab economies and policies aimed at strengthening the economies' institutional context, are seen as an expression of the desire to move in the direction of a production-oriented economy. Without even attempting to provide an exhaustive analysis of the actual drivers behind the reform process in the GCC states, it is safe to say that we can disregard the potential pressures from international financial institutions, the IMF and the World Bank, simply because the Gulf Arab states have never borrowed any significant amounts from multilateral lending institutions (Hvidt 2004).[5] Furthermore, these states have had strong financial standing from 2000 to 2010 from high oil incomes. With little reason to believe there are direct external pressures on the Gulf Arab countries to promote economic liberalization, it is argued that Gulf Arab decision-makers reckoned that economic transformation was necessary to mitigate against potential volatility of the oil market and to meet the needs of the significant demographic pressures on public spending. Thus, it is domestic factors that are the main drivers behind the

---

5   We are however aware that the neoliberal policies of such institutions indirectly exercise structural pressure on the GCC countries to conform to their policies.

economic reform initiatives enacted in the 2000s. If the Gulf Arab states were to witness volatility of oil markets where oil and gas incomes were to ever drop to 1990 levels, it would not be possible to support the Gulf Arab welfare systems. A diversified economy is better able to secure these states against the volatility of oil prices and heed off pressure in the transition away from the income of this finite resource. Furthermore demographic studies show that more than 11 million people (approximately 25 percent of the GCC population) are below 15 years of age (UN population Division 2009). With high unemployment figures and the vast number of young people entering the job market in the coming years, these states will be in desperate need of job creation.

Being an oil-poor state, Dubai has attempted to tackle diversification and populations problems since the mid 1990s, and has provided the Gulf Arab citizens and its leaders with an example of how international investments, free market orientation, innovation, country branding and openness to globalization has been able to transform the oil-poor Arab city-state into an international metropolis (Hvidt 2009; Hvidt 2007, 562ff). While the economic model applied in Dubai has lost some credibility since the 2008 international financial crisis, Dubai has no doubt acted as a significant source of inspiration to the surrounding states in preparing their current development plans.

It is however difficult to analyze to what degree a reform process has actually been undertaken. Indeed, there is a dearth of quantitative and qualitative data that could demonstrate the Gulf Arab states' shift in economic liberalization. But, we can extrapolate that there is significant economic liberalization occurring throughout the Gulf Arab states by referring to two global indexes that register changes in judicial, political and institutional frameworks throughout the GCC.

Both the World Bank's *Index of Doing Business*, and the World Economic Forum's *Global Competitiveness Index* cover the Gulf region. The first index ranks 183 countries on the basis of 10 parameters that express how easy (in terms of time and money) it is to establish, operate and close a business. The aim of the index is to measure the regulation and red tape relevant to the lifecycle of a small to medium-sized firm. As such it assesses the effort it takes to apply for and procure various licenses, to employ workers, to register property, to gain credit, to pay taxes, to engage in international trade, to enforce contracts and to close a business. A high rank (low number) indicates that the regulatory environment is conducive to the operation of businesses while a lower rank indicates the opposite. According to the 2010 index, the five states where doing business is most conducive are: Singapore, New Zealand, Hong Kong, USA and United Kingdom.

This index is relatively narrow in scope compared with the *Global Competitiveness Index*, and does not, for example, encompass items such as the macroeconomic stability, corruption, the educational level of the labor force, the underlying strength of institutions or the quality of infrastructure. According to the World Bank index, the Middle East and North Africa (MENA) region has carried through a significant number of reforms from 2004 to 2010. Two-thirds of the states are noted to be implementing reforms. The fastest pace of reforms has taken

Table 3.2 Changes in ranking of the Gulf countries, *Index of Doing Business*, 2006–2010

Country	DB 2006	DB 2007	DB 2008	DB 2009	DB 2010
Saudi Arabia	35	38	23	16	13
Bahrain*	n/a	n/a	n/a	18	20
UAE	68	77	68	46	33
Qatar*	n/a	n/a	n/a	37	39
Kuwait	40	46	40	52	61
Oman	52	55	49	57	65

Note: * Bahrain and Qatar were not included in the index prior to DB 2009.
Source: World Bank 2005, 92; World Bank 2006, 6; World Bank 2007, 6; World Bank 2008a: 6; World Bank 2009, 4.

place in Egypt, Saudi Arabia and the UAE. Saudi Arabia was also singled out by the World Bank as belonging to the Top Ten Global reformers in 2006/2007; Egypt was given the same title in four out of the last seven years; and, the United Arab Emirates made the list in 2008/2009 (World Bank 2009a).

Table 3.2 groups the GCC states into three broad groups. These include Saudi Arabia and Bahrain, who rank highest; the middle group, consisting of UAE and Qatar; and in the lower group, consisting of Kuwait and Oman. Saudi Arabia and Bahrain are ranked among the 25 most 'business-friendly' nations in the world, and as such hold a rank similar to states such as Japan (15), Finland (16), Sweden (18), South Korea (19), Switzerland (21) and Germany (25).

Viewed as a group, the six Gulf Arab states rank by far the highest among the broader group of MENA states. The average rank of the GCC group of states is 39, while the average rank of the remaining states in the MENA region is 112.[6] With exception of Israel (ranking 29), all other MENA states are ranked lower than Oman, which is the lowest ranked Gulf country with a rank of 65.

As noted in the 2009 and 2010 *Doing Business Index*, reforms have generally been undertaken in four areas: easing the procedures for starting up businesses, gaining credit or credit information, registering property; and reforms to ease trade across borders. The World Bank considers these to be the easier types of reforms to accomplish, because they can usually be carried through without any significant legal changes or difficult political tradeoffs (World Bank 2009a, 5).

As mentioned, Saudi Arabia has been implementing a significant number of reforms over the last five years. Starting a limited liability business in Saudi Arabia had once demanded the highest minimum capital requirements in the

---

6   Author's calculations using data from (World Bank 2009a, 4, Table 1.3). Note that the numbers included Israel and Iran following the World Bank classification of the Middle East and North Africa region.

world, $125,000. This amount has been significantly reduced, as has the number of procedures it takes to start a company. In previous years, 13 procedures were required to start a business; now only seven procedures are required. As a consequence, the time it took to start a company in Saudi Arabia fell from 39 days to 15.

Those and other current Saudi reforms are a part of the so-called '10-by-10' initiative. Since year 2000, a series of deliberated reforms have been implemented in Saudi Arabia in order to address the challenges that the economy was facing. These challenges included the lack of job creation in the public and particularly the private sector (Niblock and Malik 2007, 173ff). The '10-by-10' was initiated through a statement made by King Abdallah of Saudi Arabia in 2006, who stated: 'I want Saudi Arabia to be among the top 10 countries in *Doing Business* in 2010. No Middle Eastern country should have a better investment climate by 2007' (World Bank 2008, 44–46). The centralized decision-making structure in Saudi Arabia allowed the commitment to be pushed aggressively forward. The same reforms also made way for the country's accession to the World Trade Organization in 2005.

The goal for Saudi Arabia, was not only to improve its business climate but, as the King stated, to improve the country's international standing relative to other global competitors and to make it more likely to attract foreign investments. Table 3.3 illustrates the ranking, and not least the change in ranking of each of the six Gulf Arab states since 2006.

As the changes indicate, Saudi Arabia has improved its ranking significantly; it has moved from 35th to 13th place. Table 3.3 also shows that the UAE has increased its rank considerably. Both Kuwait and Oman, however, have moved down the ranks over from 2005 to 2010. Kuwaiti and Omani reforms have been too few and relatively insignificant, and consequently they lost ground in the rankings to more active reformers.

However, we should treat the ranking of Saudi Arabia with caution. No doubt significant reforms were undertaken in Saudi Arabia, but various reports and studies suggest that the Saudi Arabia General Investment Authority (SAGIA) which is charged with the task of implementing the reform program has been instrumental in painting a rosier picture of the reform process than is deserved. Since the *Doing Business Index* primarily uses decrees and written laws as data for calculating the index, it implicitly assumes that a given law is implemented after it is passed. However, in Saudi Arabia quite a number of specific laws have passed legislative steps, but have never been implemented throughout the administrative apparatus.[7] It is important to note the SAGIA employees' eagerness to please the King, and not least the eagerness to receive the personal bonuses promised to them if they could succeed in positioning Saudi Arabia among the 10 highest ranked states of the index by 2010 are corrupting variables. Saudi officials targeted the

---

7   Personal communication with Steffen Hertog, Cambridge, Canada, 28 August 2009. See furthermore (Hertog 2010a, ch. 5).

reform efforts to items that would have the greatest impact on Saudi rankings. Saudi reform programs are then understandably fragmented and only superficially implemented.[8]

The description of the reform process in Saudi Arabia thus resembles what Walter (2008, 5) calls 'mock compliance', which implies that a country might have a rhetoric and outward appearance of compliance with international standards but at the same time exhibit relatively hidden behavioral divergences from such standards.

A closer scrutiny of the data further reveals that the ranks of the Gulf Arab states are negatively affected by procedures related to the category of 'enforcing contracts'. In Saudi Arabia, for example, 44 procedures and 635 days are required to enforce a contract and the costs involved amount to 27.5 percent of the claim. Furthermore the rankings of these states are negatively affected by factors related to gaining 'credit', 'employing workers', protecting investors' and 'closing a business'. Oman also scores very low in the category of 'dealing with construction permits' (World Bank 2008, 60–76).

In summary, from the Doing Business index we see that the Gulf Arab states score relatively well at least compared to the other MENA states. It is far easier to set-up, operate and close down a business in the six Gulf Arab States than in the other Middle Eastern states and in the approximately 140 states worldwide that have obtained a lower rank. In the MENA states only Israel is on par with the GCC states. The best-ranked Gulf Arab states are raked similar to many European states. We have furthermore seen that Saudi Arabia and the UAE have improved their rank over the last five years, while Kuwait and Oman have fallen ranks. Since Qatar and Bahrain have not been ranked in earlier versions of the index, we do not know whether they have improved or fallen ranks.

Turning now to the second index, the World Economic Forum annually issues their *Global Competitiveness Report* and a biannually Arab World Competitiveness Report.[9] Competitiveness is defined broadly 'as the set of institutions, policies, and factors that determine the level of productivity of a country' and it is argued that more competitive economies tend to be able to produce higher levels of income for their citizens (World Economic Forum 2009, 4).

In calculating the Global Competitiveness Index (GCI), the World Economic Forum use 12 pillars that indicate broad descriptions of individual country economies that are more tailored and specified than those used in the Doing Business Index. These pillars are: institutions, infrastructure, macroeconomic stability, health and primary education, higher education and training, goods market efficiency, labor market efficiency, financial market sophistication,

---

8   The end-of-year bonuses of the executive staff at SAGIA were dependent upon achieving or surpassing targets set according to the rank of Saudi Arabia on the Doing Business Index (Al-Awwad 2007).

9   The latest version of the Arab World Competitiveness Report was issued in 2007 (World Economic Forum 2007). The two previous reports are from 2003 and 2005.

Table 3.3 Changes in the rank of the Gulf countries,
Global Competitiveness Index, various years

Country	Rank CGI 2006/07	Rank CGI 2007/08	Rank CGI 2008/9	Rank CGI 2009/10
Qatar	38	31	26	22
UAE	32	37	31	23
Saudi Arabia	n/a	35	27	28
Bahrain	49	43	37	38
Kuwait	44	30	35	39
Oman	n/a	42	38	41

Source: World Economic Forum 2006: Table 1, p. xvii; World Economic Forum 2008: Table 4, p. 10; World Economic Forum 2009: Table 4, p. 13.

technological readiness, market size, business sophistication and innovation (World Economic Forum 2008, 3–6). In the 2009/2010 version of the index, Switzerland, United States, Singapore, Sweden and Denmark were rated as the five most competitive economies of the world among the 134 states included. Table 3.3 shows how the Gulf Arab states were rated.

As noted in Table 3.3, the six Gulf Arab states are placed among the 50 most competitive economies in the world. They are closely ranked with New Zealand (20), China (30), Spain (33) and Portugal (43). Note, however, that the Gulf Arab states were found to be among the weakest in this segment.

The general picture is that all Gulf Arab states have improved their rank over the last four years. This is due to a combination of an improved macroeconomic standing resulting from record oil prices and from sound reform policies over the last couple of years. These policies have included business environment reform, investment in infrastructure, economic diversification, combating inflation and, not least, improvements in the educational systems (World Economic Forum 2008, 30ff). However, four of the Gulf Arab states have experienced a slight decrease in their rank in 2010.

To further explicate the rankings, Table 3.4 below highlights the rank obtained by each country in each of the 12 pillars. The scores for the United States, the second highest ranked country is included for comparison. The first noticeable caveat is the considerable variation among the six states.

Qatar is characterized by strong institutions and macroeconomic indicators, but also by weak business sophistication and a lack of innovation. In comparison, the UAE has stronger institutions, infrastructure and macroeconomic stability but weak in education and innovation. Saudi Arabia lacks a sufficiently strong education system (which leads graduates to be insufficiently trained for jobs in the private sector), is relatively insulated from foreign competition and has underdeveloped financial markets. Furthermore Saudi Arabia is characterized by restrictive labor

Table 3.4 Gulf countries ranking on each of the 12 pillars in the Global Competitiveness Index, 2009/10

Country	Overall rank	Basic requirements				Efficiency enhancers						Innovation factors	
		Institutions	Infrastructure	Macroeconomic stability	Health and primary education	Higher education and training	Goods market efficiency	Labor market sophistication	Financial market sophistication	Technological readiness	Market size	Business sophistication	Innovation
Qatar	22	9	39	13	8	25	21	14	35	28	70	37	36
UAE	23	15	6	24	20	29	10	16	33	17	54	19	27
Saudi Arabia	28	32	36	9	71	53	29	71	53	44	22	35	32
Bahrain	38	30	27	5	37	48	22	35	30	35	97	61	60
Kuwait	39	51	50	3	73	82	63	59	63	49	61	50	83
Oman	41	18	29	10	92	67	33	33	43	64	75	57	55
US	2	34	8	93	36	7	12	3	20	13	1	5	1

Source: World Economic Forum 2009: data extracted from the tables pp. 16–20.

regulations and a poor work ethic of the national labor force (World Economic Forum 2008, 31).

Bahrain boasts excellent macroeconomic stability, good infrastructure, good health care and primary education systems, as well as the most sophisticated financial market in the region. But it is relatively weak in providing higher education, labor market regulations, and has lags in business sophistication and innovation. Kuwait is characterized by weak institutions, infrastructure and education but has a positive macroeconomic situation that is rated the third best in the world, with budgetary surplus of nearly 44 percent of GDP and minimal debt in 2008. Business leaders perceive the Bahraini education system to be incompatible with the need of a competitive economy, in particular, math and science education was highlighted as needing great improvement (World Economic Forum 2008, 32). Oman has a good institutional environment and is characterized by macroeconomic stability, but has significant shortcomings in its education system; it also needs to advance liberalization in the labor market and enhance its innovative capacity.

This section further explains why the Gulf Arab states are placed among the weakest of the 40 highest ranked economies worldwide. They rank relatively well according to the 'basic requirements' of competitiveness, namely institutions, infrastructure, macroeconomic stability, health and primary education. But they rank relatively worse on the 'efficiency enhancers' indicators, namely higher education, goods markets efficiency, labor market efficiency, financial market sophistication, technological readiness and naturally market size (excluding Saudi Arabia). And finally, they are ranked comparatively lower on the 'innovation and sophistication factors', which encompass the measures of business sophistication and innovation. This is illustrated in Table 3.5, which is a summary of the rankings within the three aforementioned categories – 'basic requirements', 'efficiency enhancers' and 'innovation factors'.

At a very general level, the table above highlights that despite GCC states' success in a worldwide comparison of competitiveness, their economies have not yet progressed to a stage where they are innovation – driven. They are generally either factor-driven (they rely on their factor endowment, e.g. oil and gas) or efficiency-driven (where competition is based on efficient and high quality production). Only the UAE is classified as an innovation-driven economy, where high-income levels are being sustained by competing internationally with new and unique products (World Economic Forum 2009, 7–12).

In recognizing this, the 2007 Arab Competitiveness Report highlights three types of challenges that need to be addressed in order to improve competitive performance and maintain the growth momentum among the GCC states. These include educational reform, investment in research and development (R&D) and an overhaul of the organization and regulation of the labor markets. Improvements within these areas would both address the high unemployment, the need to diversify the economies and the current mismatch between the educational skills and the needs of the private sector (World Economic Forum 2007, 16).

**Table 3.5 Gulf countries ranking on basic requirements,
efficiency enhancers and innovation factors in
the Global Competitiveness Index, 2009/10**

Country	Overall rank	Basic requirements	Efficiency enhancers	Innovation factor
Qatar	22	17	28	36
UAE	23	9	21	25
Saudi Arabia	28	30	38	33
Bahrain	38	22	44	60
Kuwait	39	40	63	64
Oman	41	25	53	52
US	2	28	1	1

Source: World Economic Forum 2009: data extracted from the tables pp. 14–15.

In summary, all of the GCC states improved their ranking on the various competitive indexes over the last four years. This is due to progress made through economic or institutional reforms, but is not solely limited thereto. Their much-improved economic standing is also an explanation of their successes. From the more narrowly defined and more business – specific Doing Business index we saw that all of the states do relatively well in comparison with 183 states. Saudi Arabia (despite the suspected data) and the UAE have progressed considerably. However, Kuwait and Oman have been slow reformers and lost ground to more active reforms. Bahrain and Qatar are well placed at 20 and 39 in the ranking. From those figures, it can be concluded that a reform process in the direction of a more production-oriented economy is taking place.

Turning now to the issue of the success of attracting Foreign Direct Investments (FDI). One of the aims for the outcomes of reforms both in the business environment and in societies at large is an increase in FDI. Such investments are deemed important even in capital surplus states, because FDI brings both capital, but equally or even more importantly, access to new technology and modern management methods (Hill 1999).

The total amount of FDI flowing into the six GCC states has been rising significantly. In monetary terms, the increase has been made from a meagre $392 million in 2000 to approximately $63 billion in 2008. In other words, the volume has increased approximately 160 times over just eight years. Furthermore, we can see that essentially two states are responsible for this increase: Saudi Arabia and UAE. The latter experienced a gradual increase in FDI starting in 2002 while FDI inflow to Saudi Arabia has experienced a steep increase from 2004 onward. In 2008, Saudi Arabia attracted approximately $38 billion while the UAE attracted $14 billion in FDI. Bahrain and Qatar and to a significantly smaller extent Oman and Kuwait attracted the remaining $11 billion in FDI.

Table 3.6 FDI inflows to the Gulf countries, 2000–2009

	2000	2001	2002	2003	2004	2005	2006	2007	2008
Bahrain	364	80	217	517	865	1,049	2,915	1,756	1,794
Kuwait	16	-175	4	-68	24	234	122	123	56
Oman	83	5	122	26	111	1,538	1,688	3,125	2,928
Qatar	252	296	624	625	1,199	2,500	3,500	4,700	6,700
Saudi Arabia	183	504	453	778	1,942	12,097	18,293	24,318	38,223
United Arab Emirates	-506	1,184	1,314	4,256	10,004	10,900	12,806	14,187	13,700
Total Gulf countries (in million US dollars)	391	1,894	2,734	6,134	14,145	28,318	39,324	48,209	63,400

If FDI is recalculated on a per-capita basis, moreover, we find that Qatar is the by far largest recipient of FDI within the GCC group. It attracted $5.3 million per-capita while UAE attracted only $3.1, Saudi Arabia $1.5 and Oman attracted approximately $1 million per-capita.[10] These significant increases in FDI flows are likely the outcome of deliberate policies to attract such investments. These encompass not only improvements in the regulatory environment around foreign investments but, probably of more significance, the opening up for investment possibilities. In 2002, the UAE spearheaded by Dubai became the first place in the Gulf region to legalize foreign ownership of property under the so-called freehold arrangement (*Gulf News* 2007). In a similar fashion by 2004, Saudi Arabia allowed for international companies to invest in the oil sector, in public utilities (electricity and water production) and in infrastructure. Such policies evidently attracted investments in an international setting of high liquidity. It is important to note that the significant rise in the influx of FDI to the region does not necessarily contribute to the creation of a stronger private sector, as we would normally expect. For example, Saudi Arabia's FDI has contributed to oil production, public sector companies and public utilities. Data on the concrete distribution of FDI on private and public companies is however unavailable.

Conclusion

Is it possible to identify a shift towards a more production oriented economic model among the GCC states? The short answer is that 'it appears so.' From the limited available data on economic reforms it can be concluded that the Gulf Arab states seem to be in the process of reforming their economies and thus preparing their economies to become more diversified, and probably also more reliant on the private sector.

---

10 Calculated by the author from FDI data (UNCTAD 2009) and population data (UN population Division 2009).

However, a closer look at the data reveals significant differences among the GCC states. When it comes to easing the procedures around setting up, running and closing a business, both Saudi Arabia and the UAE stand out with the most intensive reform programs, even though the Saudi reform program might overstate the actual reforms implemented. Kuwait and Oman have moved to a lower rank on the indexes due to their slower pace of reforms. The analysis of the FDI data in both absolute terms and on a per-capita basis confirms the impression that Qatar, UAE, Saudi Arabia and Oman are opening up their economies and have made the latter more attractive to international investors through a reform process.

The ranking of the GCC states in the Global Competitiveness Index shows a much more uniform pattern than the rankings of the Doing Business index. Collectively, the GCC has been improving over the last four years as a result of both an improved macroeconomic standing, which has been the product of high oil revenues, and also significantly from sound policies aimed at reforming the business environment, infrastructure investments, economic diversification, combating inflation, among other policies. Judging by these changes, it can be concluded that the GCC states have been conducting economic and institutional reforms that seem to be laying the groundwork for a production-oriented economy. While this is certainly an important initial step for the states in reaching their stated aims of diversifying their economies and revitalizing the role of the private sector, rolling back 30 to 50 years of rentierism is not a process that can be either easily or hastily done.

So while one should not draw the conclusion that the allocation state model has been displaced by a production oriented model, it is fair to argue that a real process has been initiated, which – given the right political and economic circumstances – might eventually lead to the adoption of a more production oriented economic model.

Chapter 4

The Evolution of Rent Recycling During Two Booms in the Gulf Arab States: Business Dynamism and Societal Stagnation[1]

Steffen Hertog

Introduction

Rentier states are not static systems. Even in a hypothetical ceteris paribus scenario in which levels of rent accruing to government remained unchanged over time, agents who receive the redistributed rents would have the option to accumulate them over time, resulting in progressively higher levels of resources relative to current income and hence a relatively higher level of independence from the state's current allocative decisions. This fact has gone largely unrecognized in the rentier state literature, which treats rentier states as static entities.[2]

The objective of the present chapter is to demonstrate the implications of this near-deterministic process for the political economy of the GCC monarchies, cases with a long and fairly uninterrupted tradition of rent recycling. It is elaborated against the background of important changes in the rent recycling process itself which serve to reinforce the autonomy of rent accumulators.

This chapter will focus mostly on the GCC private sector, as this includes the social agents which have benefited from rent recycling the most. It will compare its role during the boom-bust cycle of the 1970s and 1980s with that of the 2000s, analyzing shifting mechanisms of autonomy from and dependence on the state. A shorter section will contrast the experience of business with that of the general national populations in the GCC, which differ from the rent-accumulating capitalist class who have mostly acted as rent consumers, explaining their stagnant position in the GCC political economies.

Based on this comparison of accumulation *vis-à-vis* consumption, the chapter will expound how the evolving linkages of business in the international political economy, and the absence thereof for the population at large, impact their respective

---

1   I would like to thank the participants of the CIGI workshop on the geo-economic of the Gulf for their comments on a first version of this paper and Nathan Hodson for his help with data.
2   For one important exception discussing rent accumulation and professionalization in the Saudi private sector, see Luciani (2005).

negotiating position *vis-à-vis* the GCC rentier regimes. I will conclude with some speculation on how these strategic positions might affect the conflict over the main socio-economic issue that will have to be negotiated between regimes, capitalists and the national population in the coming years: the integration of nationals into private labour markets.

Saudi Arabia will serve as the main empirical example, but departing from (quite) different baselines, the same causal story expounded here also applies to other GCC states, which will be discussed more briefly.

The Private Sector During Two Booms

During the 2003–08 oil boom, oil prices in real terms reached peaks comparable to those of the 1970s/1980s boom period. With GCC production levels during both periods roughly comparable, rents accruing to GCC governments returned to the heights of the first boom. But while during the 1970s the oil sector crowded out most of the rest of the economy in relative terms, during the second boom period, both government and private sector have kept larger shares of GDP (see figures 4.1 and 4.2 for Saudi and Kuwaiti data). On the face of it, even in boom times, the non-oil economy remains more important. Much of the rest of the chapter will demonstrate that economic activity by government as well as business has undergone important changes also in qualitative terms.

Even if the private sector is relatively larger, it could still rely mostly on rent-driven government spending. Could it be that the larger share of business in GDP is simply driven by larger government activities? Figure 4.3 provides for a first eyeball test of this hypothesis on the Saudi case. We see that in the 1970s and 1980s, the higher oil price was correlated with a relative expansion of typical 'boom-time' sectors like construction and ownership of dwellings. The immediate transmission mechanism probably was that oil prices allowed for higher levels of current and capital government spending as evidenced in Figure 4.4.[3]

During the second boom period in the 2000s, however, the composition of GDP has changed much less drastically. This seems to indicate that higher oil prices and greater government spending do not lead to the kinds of sectoral distortions witnessed three decades before (and sometimes associated with the Dutch Disease in terms of an unsustainable boom in non-tradables). The impressionistic reading is that the structure of the economy is more robust to short-term demand shocks and on a steadier growth path. On the same grounds, the recent boom, even if it should be followed by a period of reduce spending, is unlikely to be followed by a collapse of real estate-related sectors as happened in the second half of the 1980s in the wake of rapidly decreasing government project spending.

---

3   Current spending is used mostly for salaries, transfers, subsidies, operations and maintenance, while capital spending goes into physical assets such as roads, building, machinery etc.

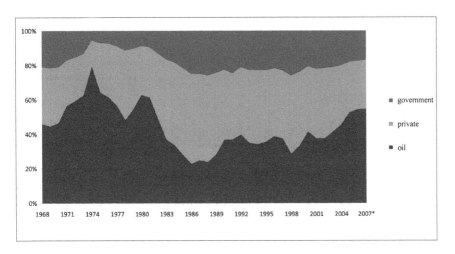

Figure 4.1 Composition of Saudi GDP (current prices)
Source: SAMA.

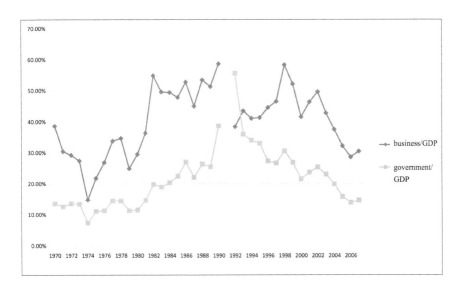

Figure 4.2 Composition of Kuwaiti GDP (current prices)
Source: Central Statistics Office.

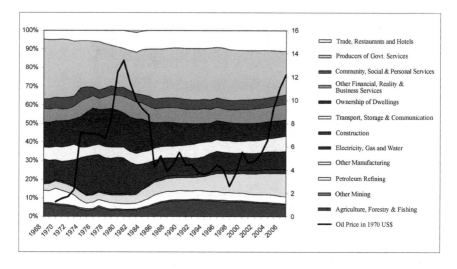

Figure 4.3 Oil price vs. composition of non-oil GDP in Saudi Arabia
Source: SAMA.

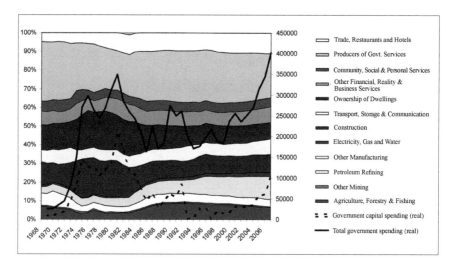

Figure 4.4 GDP composition vs. government spending in Saudi Arabia
Source: SAMA.

The evidence is graphical, not statistical. Moreover, while the relative composition of economic activity might be less affected by state spending, perhaps the absolute level of business activity still is? Has the impact of state spending on business growth changed from the previous boom to the recent one?

Impressionistically, the absolute size of the private sector seems to closely follow state spending in both Saudi Arabia and Kuwait:

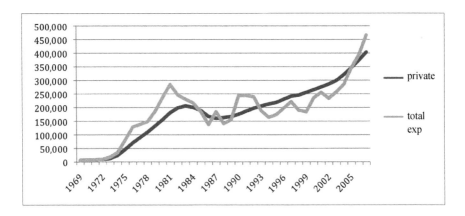

Figure 4.5 Private sector contribution to Saudi GDP vs. total government expenditure
Source: SAMA.

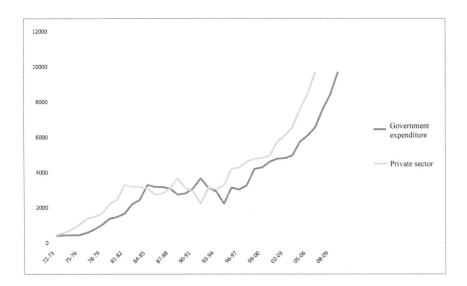

Figure 4.6 Private sector contribution to Kuwaiti GDP vs. total government expenditure (million KD)
Source: Central Statistical Office.

But to gauge the causal impact of state spending – at least in the short run – we rather have to look at growth rates. Figure 4.7 seems to indicate that Saudi business growth tracked the growth of state spending only up to the mid-1980s, with subsequent fluctuations in state spending affecting business growth rates much less.

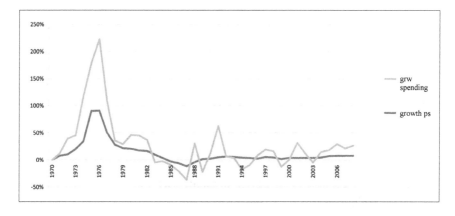

Figure 4.7 Growth rates of Saudi private sector contribution to GDP and total government

To make sure annual fluctuations do not obscure mid-term effects, we can look at a three-year moving averages of spending and business growth (Figure 4.8):

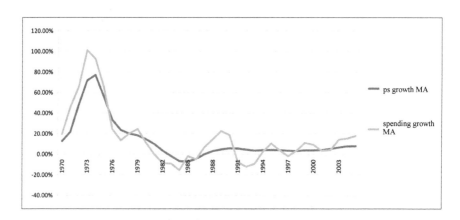

Figure 4.8 Three year moving averages of growth rates, Saudi private sector contribution to GDP vs. total government expenditures

The same pattern seems to be obtained: a tight correlation during the first boom period and a much steadier, more autonomous private sector growth path after the mid-1980s. The graphical evidence for Kuwait is less clear when it comes to year-on-year changes:

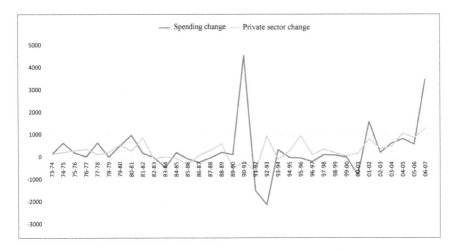

Figure 4.9 Annual changes of Kuwaiti private sector contribution to GDP and total government expenditure

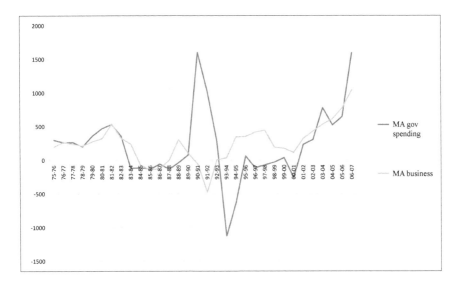

Figure 4.10 Three year moving averages of growth rates, Kuwaiti private sector contribution to GDP vs. total government expenditures

The pattern for three-year moving averages is somewhat clearer: An obvious correlation seems to emerge in the pre-Gulf war period, while the correlation afterwards is less straightforward. The argument has, again, been impressionistic. Ordinary least squares time series tests on the Saudi data show, however, that the short-term per unit impact of change in government spending on business activity is indeed much lower in the post-1985 period than in the 1971–1985 boom era. This is true for both current and capital spending, and for the impact of the two on both total business activity as well as on individual sub-sectors such as the ones illustrated in figures 4.3 and 4.4. Interestingly, the impact of the 'lagged' change in business growth is much larger in the post-1986 period, i.e. in any given year, business growth is strongly influenced by where it was in the preceding year. There hence seems to be a much stronger, continuous momentum of business growth that is less affected by short-term fluctuations of state spending.

In the Kuwaiti case, the statistical evidence is somewhat weaker, but again in line with the results of the 'eyeball' tests on the above graphs: Year-on-year changes in government spending seems to have no statistically measurable effect on business growth either before 1989 or after 1993,[4] possibly because the Kuwaiti budget year is out of sync with the calendar year in which GDP figures are reported. By contrast, the three-year moving averages however are strongly correlated, but more so before 1989 than after 1993. The general conclusion seems to be that the immediate impact of state spending on business growth has attenuated since the 1980s. Existing statistical research on (somewhat older) Saudi and Omani data reaches similar conclusions (Kireyev 1998; Treichel 1999).

The Private Sector and the Demand Structure of the GCC Economies

Although it is likely that long-term business growth is driven by government spending to a significant extent, business is less sensitive to short- to mid-term fiscal policy decisions. As most politics – particularly of fiscal issues – is negotiated in the short term, this appears to be an important finding. Business is no more all-dependent on government spending decisions and seems to cater to a more significant private demand at least in the short run.

Private demand in the GCC rent economies is a curious beast, as much of it is in fact indirectly fed by the state: In most cases, the majority of national employees – who tend to be the best earners among the total population – are on the public payroll, and public sector salaries with average are better than private sector salaries on all levels of education.

---

4   Due to the Iraqi invasion in 1990 and the idiosyncrasies of post-war rebuilding (high state expenditure accompanied by business caution), the years 1990–92 have been left out of the tests.

The statistical results on Saudi Arabia cited above indicate that even current spending – which consists to a significant extent of wage spending – has a much reduced impact on business growth in the post-1986 period. This could be for two reasons:

1. As current spending in the last three decades has grown fairly gradually, without much variation in its growth rate, its potential impact is not picked up well by statistical tests, which would require more variation on the current spending as independent variable; or
2. Current spending feeds to business activity mostly through the (re-) spending of salaries, which is not instant and does not track current spending closely in the short-run, but rather smoothens it over time.

Both reasons are quite plausible but cannot be established with certainty. The more certain, and arguably more important, variable is the ratio of GCC governments' current to capital spending, which in the 2000s has been considerably larger than during the 1970s boom, when payrolls were smaller and public sector maintenance costs lower, meaning that most available money could be spent on projects.

Much of business growth during the 1970s was indeed driven by government capital spending, which is usually translated into business activity through direct procurement of capital goods and various types of contracting arrangements. While GCC capital spending has increased again with the second oil boom, it is in most cases still much smaller relative to current spending than in the 1970s, the lion's share of which in turn consists of civil servants' salaries (see Figure 4.11).[5]

The extent to which the Saudi government in particular is willing to distribute resources through public sector salaries becomes salient when we look at the share of Saudi civil servants in the total population (Figure 4.12), which has continuously increased since the 1970s, despite the rapid growth of the population from about 6 million in 1974 to 18 million in 2008 – and despite uninterrupted fiscal deficits from the 1983 to the year 2000. Even in 2009, when government capital spending had picked up strongly, a full 43 percent of total government spending were estimated to go to salaries.[6] By contrast, the international average is closer to one fifth of total spending; for mid-income countries, the category in which Saudi Arabia has traditionally been placed, it is even lower (IMF 1995).

The majority of Saudis still work in the public sector. Expatriates in Saudi Arabia, which constitute about a third of the total population, are mostly employed in the private sector. This means that their consumer spending is mostly derived from private salaries. Average salaries of expatriates however are much lower than those of Saudis – less than a third on average according to Ministry of Labour data – and they tend to save and remit abroad a large share thereof, making them less

---

5   The one case with the highest ratio, Qatar, is incidentally the one with the least developed private sector and an economy that is mostly driven by state activities.
6   In the austere late 1990s, the figure was above 50 percent (Sfakianakis 2009, 7).

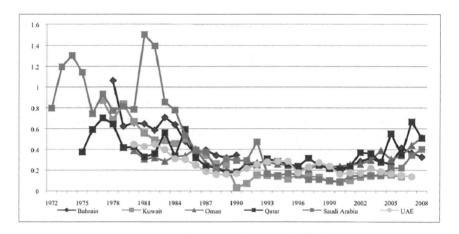

Figure 4.11 Ration of government capital to current expenditures in the GCC

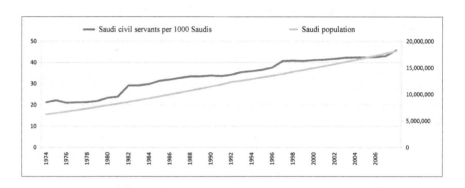

**Figure 4.12 Density of Saudi civil service employment (left-hand side)
vs. total population (right-hand side)**

important for consumer demand on the Saudi market. The situation in other GCC countries is comparable.

Given better pay and local recycling of public sector salaries, consumer demand in Saudi Arabia hence is still predominantly fed through state employment. The official figure of about 900,000 public sector employees is slightly larger than the official figure of registered Saudi workers in the private sector. The former only includes individuals registered with the Ministry of Civil Service however; the actual number of state employees, including security services and the religious sector, has been estimated as twice as large, at 1.8 million individuals (Sfakianakis 2008).

This means that even if government spending decisions have a much attenuated short-term impact on business growth patterns, indirectly most of the demand on the Saudi private market still is fed through state spending. The economic character and political implications of this spending have changed significantly, however: First, current spending tends to fluctuate much less dramatically, as most of it is on de facto non-discretionary items.[7] While the Saudi government managed to reduce capital spending radically in the 1980s (see Figure 4.11), thereby wreaking havoc with the Saudi contracting sector, it did not manage to do the same with politically sensitive current spending – which directly affects the livelihood of the Saudi populace through salaries, subsidies and public services (see Luciani in this volume).

So even if we ignore the statistical results cited above and assume that reduced current spending could theoretically have a strong negative impact on business growth, in the absence of an existential fiscal crisis, actual current spending is likely to remain on a high plateau. Capital spending will probably remain subject to stronger fluctuations, but is less important for business than in the 1980s. A repeat of a business crisis of 1980s proportions therefore remains unlikely for many years.

The second important implication of the different state spending mix is that although the GCC economies might fundamentally remain driven by rent-fuelled state spending, the state tends to have less control over how the rents are recycled: While capital spending almost by definition requires discriminatory decisions of which private contractors to choose, and which ones not to, at the point when public salaries get recycled into the private economy through diffuse, private consumer decisions, the regime has much less control over which private actors benefit. So while significant segments of the general population remain directly dependent on the state through its (sometimes discretionary) employment decisions and salary payments, much of business is one step removed from direct distributional decisions by the state, instead catering to private if ultimately state-caused demand.

Hence, the GCC monarchies still are rentier economies; but politically speaking, there is less of a direct rentier relationship between government and business. This is a distinction of degrees and the extent to which direct state dependence has been attenuated differs strongly between the six countries, arguably most in Saudi Arabia and least in Abu Dhabi and Qatar. The trend since the 1970s has been the same everywhere, however. To the extent that consumer spending is more important for business than direct contracting with the state, markets are likely to be more competitive and contestable due to the diffuse and less political nature of consumer decisions.

This is arguably one of the main processes that has led to the managerial maturation of the main Saudi business groups that survived the 1980s bust, and which has prepared the leaders among them to compete in neighboring markets and, sometimes, overseas. None of this is to say that a large business group could thrive in the GCC if it drew the ire of regime leaders; there remain many non-fiscal, bureaucratic and regulatory instruments with which regimes can influence a

---

7   On the 'stickiness' of entitlement spending in Saudi Arabia over the decades see chapter 4 of Hertog (2010).

company's fortune. Nonetheless, today it is a lot easier to compete when the ruling elite is *indifferent* to a business group, as the state contracts traditionally used to mete out favours have ceased to be the sine qua non of success.

Capital Accumulation and the Private Sector's Return to Public Services

We have shown that structures of rent distribution by GCC regimes have changed significantly since the 1970s oil boom. Business at least in the short run seems to be less vulnerable to fiscal policy decisions than it used to be, for at least three reasons: reduced public spending, elasticity of business growth, more stable government spending patterns, and the predominance of current spending, which feeds into business growth diffusely and indirectly rather than through direct, discretionary regime decisions. Consequently, business has significantly improved its relative autonomy.

There is a further, more general and less contingent mechanism through which business has improved its autonomy over time: its gradual accumulation of capital by virtue of its position in the rent recycling circuit. Due to its generality, this mechanism is probably the most relevant for the broader debate about changes in rentier state structures (see also Hvidt in this volume).

Even if we presumed that rent-seeking and distribution structures remained fixed, the distribution of resources in a rentier system is bound to change over time: While the allocation state is forced to continuously disburse its largesse, the recipients of state-provided rents can in principle accumulate resources to the extent that they receive rents above their mundane consumption needs. In the absence of major social unrest and existential economic crises, privileged rent recipients should hence become progressively wealthier, while the state's fiscal situation is subject to the vagaries of the oil price and of past, politically locked-in spending decisions.

Note that while state income in 'production states' will tend to grow with the riches of society thanks to a system of taxation, this is not the case in rentier systems, where in principle, and paradoxically, societal riches can outgrow the resources of the state. Conspicuous consumption and bad investment decisions mean that this process of private rent accumulation is not automatic for every individual rent recipient, but given basic political and socio-economic stability, it is hard to see how it should not obtain in aggregate and in the long run. It has important political ramifications.

Let us imagine a business partaking in the rent recycling process over several decades and, for the sake of simplicity, let us assume that the government-provided rents accruing to it on an annual basis are stable over time.[8] Let us further

---

8   This is less unreasonable an assumption than it might seem given the instant riches created in many cases by the 1970s boom and the long-term privileges and stability that many businesses have enjoyed subsequently.

also assume that the annual profit of the business is re-invested, either locally or internationally, but the annual returns on these reinvested profits are used for consumption purposes by the business owner; the two hence cancel each other out.[9] In such a scenario, after a few decades of rent-seeking, the immediate access to rents would be much less important than in the first year. The returns on the total accumulated assets after three decades – equivalent to 30 years of profits – are very likely higher than the annual, rent-based returns of the business.

This is of course a highly stylized example, but it illustrates the basic process at work: The longer one accumulates rent, the less important access to the government-supported rent recycling process becomes, especially if one lives frugally, which many Gulf Arab business families do. It also illustrates the main variables determining how quickly this process unfolds in practice: levels of private consumption, rates of return, as well as changes over time in rent flows (decreasing rent flows – as after 1983 – accelerate it, while increasing rent flows – after 2000 – slow it down or reverse it).

Above we have argued that accumulation, though still rooted in rent recycling processes, has increasingly been a result of businesses' catering to private consumer decisions. This augments the autonomy of businesses from government to the extent that they operate on private, generally more competitive markets. The accumulation argument presented here is more general in the sense that it applies no matter whether the rent circuit is accessed thanks to competitive activities or through pure, government-oriented rent-seeking. Even for pure rent-seekers, rents can become less important over time if they incrementally stash away their returns, preferably in overseas accounts.

In fact, many Gulf business families have kept much of their money in the local economies and have reinvested it actively – indeed, Luciani (2005) finds a relatively high level of patriotism among the Gulf business classes. This corporate reinvestment process, together with the increasing orientation to private markets, has led to a gradual professionalization of many business groups. The increasing contribution of the private sector to national gross fixed capital formation (see Figure 4.13) is a natural result of this process. Much of this investment goes into fairly straightforward real estate projects that require limited expertise, but an increasing share has gone into more demanding projects that had been almost the sole domain of the public sector.

Outside of the trade sector, the rentier state had steamrolled over traditional business activities soon after the onset of oil production, marginalizing or putting an end to the private provision of education, health, infrastructure, water and electricity services that had started to unfold in the pre-oil age.

---

9 This would of course mean passing from a very frugal initial existence to a lavish life further down the road; in a more realistic scenario, the business owner would first consume more than the returns on reinvested capital, but as his reinvested capital grows, sometime reach the point where consumption would be less than returns on reinvested capital. Such nuances are irrelevant for the basic argument.

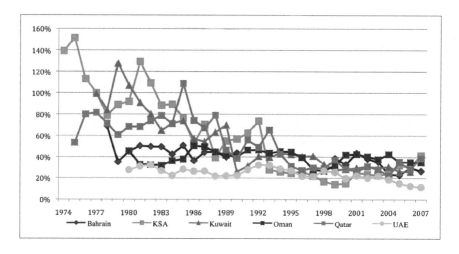

Figure 4.13 Share of government capital spending in national gross fixed capital formation
Source: ESCWA, National Sources, IMF.

Since the 1980s, and more so the 1990s and 2000s, Gulf business has been gradually returning to such public service and infrastructure provision, having acquired capital resources as well as managerial capacity to once again rival the state apparatus. The independent water and power projects, private schools, universities and hospitals that have been burgeoning all over the region are testimony to this gradual rebalancing of capacities. In several service sectors, veritable multi-national enterprises have emerged in the Gulf, including Zain in telecoms or Agility and Aramex in logistics.

The 2008 international financial crisis has led to the cancellation or postponement of many private projects, as businesses became risk-averse and local banks even more so, but it has not reversed the fundamental trend towards private provision. Governments remain committed to the increasing delegation of public service functions to the local capitalist class. Full state funding for recent utility projects during the crisis has been explicitly framed as a stopgap measure to give way again to public-private partnerships once the storm has been weathered.

The competition for utility partnerships and public service licenses has generally become stronger and even if the playing field is not fully leveled, no local business groups can hope to obtain a major deal unless it brings significant expertise to the table. While short-term direct dependence of business on government spending has decreased, government in turn has developed a greater need for the cooperation of the private sector, reflecting a gradual but discernible shift of the respective political bargaining positions.

The Private Sector's Exit Option

In a world of international capital mobility, capitalist accumulation in the GCC has a further political dimension that works out in favour of business: The 'exit option' for private capital in the GCC has become much more important since the 1980s.[10] Private players can threaten to withdraw their resources from local markets if they are unhappy with local policy, and the more important these resources are relative to the current income created by the quotidian rent circuit, the more credible this threat is. It can be 'instrumental' in the sense that businesses and private sector associations explain to governments the impact that undesirable regulations have on their willingness to invest, as has happened repeatedly through policy statements emerging from business meetings such as the Riyadh Economic Forum. It can also simply be 'structural' in the sense that businesses silently vote with their feet by withdrawing or not reinvesting capital, even if this is not intended as a political statement.

In the 2000s, GCC governments have explicitly recognized this threat and bargaining chip. Consequently, capital flight to neighboring countries and the risks of falling behind in terms of regulatory reform are often referred to in public reform statements as well as internal policy reports (for example, see SAGIA 2003). In this context, Dubai – despite all its excesses – is often mentioned as a model and benchmark and has indeed become a haven for GCC business players seeking refuge from heavy regulation in their home markets. Probably the highest-profile case of a (mostly) private company voting with its feet however was the relocation of telecoms giant Zain's headquarters from Kuwait to Bahrain in 2007: a slap in the face of the Kuwaiti government which had been struggling to update its business regulations at the same pace as its neighbours. A similar move by an enterprise of this scale would have been inconceivable two decades earlier.

As Gulf business families' ratio of overseas resources relative to local current income has grown over time, some of the large families have taken to actively managing their overseas resources and are increasingly engaged in foreign direct investment. The more this internationalization proceeds, the less potent threats and demands from local governments are. There are no good estimates of the total volume of the Gulf's private overseas assets, but they are clearly much more significant this time around than during the first boom and are increasingly rivalling sovereign wealth funds' overseas assets.

Behind closed doors, some major players have been heard saying that they are ready to abandon their local operations altogether if the business environment turns too inhospitable. This is effectively what some business actors in more less-business friendly (semi-) rentier environments such as Libya and Syria have already done, where parts of the bourgeoisie keep and manage their resources almost completely overseas. The rate of capital repatriation is effectively a vote of confidence in the local political system.

---

10   On the concept of 'exit' see Hirschman 1970.

Private GCC capital has also become a factor of soft power in the wider Middle East region; it has played an important role in the economic revival in Jordan and Egypt, and some of the more venturesome Gulf groups are committing increasing resources to the capital-starved Syrian real estate, industrial and banking markets (see Momani in this volume). Investment agencies of poorer Middle East states have taken to organizing roadshows in the Gulf to attract Gulf capital to their liberalizing markets.

This process of regional integration has been put on hold by the 2008 international financial crisis, but is likely to resume with time passing. Demographic growth and infrastructural deficits, combined with an immature local capitalist class, make neighboring countries a natural destination for Gulf capital. The channels for intra-MENA capital movements are far more variegated than in the 1980s or 1990s: Most currencies have become convertible; most service and manufacturing sectors have been opened for foreign investment; banks and utilities are slated for privatization; stock markets have been created or re-opened; and a regional private equity industry as well as a new class of regionally-oriented investment funds have come into being.

All these domestic and regional factors have given business a stronger role in economic policy-making; consultative structures between government and business have become increasingly formalized through the integration of chambers of commerce and individual business representatives in the debate of drafts laws. This does not mean that business is ready to play a political role in a strict sense, however: It appears to have no interest in political change whatsoever and largely abstains from electoral politics in the cases where meaningful elections take place. Even in economic policy matters, it remains a policy-taker on most issues, usually acting as a veto player rather than developing its own policy proposals. It tends to leave the development of new sectors to less risk-averse state-owned enterprises. Despite its general managerial maturation, its own governance structures – just as those of GCC ruling elites – have changed little at the core, which remain family-dominated and informal in most cases.

Perhaps the absence of major state-business fault lines and the generally pro-capitalist policies of GCC regimes explain this relative passivity. In the case of a major conflict, however, a professionalized capitalist class with large overseas capital resources would have a very different bargaining position compared to the 1970s.

The one policy area in which serious state-business conflict appears to be brewing is that of labour nationalization: With state bureaucracies overstaffed and current spending on wages already locked in on a very high level, regimes demand that businesses share more of the burden of employing nationals. With higher reservation wages, much better de facto labour rights and little by way of practical education, the employment of nationals threatens to impose a significant burden on a private sector used to an almost unlimited influx of cheap and pliable foreign workers. Due to continuing demographic growth and pervasive underemployment of nationals, the battle over labour nationalization is likely to be the main socio-economic issue for decades to come.

As the problem is only going to become more pressing, labor nationalization could prod GCC businesses into serious collective policy bargaining. Structurally, forcing the employment of nationals on private business is equivalent to taxation: It increases business costs, while alleviating pressure on the public purse, which needs to spend less on over-employment of idle citizens.[11] This logic, independent of whether business players are fully aware of it or not, makes labour nationalization a fundamental challenge to existing rentier state structures and will make it a highly political issue. Although no formal imposition of taxes would have to take place, successful nationalization of labour markets could to some extent make 'production states' out of the GCC allocative states, through: a) a de facto shift of the fiscal burden from government to business; and b) through the growth of 'real' private demand, i.e. a demand fed by wages that are paid to increasing numbers of nationals in the private sector. This would in turn attenuate even the indirect and long-run dependence of local business on government spending.

It is not clear what, if anything, business could demand in return for a larger contribution to national employment. A deeper integration into policy-making structures with a more formalized veto role, and the delegation of certain regulatory functions to business associations are conceivable demands. Gulf business would however have to get its own organizational act together before any such steps could be undertaken. In any case, if nationalization is imposed in a ham-fisted and top-down way – as it has been thus far – it is more likely to lead to capital flight than to any new political dispensation between state and business. In this sense, the exit option of Gulf capital could have important economic consequences, but a limited impact on political outcomes.

The Populace during Two Booms:
The Political Economy of Current Expenditure

We have seen that Gulf business today has a position in the local and international political economy that is fundamentally different from the one it occupied in the 1970s. This is largely attributable to its opportunity to accumulate rents over a prolonged period. The following section will show that the position of most other rent recipients in the GCC countries has remained static by comparison: As the general population have acted mostly as rent consumers, their position in the Gulf political economy is essentially the same as three decades ago.

---

11   This is the case independent of whether nationalization is enforced by sectoral or national quotas, by limiting certain jobs to nationals, through quantitative limits on foreign labour, or through fees on imported workers (while only the latter amounts to formal taxation).

The bulk of the GCC national population remains directly dependent on the state through public employment and its consumption of various subsidized goods and services. Table 4.1 shows that in most cases, the majority of employed nationals in 2005 were still on the public payroll, while expatriates dominated private labour markets. Low-quality education and uncompetitive wage expectations keep most GCC nationals out of the private labor market: International education benchmarking exercises such as PISA and TIMSS have placed the GCC countries considerably below the global average and far below other countries with comparable per capita GDP.[12] At the same time, they have to compete on a de facto internationalized labour market where low-skilled expatriate workers earn as little as $150 per month. While international capital market liberalization has by and large benefited the local business class, the integration of the GCC into the international labour market has had disastrous consequences for national labour.

Against this background, the paternal GCC state still feels compelled to care for its citizens through public jobs and other types of handouts. However, at least in Saudi Arabia, Bahrain, Oman and the poorer emirates in the UAE, resources today are insufficient to provide a job to every male national of working age. Dependency ratios – the number of individuals depending on one salary – remain high, as relying on relatives' salaries is often preferred to entering the private labour market. As real wages in the civil service have often eroded in the course of the 1980s and 1990s, most families are left with limited savings, increasing their day-to-day dependence on government munificence.

Attempts in the 1980s and 1990s to increase utility and public service prices have met stiff business and popular resistance, meaning that most services are still provided free or below cost. In contrast to GCC business, the rentier bargain between GCC regimes and their populations at large remains unchanged, in terms of both the mechanisms of distribution and the level of dependence. Paradoxically, the continuing dependence of a growing population on government spending increases the short-term autonomy of the private sector, as it implies distribution of rents through salaries rather than through capital spending.

International economic integration of the GCC has not worked out to the general citizenry's advantage: While suffering from international labour competition, it has no credible exit option. This is the case with labour in most other parts of the world as well – but different from non-rentier countries, national labour inputs are not needed for most production processes in the Gulf. National labour's economic negotiating power *vis-à-vis* the GCC regimes is therefore restricted.

The second oil boom has tempted most GCC regimes to increase redistribution to national consumers: Wages, pensions and welfare payments have been increased; in 2006, Saudi Arabia further decreased its petrol prices. This would not be a

---

12   PISA refers to the OECD's 'Programme for International Student Assessment' (PISA) which surveys reading, mathematical and scientific literacy levels; TIMSS is the 'Trends in International Mathematics and Science Study', which assesses student performance in math and science.

Table 4.1 Employed individuals in the GCC in 2005 ('000)

	Bahrain	Kuwait	Oman	Qatar	Saudi Arabia	UAE
Nationals	*106*	*319*	*208*	*64*	*1336*	*262*
% of total labor force	31	18	32	8	22	9
Private sector	72	43	99	9	623	70
Public sector	34	276	109	55	713	192
Expatriates	*231*	*1495*	*446*	*768*	*4809*	*2738*
% of total labor force	69	82	68	92	78	91
Private sector	227	1401	423	601	4739	2538
Public sector	3	94	23	167	70	200
Total labor force	*337*	*1814*	*654*	*832*	*6145*	*3000*
% of total population	47	61	26	71	27	63

worry if populations were still as small as during the 1970s boom. Population growth has been rapid however, putting distributional arrangements under strain at least in the lower-rent economies. GCC governments have generally been more cautious with their fiscal expansion during the 2000s boom, expanding government employment only modestly. But in fact, they have also had much less rents available *per national* than during the first boom. Figure 4.14 compares per capita oil rents in Saudi Arabia in current and real terms, showing that the annual resources available per capita in the 2000s have been about half of what they were in the 1970s and early 1980s.

Lower rents per capita will in turn increase the pressure on the relatively poorer GCC regimes to nationalize their private labour markets. It is here that the continuing dependence of national populations on current rent disbursals will come to haunt the private sector. For the time being, the reserves prudently accumulated during the 2000s have allowed GCC regimes to shield national populations from the 2008 international financial crisis – different from the business class, which due to its greater autonomy from the state and its larger and more internationally integrated resources was dealt a heavy blow.

In the mid-term, however, the rentier bargain for national populations in Saudi Arabia, Oman and Bahrain is likely to come under strain. The high levels of current spending that have been locked in over the years could create serious fiscal pressures within a decade or so. If Saudi Arabia continues to expand its spending by 3 percent a year and oil prices remain at 2006 levels, it will have expended all of its official reserves by 2026. If it continues to expand spending by 15 percent a year, as it has been doing during much of the 2000s, its reserves would be gone by 2015 already.

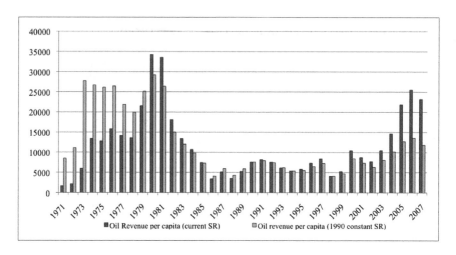

Figure 4.14 Oil income per Saudi citizen, nominal and real
Source: SAMA, based on Hodson 2010.

It is this long-term fiscal logic that could involve regime, population and business class in a renegotiation of the rentier bargain in which the state would provide a lesser share of national employment, the population would enter the private labour market in larger numbers, and business would content itself with a costlier and, in the short run, less qualified workforce. The GCC economies would move further away from the pure rentier model. In the ensuing give and take, the state would lose some political control, and population and business some of their privileges. For a long list of reasons elaborated above, business likely would have the strongest bargaining position

Chapter 5

Institutional Competition and Symbiosis in the Gulf: The Politics of Efforts to Establish an International Islamic Financial Policy Forum

Andrew Baker

Introduction

How and in what ways do political and institutional relationships, shape and influence the Gulf Arab states' engagement with the wider international political economy? How do different forms of political contestation drive strategic decisions on economic and financial development strategies in this region? This chapter seeks to shed light on these important questions through a case study of one particular institutional episode that the author has had direct exposure to.

On 28 February 2008, the United Arab Emirates' Ministry of Finance and Industry, issued a press release following a meeting of representatives from predominantly Gulf Cooperation Council (GCC) states, the Islamic Development Bank (IDB), and a range of other multi-lateral financing and standard setting bodies at the Movenpick Hotel, Bur Dubai. The statement announced that a proposal to establish an International Islamic Financial Policy Forum (IIFPF) would be presented to the annual meeting of the Islamic Development Bank (IDB) for formal approval in June 2008. However, the proposal to establish the IIFPF is yet to come to fruition and has been successfully opposed by central banks in the region and by the Islamic Financial Services Board (IFSB) based in Kuala Lumpur, Malaysia. The tale of the bid to establish an International Islamic Financial Policy Forum is emblematic of the Gulf Arab states' attempts to establish institutional leadership over the ultimate social purpose and defining characteristics of Islamic finance. It provides fascinating insights into the politics surrounding money, finance and economic development in the region. This chapter provides an account of the politics surrounding Gulf Arab states' efforts to establish an International Islamic Financial Policy Forum (IIFPF) emphasizing the contingent nature of Islamic finance and the perilous, ubiquitous and episodic nature of International Organization (IO) agency in the context of the Gulf Arab region.

The first section discusses the idea of an apex policy forum for Islamic finance. Section two covers the areas of contestation at the forefront of the proposal, including competing regional visions of Islamic finance; a geographical struggle between GCC countries and South East Asian economies, principally Malaysia, concerning global leadership in the field of Islamic finance; and institutional competition between the Islamic Financial Services Board located in Kuala Lumpur, Malaysia and the Islamic Development Bank located in Jeddah, Saudi Arabia, and between finance ministries and central banks in the GCC states. The final section of the chapter discusses the IDB's role as policy entrepreneur and considers the innovative agency IDB displayed in driving the proposal.

The Idea of an International Islamic Financial Policy Forum

Dr Mohammad Khalfan Bin Khirbash, the UAE Minister of State for Finance and Industry first mooted the idea of an International Islamic Financial Policy Forum in December 2006, although staff at the IDB had been considering such a proposal privately for some time. The proposal was submitted to the 32nd annual meeting of the Board of Governors of the Islamic Development Bank (IDB) in Dakar, Senegal on 29–30 May 2007. The Board instructed IDB officials to follow up with expert consultations and further studies before re-submitting recommendations to the next IDB annual meeting in 2008 in Jeddah. While the UAE government formally initiated the proposal, the real driving force behind the idea appeared to be the staff of the IDB, who cultivated the UAE government as a sponsor, or agent for the proposal, as formal IDB decision-making procedures required policy initiatives to be proposed by member states. Notably, the first reference to an agenda setting apex policy body is to be found in an internal IDB working paper dated November 2005. From the outset IDB officials were in the lead, formulating the rationale for and details of the proposal, while proactively seeking to mobilize a consensus in favor of the proposal amongst the organization's membership.

The Islamic Development Bank (IDB) is a 56-member country multi-lateral development-financing institution located in Jeddah, Saudi Arabia, with its own full-time salaried staff and secretariat, and has been in operation since 1975. The purpose of the Bank is to foster economic development and social progress of member countries and Muslim communities in accordance with *Shari'ah* law. The Bank participates in equity capital and grants loans for productive projects and enterprises, while granting financial assistance to member countries to fund other forms of social and economic development, and operates a special fund for assistance of Muslim communities in non-member countries. These functions are performed through the acceptance of deposits and the mobilization of financial resources through Shari'ah compatible modes. The Bank also provides training facilities for personnel engaged in economic development activities in member countries in an effort to ensure those activities conform to *Shari'ah*. Member countries pay a contribution to the capital of the Bank (currently 15 billion Islamic dinars, which is divided into shares of a value of 10,000 Islamic dinars each).

The aim of the UAE proposal was to create an 'apex policy forum' for Islamic finance, comprised of a relatively small group of finance ministers and central bank governors, to engage in what IDB officials described themselves in background documents as 'senior deliberative transgovernmentalism' modelled on the G-20 – a term derived from Baker (2006, 2009) on the interactions between senior finance ministry and central bank personnel. According to the IDB, apex policy forums forge consensus amongst like-minded agencies, who then act together to steer international policy in particular directions, by setting agendas and establishing priorities for a range of other decision-making bodies. For IDB, the putative Islamic financial architecture (the collection of markets, institutions and practices employed by governments, businesses and individuals) had developed in a somewhat ad hoc fashion and was characterized by the absence of a senior or apex agenda-setting body.

Some prominent examples of apex policy forums, in the context of global finance, include the G-7 and G-20 groups of finance ministers and central bank governors (Baker 2009, 2010). As argued elsewhere these apex policy forums enjoy powers of initiation, endorsement and veto (Baker 2008, 2009). Following deliberations between senior figures, these apex forums release statements or communiqués, which represent an effort to convey any collective consensus that exists amongst these groups of national officials on priorities, agendas and broad policy orientation. This activity represents the formulation of a collective political will among national authorities, who then strategically signal this to other governments, to markets, the financial press, but also to an array of other more specialist bodies and committees that make up the current global financial architecture – the IMF, World Bank, Basle Committee, IOSCO, the Joint Forum, the Financial Stability Forum, the Financial Action Task Force. In effect, apex policy forums reach normative and ethical judgments about what the global financial system should look like, how it should function and which values it should represent in its overall operation and organization. Apex policy forums use the seniority of their members and their status as representatives of sovereign authorities with jurisdiction over systemically significant territories, to essentially define the terms on which international financial governance is conducted, the language used, the assumptions on which it is based. Consequently, they set priorities and agendas for the entire global financial architecture. In this regard, apex policy forums seek to raise consciousness, set agendas, create networks and 'light fires under civil servants and bureaucrats' (Hodges 1998) so as to give a sense of urgency to their ongoing work. Ultimately, apex policy forums seek to reach agreement on certain strategic objectives and priorities that should inform the governance of finance. It was this role that IDB officials envisaged for an International Islamic Financial Policy Forum, as their analyses of the Islamic financial architecture revealed that there was no agenda setting equivalent of the G-20, for the niche Islamic financial services industry and its emerging architecture.

Two motivations appeared to be driving IDB officials. The first was the altruistic calculation that cross border policy challenges, such as the diversity of

Shari'ah related interpretation, standards and practices, have created uncertainty in structuring *Shari'ah* compliant cross-border transactions and product standardization, resulting in market segmentation that has worked against the development of an efficient functioning Islamic financial system and has retarded the further growth of the sector. One internal IDB working paper drew on the institutional economics of Douglas North to argue that 'unresolved foundational gaps' and 'persistent cross sectoral issues, including the lack of formal or informal functional relationships can be expected to increase transaction costs in the Islamic financial industry'. Some sort of apex oversight body it was believed could aid the further growth and development of Islamic finance, by acting as a catalyst to coordinate the task of addressing such discrepancies, and providing strategic direction to more functionally specialist bodies such as AAOIFI (Accounting and Auditing Organization for Islamic Financial Institutions – a private sector body located in Bahrain) with its focus on accounting and auditing, and IFSB with its focus on banking supervision. The second motivation reflected IDB's own status. A number of officials feared that a lack of strategic direction involving the absence of clear paradigmatic goals for Islamic finance could damage the reputation of the IDB, given that the IDB's mandate has been to assist and assume a leadership role in the development and promotion of the Islamic financial services industry and its various segments. From the perspective of Gulf Arab decision-makers and the IDB, the growth of Islamic finance had also been accompanied by a form of drift involving a lack of strategic direction and macro level purpose. An agenda setting body comprised of high level Gulf Arab political figures it was believed could give political urgency to the work of IDB, and provide the necessary political consent and crucial strategic direction required to achieve clearly defined objectives for Islamic finance. In other words, Gulf Arab and IDB officials calculated that the creation of an International Islamic Financial Policy Forum (IIFPF) could empower the institution by providing strategic direction, clear mandates and political endorsement for ongoing work, as well as identifying new issues and challenges that needed to be addressed and required political leadership. The proposed forum was intended to assist in the development of four pillars of an Islamic financial architecture: agreeing on strategic goals and priorities for Islamic finance; defining functional relationships; setting directions in developing functional specialization; and encouraging greater compliance with international standards and harmonization across countries. Consequently, the proposal that emerged from the experts consultative session in Dubai outlined the mandate of the International Islamic Financial Policy Forum as follows: to build cross border consensus on the strategic vision and priorities for Islamic finance; to encourage and consider support enabling policies that would align Islamic finance with the objectives of social and economic development; discuss policies to support public finance, microfinance, *Zakat*, *Awquaf* and private philanthropy as pro-poor instruments for promoting socio-economic development; facilitate the development of cross border mechanisms which could lead to cross-border *Shari'ah* convergence and standardization on the basis of *maqasid*; encourage functional and operational relationships between Islamic standard setting bodies and the relevant national authorities to facilitate adoption of standards. Ultimately, despite the success that Gulf Arab and IDB officials enjoyed in building an initial coalition of support amongst states for the proposal, in which IDB officials played the lead role in orchestrating a range of mainly GCC states, the proposal has not come to fruition. The impressive leg work and policy innovation of Gulf Arab and IDB officials was thwarted when Dr Khirbash, the UAE minister of finance, who had effectively acted as an agent of IDB, in agreeing to forward and sponsor the proposal, left office and was replaced by Obaid Humaid Al Tayer. New in post, Obaid Humaid Al Tayer was susceptible to political pressure from more experienced domestic colleagues. Following consultations with IFSB colleagues, the UAE Central Bank Governor Sultan Bin Nasser Al Suwaidi, pressed Al Tayer to withdraw as sponsor of the proposal. Once Al Tayer agreed to abandon plans to formally submit the proposal to the IDB board, the recommendations of the experts consultative session did not reach the annual meetings of the IDB in Jeddah for approval. IFSB opposition appeared to be motivated by a combination of institutional jealousy and not entirely rational fears of institutional competition, and possible concerns over some of the priorities the new forum was to be mandated to address, which did not fit entirely comfortably with its own vision of the principal challenges facing Islamic finance. Further, sections of this chapter will examine in closer detail the politics and patterns of power at work in this failed attempt to establish an International Islamic Financial Policy Forum.

Competing Visions of Islamic Finance?

The above narrative raises the key question – what was really at stake in the proposal to establish an International Islamic Financial Policy Forum, in relation to the future of the Islamic financial services industry as a whole, given the determined and concerted positions of some key actors? Finance, Philip Cerny once informed us, is the infrastructure of the infrastructure (Cerny 1993). Money and finance have an inherent fungible quality. It links economies and nations, lubricating cross border exchanges. As the recent 2008 international financial crisis has illustrated, the fungible quality of finance has also given it a contagious quality, which means problems in finance can easily spill across state borders, across sectors and into the real or productive economy. As political economists have long argued finance and the features and structures of a financial system can largely determine the characteristics of a society and its entire political economy (Zsyman 1983; Story and Walter 1998). This chapter rests on the observation that a financial system is also an expression of power relations and social purpose. If it were based on western political economy, such an assertion would be relatively straight forward and uncomplicated, and this was certainly something understood by luminaries such as John Maynard Keynes and J.K. Galbraith. But in an Islamic and Gulf Arab context such an assertion is less straightforward and requires further clarification.

My argument is that Islamic finance constitutes a strategic, structured, but contested field of action in which different visions and conceptions of the social purpose of Islamic finance compete for supremacy, and in which institutions also compete for supremacy, partly out of a concern with institutional or bureaucratic prominence, but also partly out of their attachment to these differing conceptions of the appropriate social purpose for Islamic finance. The case of the International Islamic Policy Forum proposal is in part a reflection of a Gulf Arab determination to realize their vision and concept of Islamic finance and has its roots in the region's self-identified claim to be the birthplace of Islam.

Islamic finance is a complex and arcane area to the uninitiated. Its basic concern is with the avoidance of usury (*riba*), or the payment of interest. It involves the structuring of a variety of complex financial products that substitute for the payment of interest in a variety of ways. The technical details of these practices and how they substitute the payment of interest is, I would suggest, less important than the rationale, justification and underlying social purpose accompanying them. However, this chapter is not the place for a detailed discussion of the nuances of Islamic finance. Because 'Islamic finance', or claims by financial institutions and banks to be offering 'Islamic financial services' are based on and derived from an interpretation of the teachings and writings of the Koran, and depend at least in part on the judgments of Islamic jurists or *fuqha* (experts on classical juris-prudence), Islamic finance itself is an inherently contested and contingent domain. For example, Bakar (2002) distinguishes between *Shariah* principles based on *maqasid*, objectives of Islamic law, and the practice of *tarjih*, where one perspective is preferred over another based on a more appealing or convincing argument. Therefore, disagreement is one of the defining features of Islamic finance.

Even when it comes to fundamentals of the size, scope and importance of Islamic finance, there is little in the way of a widely accepted consensus. The absence of reliable data sets on Islamic finance compounds this problem (El Gamal 2006). For some for example, Islamic finance is little more than a niche industry that remains a relatively minor part of the financial sectors of most Islamic countries and remains only a minor issue confronting these countries (El Gamal 2008). Perhaps unsurprisingly, in its role as champion and pioneer of Islamic finance, the staff of the Islamic Development Bank, have taken a quite different view. They point to over 240 institutions operating in 48 countries with total combined assets in excess of US$200 billion, with an estimated annual growth rate between 12–15 percent, and to estimates that suggest Islamic financial institutions will attract between 40 and 50 percent of all savings of the Muslim population in some areas, within the next few years. What is clear is that Islamic financial services have been growing and that growth has brought with it challenges and tensions that need to be resolved. My intention here is not overstate the size and significance of Islamic finance as a constituent part of the global financial system, or of the economies of Islamic countries, but to emphasize and draw attention to how Islamic finance is becoming a strategic battleground in which Gulf Arab states wish to lead. This struggle will in turn act to shape the question of what it is to be an Islamic society and the characteristics such a society should display, the relationship between state and market, the kind of economic and social development strategies to be pursued, and the competing projects and visions this entails. In other words, Islamic finance remains a contested domain that is integral to the future development trajectories and defining characteristics of Muslim countries. Gulf Arab officials' initial efforts to create an Islamic International Financial Policy Forum reflected this contest along three principal dimensions.

First was the struggle over the appropriate social function and purpose of Islamic finance. Some academic writings have emphasized that the paradigmatic goal of Islamic finance should be distributive justice, defined as the equitable distribution of the benefits of deposits provided by a wide spectrum of the population by helping to eliminate poverty, expand employment and self employment opportunities, while reducing inequalities of income and wealth (Chapra 2005). This is derived from a macro-level understanding of *Shari'ah*, which asserts that all of *Shari'ah*, especially in the area of financial transactions, is intended to maximize benefit and minimize harm and that the permissibility or impermissibility of particular financial instruments should be subordinated to these particular macro concerns. For IDB this translates into the view that, 'the overarching goal of Islamic financial intermediation must be to finance economic growth with distributive justice, as a means of contributing to development'. As a development institution, IDB official documentation naturally gravitates towards a more development oriented vision of Islamic finance, rooted in conceptions of social justice and collective good. For IDB therefore, the growth of Islamic finance, presented a pivotal challenge relating to the limited contribution of Islamic finance to socio-economic development and poverty alleviation. Recommendations from the experts' session discussing the establishment of an IIFPF reflected this view. These recommendations emphasized the paramount need for a strategic reorientation of the industry by addressing the needs of financially poor households and SME sectors. In this respect, Gulf Arab officials' recommendations noted that an apex policy forum should seek to 'scale up' the contribution of Islamic finance to charitable and philanthropic sectors through instruments such as *Zakat* and *Awqaf*.

The IDB position, evident in their effort to establish an International Islamic Financial Policy Forum (IIFPF), was that the principal challenge facing Islamic finance was the need to establish a shared vision for the Islamic financial sector. The focus was on the need to enhance the sector's contribution to socio-economic development by integrating Islamic finance with pro-poor policies, including the honouring of some sense of philanthropic obligation. As one IDB official intimated, Islamic finance has 'no purpose, or reason for its existence, as an alternative to conventional finance, if it is not delivering in these areas'.[1]

---

1   Confidential off the record remark to the author. Such a perspective rather negates the critique that Islamic finance is simply a convenient way of coloring conventional financial practices with an Islamic hue, which sees 'fees' as interest under other name,

IDB authored background documents on the IIFPF proposal emphasized that the growth of Islamic finance had been characterized by the private sector's failure to perform in these areas, citing academic literature that identifies the absence of a linkage between conceptual models of Islamic finance and the actual practices of Islamic banks (Chapra 2005; Archer and Ahmed 2003; Ahmed 2002; Iqbal and Mirakhor 2002). In this respect, Gulf Arab and IDB officials highlighted the problem of genuineness in the sense that some industry innovation has been aimed to get around *Shari'ah* precepts and has been based on mimicking features of conventional finance. In other words, the Gulf Arab and IDB position was that Islamic finance had neglected a sense of public good and wider social purpose and had been too oriented towards private and individual accumulation and reward. According to this perspective, the lack of a sense of wider social purpose has consequently resulted in Islamic finance losing its distinctiveness and therefore the reasons for its existence – a view not held in the IFSB and its regional supporters in East Asia. IDB officials persuaded Gulf Arab officials that an apex policy forum was the solution to this lack of direction, which could potentially re-inject a sense of social purpose into the operation of Islamic finance through high level political deliberation, designed to establish a consensus on normative priorities and objectives.

Immediately this should alert us to a potential state-market tension in the proposal to establish an International Islamic Financial Policy Forum. The proposal involved establishing a forum of state policy-makers seeking to re-orient private market activities in a more socially aware, less individually oriented direction. Inevitably this would entail state policy-makers and possibly religious scholars seeking to exert more control and direction over the activities of private industry representatives and participants than had hitherto been the case, and to correct private market wrong doing, or un-Islamic behavior and activity. In this context, it is easy to understand how this form of authoritarianism with a social conscience, or social purpose would chime with the social settlements, or benevolent rentierism evident in Gulf Arab states (Beblawi and Luciano 1987; Sharabi 1988; Davidson 2005; Brumberg 2003; Crystal 1995; Nooneman 1996). It is perhaps unsurprising therefore that the most receptive audience to the IDB proposal appeared to be Gulf Arab ministries of finance. Ensuring that private sector financial institutions had an obligation to contribute to the delivery of some degree of distributive justice would not only resonate with Muslim sentiment amongst their domestic populations, but would also buttress their own efforts to deliver political and social stability through fiscal re-distribution.

The IDB views of the challenges facing Islamic finance were by no means universally shared by all experts in the field, or all policy-makers. Others place a far higher attachment on efficiency concerns, and good, sound regulatory practice in terms of how that regulatory practice feeds into and contributes into wider

---

because it is not the technicalities of avoiding usury that defines Islamic finance, but the social purpose attached to it by jurists, private practitioners and regulators.

global systemic stability, and the competitiveness and international credibility of the industry (Sundarajan 2005; El Gamal 2006). These differences reflect one of the principal tensions that characterizes Islamic finance as it has grown. On the one hand, Islamic finance consists of markets, like any other. From this perspective, there is an impulse and need to compete with conventional finance and attract investors and customers, by demonstrating financial value and returns and sound regulatory practice. On the other hand, the industry's survival has depended on the capture of pious Muslims who had previously shunned the conventional financial sector and may abandon their investments, if Islamic finance simply becomes a pale imitation of conventional western finance. In effect, struggles over Islamic finance can be portrayed as efforts to attain a suitable balance between these contrasting impulses and the different routes to attaining such a balance, which in turn begin from a differing sense of priorities.

While the perspective of the Gulf Arab and IDB officials, discussed above, placed a greater importance on the genuineness of Islamic finance and a *Shar'iah* derived sense of social purpose, an alternative perspective places a greater emphasis on market efficiency and international acceptability, to which the Islamic elements of Islamic finance should be subordinated and adapted. Here the principal challenge is to continue the process of understanding modern financial practices and developing an Islamic jurisprudence that is appropriate for today's legal, regulatory and financial realities. According to such a view, Islamic finance's ability to adapt to existing international regulatory frameworks is seen as positive and a commendable strength, but is one that still requires further development (El Gamal 2006). It is precisely this kind of role the Islamic Financial Services Board (IFSB), comprised of central bankers, regulators and international institutions such as the IMF has played. IFSB has interpreted agreements such as the Basle capital accord on capital adequacy for Islamic institutions and also issued recommendations in the areas of corporate governance and risk management. In this respect, the IFSB's role is to promote the transparency of Islamic finance and therefore its international market competitiveness by introducing existing international standards in a fashion that is consistent with *Shari'ah* principles. El Gamal predicts that one of the consequences of this will be to change the very Islamic jurisprudence upon which the industry is built, but this itself is seen as a natural almost Darwinian market led evolution towards a more efficient and less anachronistic financial model (El Gamal 2006). In contrast to the distributive justice vision of Islamic finance discussed earlier, this vision, based on evolving modernization, involving the incorporation of a series of more efficient market practices, and adjusting *Shari'ah* accordingly, is largely viewed as a technical enterprise. In other words, this is a vision of Islamic finance that involves far more freedom for major market players, invokes the logic of market efficiency and therefore tends to find more favor with major industry players, than the IDB vision which came to the fore in the proposal to create an International Islamic Financial Policy Forum. While neither of the two visions of Islamic finance discussed here necessarily wants to abandon, or completely dilute the key features of alternative visions – the Islamic elements of Islamic finance, or profitability, competitive efficiency, market presence and financial success – they do reflect a differing sense of priorities and different routes to attaining a balance between market efficiency and Islamic obligation.

The second element of contestation that emerged in the bid to create an apex policy forum for Islamic finance, involved a geographical struggle. The initial IDB/UAE invitation to attend the experts' consultative session to discuss the IIFPF proposal was extended to government officials from nineteen Islamic countries, but by the time of the eventual meeting those attending the meeting included the GCC states of UAE, Saudi Arabia, Kuwait, Bahrain, Qatar and a sole African representative in the form of Sudan. Despite the IDB invitation originally being sent to Indonesia, Malaysia, Singapore, Bangladesh and Pakistan, no South or South East Asian representative attended the meeting. The strong presence of Gulf Arab states was of course due to the fact that a fellow GCC state – the UAE – hosted the meeting and acted as formal proposer of the prospective forum, but it also reflected a far greater degree of consensus among Gulf Arab states for the IDB proposal and the vision of Islamic finance it represented. Notably, IDB itself is headquartered in a GCC state – Saudi Arabia, suggesting, that as the 'Washington consensus' would indicate, the geographical location of an organization does matter when it comes to that organization's preferences and world view. Such a contention is further strengthened when we consider that IFSB, which opposed the proposal and ultimately mobilized against it, is located in Malaysia, and has been far closer to a Malaysian model of Islamic finance. Certainly there appeared to be a lukewarm and unenthusiastic reaction from South East Asian states to the apex policy forum proposal, as evidenced by their non attendance at the consultation session. In other words, the IIFPF proposal also involved geographic rivalry and struggle for ascendancy in the domain of Islamic finance.

In this regard, Malaysia emerged as one of the earliest mature Islamic financial markets in the mid 1980s, with conventional Malaysian banks being allowed to offer Islamic financial products through 'Islamic windows'. From the outset, the Malaysian central bank began supervising Islamic banking practices, which made it a technical institutional leader in the field. Malaysian Islamic finance relied on the opinion of Malaysian Islamic jurists who allowed the trading of debts and pure debt instruments, which was not approved of by Islamic jurists in other regions, particularly in GCC states. The Gulf Arab model of Islamic finance has therefore evolved in a more conservative fashion, than the South East Asian model, which has generally followed the Malaysian example and evolved in a more liberal direction. The conservative bent to the Gulf Arab model has actually proved a spur to investment from many more conservative Muslims and to some extent has acted as a competitive advantage for Islamic finance in GCC states. Bahrain for example, has made a concerted attempt to promote itself as a global center for Islamic finance, which brought a reaction from Malaysia in the form of efforts to harmonize its Islamic financial practices with those in operation elsewhere. There is also amongst Gulf Arab states, a sense that they are home to the true Islam and this more conservative approach, would certainly be consistent with this sense of identity. The rent and wealth accruing to Gulf Arab states, from plentiful oil supplies might also explain why their authorities take a more expansive view of the ethical obligations and social purpose attached to Islamic finance, because they are in a financial position to do so.[2]

When the Malaysian central bank led efforts to create the IFSB in 2001,[3] housed it in Kuala Lumpar and provided contributions for running expenses, this was in part an effort to emphasize Malaysia's leadership role in Islamic finance. In this respect, the efforts to establish an IIFPF and the politics surrounding it can be interpreted as a struggle between GCC state's bid for a leadership role and Malaysia's claims as the principal representative of SE Asia to lead in this domain, involving a contest for supremacy between a more conservative Gulf Arab model revolving around a more expansive interpretation of *Shari'ah* principles and a supposedly efficient more market-oriented Malaysian model. The IIFPF can be interpreted in this regard, as an effort to reassert the role of the state and Islamic jurists in reigning in private market actors, and to promote the dominance of a model based on social purpose, with a genuine commitment to *Shari'ah* principles, which had more resonance with the Gulf Arab model than the Malaysian model in which market actors enjoyed a greater degree of freedom. For this reason, the IIFPF proposal appealed more strongly to Gulf Arab states than to South East Asian states, especially Malaysia and this as we shall see was reflected in the position of the Malaysian based IFSB.

However, the IIFPF proposal was not a straightforward case of inter-state and inter-regional geographical rivalry based on a bid for leadership in Islamic finance. It was also based on inter-institutional and bureaucratic rivalry that cut across states and added an additional element of complexity to the struggle over an apex policy forum. Institutional rivalry was a third area of competition overlapping with the previous two. The IFSB reacted badly to the proposal and mobilized its membership in an effort to prevent it from coming to fruition, despite the fact that the proposal involved an IFSB representation in the prospective apex policy forum. As the earlier discussion illustrated, IFSB's functional responsibility as a standard setting body based on market transparency and efficiency gave it good cause to oppose the notion of a social and moral purpose being attached to Islamic finance. However, there were institutional dynamics and motivations at work. IFSB has viewed itself as the prominent standard setting body in Islamic finance and wishes to preserve and consolidate that position. Establishing an apex policy forum, although not subordinating IFSB, would subject it to strategic

---

2   I am grateful for comments from participants at the GeoEconomics of the Gulf Workshop, held by the Centre for International Governance Innovation, Woener House, University of Waterloo, Ontario, Canada, 28–29 August 2009, for these points.

3   The Islamic Financial Services Board is located in Kula Lumpar and is comprised of central banks and financial regulators. It effectively acts a Basle Committee on Banking Supervision for Islamic finance.

oversight from finance ministries, allowing external actors to set priorities and seek to coordinate its activities. Despite evidence from the wider global financial architecture which illustrates how apex policy forums have usefully energized, catalyzed, publicized and legitimated the work of groups such as the Basle Committee on Banking Supervision, as well as providing political will and endorsement, which has enhanced implementation of its initiatives, these potential benefits were not explicitly recognized by IFSB. Instead, IFSB viewed an apex policy forum as a potential institutional threat that might restrict its own room for manoeuvre and undermine its prestige, and consequently took action to block the proposal. Central banks appeared particularly keen to repel finance ministry oversight of their activities and were far less comfortable with the IDB's development and justice oriented vision of Islamic finance, than with an approach based on technical and market efficiency and transparency. The IIFPF proposal can therefore also be interpreted as a struggle between IDB and IFSB, and a Gulf-centred and South East-Asian centred vision, for the role as the ascendant institution and primary voice of Islamic finance.

Notably, the two institutions perform different roles and have very different characters. IDB is more akin to a multi-lateral development bank, and IFSB is closer to a technical transgovernmental policy network (Baker 2009), or a transnational policy community (Tsingou 2008), made up primarily of national technocrats, concerned with voluntary regulatory standards and codes and definitions of best practice, with only a small secretariat compared to the IDB's more expansive bureaucracy. IFSB is generally the sum of its national member parts, whereas IDB tends to be more than that, due to an active and sizeable bureaucracy, which as this case demonstrated, has the potential to exercise its own agency. IDB has been far more attuned to a sense of social purpose derived from Islamic teachings, which would if necessary be upheld by the state as the ultimate arbiter. IFSB has been far more sympathetic to private market interests, seeking to translate international standards, institute greater market efficiency, and has been subject to pressures from private lobbies to a far greater extent. Reflecting these differing visions there is also some institutional rivalry between the two institutions, and certainly a sense amongst IDB officials that there is some competition and mistrust from IFSB towards IDB initiatives, while this is reciprocated in IDB suspicion of IFSB intentions and orientation.[4]

Ultimately, what was at stake in the IIFPF proposal was the question of what Islamic finance is and should be, including whether it should have a social purpose – as the Gulf Arab states envisioned, or whether it is simply a commercial opportunity and enterprise like any other, that should be determined and driven by considerations of market efficiency – as South-East Asian countries envisioned, as well as the all important question of how to attain a desirable balance between these different visions.

---

4   Personal confidential communication with IDB officials.

Policy Entrepreneurs and the Innovative Agency of the
Islamic Development Bank

By proposing an apex policy forum for Islamic finance, IDB was effectively seeking endorsement and a mandate for its own development-oriented vision of Islamic finance, while simultaneously imbuing Islamic finance with a distinct sense of social and moral purpose. The calculation here was that this would carve out policy space for the institution itself and re-inject a developmental role into the functioning of Islamic finance, thereby allowing IDB to better perform its own role and fulfil its mandate. In this sense, IDB was seeking to create a state based governance mechanism to increase strategic direction of its own activities, in recognition that IOs need states to direct and take an interest in their activities, in a situation of mutualism.

The problem with Islamic finance from an IDB perspective was that it had come to resemble western finance far too closely and in the process had become too concerned with balance sheet positions and bottom line profits, neglecting its socio-economic development function and its moral and ethical obligations. Creating an apex policy forum, was, from the IDB perspective, a means of potentially addressing this, while simultaneously re-energizing the institution and giving it a clearer sense of direction and a greater capacity to achieve development targets using Islamic finance as a utility for achieving this end. From an institutional perspective therefore, IDB had a great deal to gain from the creation of an apex forum for Islamic finance and therefore acted as the principal architect and orchestrator of the proposal. IDB officials first formulated and developed the idea of an apex policy forum through internal research and working papers. They then planted and cultivated the idea outside of the organization, selling it to a member government and allowing one member government to assume ownership and take credit for the proposal, as formal proposer of the forum – The Ministry of Finance and Industry, UAE.

In the first instance this role as orchestrator involved the drafting of working papers and background documents, which informed the proposal and built the detail on the UAE's proposal. The agenda for the expert's consultation session was also formulated by IDB officials, while the invited experts were carefully selected by IDB officials and funded from the IDB's budget. Notably, the IDB officials who played the prominent role in cultivating this proposal are non-Gulf citizens, western-educated and very able and politically astute technocrats. The format and tone of debate at the experts session was therefore, largely defined and shaped by IDB, even if IDB officials contributed little to the open sessions. More prominent voices in these sessions were the invited experts and the chair of the session, the IMF's Middle East director. The IMF's Middle East director was briefed behind the scenes by IDB officials and viewed his role of chair, as establishing a consensus amongst states to endorse the proposals favoured and drafted by IDB.[5] Moreover, in the break out session, in which the recommendations to be presented to the IDB's annual meeting were formulated, IDB officials authored this document in conjunction with the IMF director. The outcome closely resembled the IDB background document, which was circulated ahead of the meeting. GCC state representatives had little input to this proposal at this stage, with the exception of some consultations with the UAE as host. The proposal was then presented to the finance ministry representatives for their approval. In short, IDB largely authored the IIFPF proposal, and exercised a leadership role, albeit from behind the scenes, mobilizing the GCC coalition in support of the proposal. In other words, IDB displayed the characteristics of a 'policy entrepreneur'. In this respect, individual IDB officials were innovative and creative in developing the idea of an IIFPF, they were also skillful, resourceful and determined, in cultivating the proposal with a member government, planting the idea and then mobilizing IDB formal decision-making procedures and outside expert opinions to support the proposal. IDB officials identified the need for an apex policy forum and the benefits it would bring to their organization and Islamic finance, and then sought to pursue the idea further by not only drafting the proposal and enlisting a sponsor, but also designing a strategy and managing the procedures that had to be followed in order to bring the proposal to fruition.[6]

Conclusion

The proposal to establish an apex policy forum for Islamic finance was politically important and interesting for two principal reasons. Firstly, the proposal involved three areas of contestation. The first of these was between contrasting visions of Islamic finance one emphasizing the genuineness of Islamic finance including its obligation to deliver social justice and work for low income groups, or poorer households, and a more market oriented vision placing an emphasis on international competitiveness, efficiency and compatibility. The second area of contest involved a geographical struggle for leadership in Islamic finance between Malaysia, which has sought to cultivate itself as a modern center for Islamic finance and the GCC states that have a more conservative approach, but have similarly viewed themselves as the global hub of Islamic finance. The third area of contest was between the IDB and IFSB who have both sought to

---

5   Confidential remarks to author by officials present.

6   For some the prominent role of an IO in this case might suggest that governments and states were simply not that interested or concerned by the proposal attaching little importance to Islamic finance. However, the actions of the UAE central bank in pushing for withdrawal of the proposal would suggest that this was not the case and something of importance was at stake. Furthermore, it is likely the proposal would have been killed off and rejected at an earlier stage, if governments were completely disinterested.

establish themselves as the principal multi-lateral organization in the area of Islamic finance, and between finance ministries and central banks. Secondly, the episode revealed that inter-bureaucratic rivalry is becoming a more prominent political trend and pattern in GCC states and that this is directly related to future economic development and management strategies, involving the appropriate balance between state and market, and between the objectives of international market efficiency, competitiveness and acceptability, and social cohesion and justice, including the question of the extent to which *Shari'ah* principles should be respected in economic development and management. This case provided some hints as to some of the bureaucratic struggles within GCC states, but future research should probe these struggles further and seek to come to a better understanding of the differing priorities of different bureaucracies and the interplay between agencies such as finance ministries and central banks, which will have a major impact on the future political economy of GCC states, as their economies become more diverse and complex and their societies more pluralistic.

Chapter 6

Oil and Financialization in the Gulf Cooperation Council

Samer N. Abboud

Introduction

The 1970s oil boom placed enormous financial resources at the disposal of the oil producing states of the Gulf Cooperation Council. These petrodollar revenues generated substantive and long-term structural shifts in the economies of the GCC member states. More specifically, petrodollars underpinned rentierism as the model of state-society relations in the region. This model was based on the state's centrality in economic planning and its allocative function in the economy (Luciani 1990). The primary function of the state was to allocate or distribute petrodollars throughout the economy to support social welfare programs, infrastructural development, and the non-oil sectors of the productive economy. The circulation of petrodollars would also have considerable structural impacts on the global economy, as large petrodollar resources were channelled through Western banks and into non-Western economies in the form of loans and debt.

Since then, a number of structural shifts within the global political economy have occurred, including the collapse of the Bretton Woods monetary system, the liberalization of capital and trade flows, and the spread of privatization policies throughout the Western and non-Western worlds. Thus, the global context of the post-2003 oil boom was markedly different than that of the 1970s that was described above. In particular, one of the most dramatic shifts in the global political economy was the increase in financial activity, services, and assets. The liberalization of the international monetary system contributed to this increase, which gradually shifted financial services away from bank-based activity towards market-based financial instruments.

This changing global context was mirrored in the GCC region, as there has been considerable growth and expansion in the size, capacity, and political agency of the regional private sector (see Hertog; Momani in this volume), the development of regional economic institutions, increasing non-oil linkages with the global economy, and the widening of economic activity throughout the entire GCC region. At the same time, the GCC region's financial landscape has changed dramatically, as regional financial markets have grown considerably in their services, capacities, and linkages with global markets. One of the major reasons why petrodollars were circulated outside of the region in previous boom periods was because of the inability of domestic economies to absorb so much capital for productive use. Thus, the growth in the GCC's financial capacity suggests that the circulation of petrodollars in the most recent period would be markedly different than previous oil booms.

With this in mind, this chapter is interested in asking how oil revenues have been marshalled in support of the economic policies and strategies of GCC member states to generate finance-led growth, and how these policies and strategies have initiated structural changes away from oil dependence. I take structural change here to refer to changes in the organization and operation of GCC economies. I consider that the underlying goal of structural change in the GCC is to generate long-term diversification that supports the transition away from dependence on hydrocarbon revenues and the distributive functions of the state. While this process was clearly underway prior to the 2003 oil boom, the revenues accrued to the state since then have accelerated this transition considerably. Thus, the substantive questions raised here concern the relationship between oil revenues, financial services, and structural change. My line of inquiry is, then, similar to that of Hvidt (in this volume) and others who demonstrate an interest in structural change. However, while Hvidt addresses the shift towards the productive sectors of the economy, I am interested in developments in the financial services sector.

In order to examine the relationship between finance and structural change in the GCC, I draw on the financialization framework. Financializaton can be defined as 'the increasing role of financial motives, financial markets, financial actors and financial institutions in the operation of the domestic and international economies' (Epstein 2005, 3). Furthermore, I make the argument that financialization – understood broadly as the increasing shift towards financial services – is central to policies of diversification. Thus, my intention in this chapter is to demonstrate the relationship between diversification and financialization. Since financialization is defined as a shift towards market-based financial services, I begin with a discussion of the meaning of the term. This is followed with a brief assessment of the circulation patterns of previous oil booms in order to draw contrasts with the recent oil boom. The subsequent analysis of the growth and expansion of the financial services sector in the GCC will demonstrate how economic agents, government policy, and the shifting structure of financial markets, all reflect financialization in the region. The chapter then concludes with an assessment of the relationship between diversification and financialization.

Financialization

Financialization is a term that is sometimes carelessly employed to explain a range of phenomenon and patterns in financial sectors. Indeed, Dore is correct to point out that: '"financialization" is a bit like "globalization" – a convenient word for a bundle of more or less discrete structural changes in the economies of the industrialized "world"' (Dore 2008, 1097). A sufficient literature review of the term is well beyond the scope of this chapter (see Engelen 2008), suffice to say that different scholarly communities have conceptualized financialization in multiple ways, leading to ambiguities and perhaps diluting the term of conceptual and analytical value. Despite this, the framework can have significant value in helping us understand structural change in the GCC region. The growth of the financial sector in the region, and its relationship to the oil sector, is a subject of considerable research, interest, and debate (see Nugée and Subacchi 2008; House 2008; Maloney 2009). However, the majority of this literature is concerned with describing the growth of the financial services sector in the GCC, without elaborating on relationships between financial services and the broader issues of structural change. The more salient arguments of the financialization literature can contribute to our framing and understanding of these debates, and our understanding of long-term structural change in the region.

Watson's delineation of the literature on financialization into microfoundations and macrofoundations accurately captures the breadth of research that draws on the financialization framework (Watson 2009). Broadly speaking, the microfoundations literature is concerned with the relationship between household and corporate economies (ibid.). For example, on one end of the scale, financialization research has examined household and individual patterns, including wages, consumption, debt, and investment. On the other end of the microfoundations literature, research focuses on corporate activity, which is primarily concerned with issues of shareholder value strategies, financial management, institutional investment, and corporate governance.

In contrast to this literature, this chapter is interested in the macro-foundations of financialization. This level of analysis refers to government attempts to support finance-led growth through the expansion of market-based financial services and instruments. While the term has been used throughout a range of literature, it remains important to stress that virtually all definitions emphasize that financialization refers to the growth of financial markets, actors, institutions, and motives in domestic and regional economies (Epstein 2005, 3). Thus, I take financialization to refer to the policy, institutional, and investment strategies of governments to support market-based, finance-led growth. This is distinct from bank-based activity undertaken by central monetary authorities, such as the acquisition of bonds, deposits, foreign debt, foreign exchange, and savings. In contrast, financialization refers to market-based activity in financial assets that are largely outside of the formal banking system, and instead concentrated in private markets. This understanding of financialization helps us think about how growth in financial services shifts the underlying structures and operation of economies.

Three interrelated conduits broadly define financialization: changes in the structure of the economy; economic policy; and corporate behavior (Palley 2007, 11). These conduits are central to understanding how patterns in the financial services sector impact broader structural economic change. First, economic policy has been central to changes in financial markets. The deregulation of the financial sectors across the world and capital liberalizations have given rise to such financial instruments as derivatives and asset-backed securities. These new instruments have dramatically reshaped and expanded global finance. Thus, a measure of financialization is in the organization and operation of financial markets. For example, most of the petrodollars in the 1970s were intermediated through banks. These assets were held as reserves, and had restricted impact on economic activity in oil-producing economies, primarily because these reserves were held to fulfill the state's distributive function. This contrasts significantly with the current period where financial markets are crucial to economic growth. The second conduit is economic policy, specifically government attempts to create a policy and institutional framework that supports financial market activity and expansion. This also refers to governments' active encouragement and facilitation of public and private sector agents' financial market activity. The final conduit of financialization is corporate behavior. This concerns how economic agents increasingly acquire profits and conduct economic activity through financial markets.

In the majority of literature on financialization, the US, UK, and Western Europe serve as the primary case studies. This is in large part because these economies have undergone the most dramatic financial changes since the 1970s. By drawing on the macrofoundations of the financialization literature, I do not wish to suggest parallels between the experiences of the GCC and these countries. Nor is it my intention to suggest that the GCC has, overnight, been transformed into a financialized economic unit. The overwhelming majority of revenues continue to accrue from hydrocarbons (Hvidt 2010; Toksov 2008, 89–90). Thus, instead, I draw on the financialization framework to support the argument that finance is playing an increasingly important role in economic activity in the GCC on the one hand, and on the other hand, that this increasing share of economic activity is reflective of structural economic change within the region. As I will argue below, this is evident by the expansion of market-based investments, the growth of SWFs and other public investment agents whose investments are concentrated in finance, the increase of inter-regional investments in the financial sector (Eid 2008), and the expansion of both the regional financial sector and of Islamic financial instruments. These developments have not necessarily come at the expense of investments and growth outside of finance. Thus, my central argument here is that financialization is crucial to economic diversification and the structural transition away from oil dependence – a transparent, strategic, and desired goal of all GCC states.

Petrodollars in the 1970s

During the 1970s and into the 1980s, oil producing states enjoyed massive financial surpluses as a result of high oil prices. Financial surpluses accumulated during this period were paralleled by deficits in the oil importing countries, creating imbalances in oil importers' current accounts. However, because of weak financial intermediation and limited regional absorptive capacity in oil exporting countries, these surpluses were largely recycled through the global commercial banking system, and global imbalances were largely corrected through the re-circulation of oil revenues into the major oil importers' economies.

Many of the Gulf Arab oil producing countries adopted policies that facilitated the recycling of oil revenues in the global system (Abed 1983, 48–51). During the booms of the 1970s, there were seven identifiable ways in which these oil revenues were circulated. First, most of these countries followed rather conservative foreign investment strategies, including investment in US government bonds and overseas deposits. Although most assets were held in US dollars, there was enough diversification so as not to destabilize other currencies. This circulation strategy had the effect of sheltering oil producing countries from any shocks to the dollar. Second, oil-producing countries embarked on a spending bonanza, absorbing exports from both the industrial and industrializing worlds at rapid rates. Such an increase in spending also had the effect of correcting some of the imbalances generated by the transfer of wealth from oil importers to oil exporters. Third, exchange rates and capital flow restrictions were liberalized, facilitating the re-circulation of money into all importers' economies. Fourth, during this time, foreign aid levels were between 2.5 and 5 percent of total GDP, an exceptionally high figure. Fifth, the Gulf Arab oil producing countries transferred revenues through the purchase of bonds and the provisions of loans to international financial and aid institutions. This facilitated the process of transferring financial resources in the form of debt to the industrializing countries. Sixth, several regional institutions created to support development in Gulf, African and Islamic regions were also injected with petrodollars. Finally, despite the high oil prices in the 1970s, most oil producing countries pursued moderate positions on price increases, 'thereby easing the burden of adjustment by the industrial, as well as the developing, oil-importing countries' (Abed 1983, 49). The policies pursued by the Gulf Arab oil producing countries were primarily aimed at correcting global structural imbalances.

Circulation of these revenues happened primarily through bank-based instruments, thus commercial banks became the primary intermediary for petrodollars. By 1974, half of all oil revenues spent were in the form of bank deposits and money market instruments (International Monetary Fund 2006). Furthermore, monies (around $25 billion) were circulated into long-term investments such as loans to governments and government bonds.

The nature of these investments reflected the architecture of the global financial system in the 1970s. During this period, a number of liberalizing measures were adopted in the US and Europe to facilitate the circulation of capital. For example, in the 1960s, Eurocurrency markets were created. These markets provided a regulatory momentum towards capital liberalization that would eventually lead to the creation of new asset classes and financial instruments. Since such deregulations were most advanced in US and European economies, these banks had strong intermediary capacities. As a result, they represented the major intermediaries of oil revenue circulation in the global economy.

A defining feature of the global political economy since then has been the gradual spread of deregulation and liberalization policies throughout the world.

Not only have capital liberalization policies secured the flow of capital across borders, but they have also contributed to the growing importance of finance in the profit-generating activities of companies. Indeed, financial services and operations such as hedge funds, private equity, insurance houses, fund managers, derivatives, investment banks, and other, more obscure, financial instruments, have increasingly become the core of profit-generating activities for financial and non-financial firms. Epstein states, 'sometime in the mid-to-late 1970s or early 1980s, structural shifts of dramatic proportions took place in a number of countries that led to significant increases in financial transactions ... the profitability of financial firms, and the shares of national income accruing to the holders of financial assets' (Epstein 2005, 4). These shifts, however, had not demonstrated an impact on the circulation of oil revenues, as they continued to be channelled into bank-based instruments.

The global context of high oil prices was considerably different in the 1970s than it was during the post-2003 oil boom. In the context of the GCC, both the global trend towards capital liberalization and economic deregulation and the domestic liberalization initiated in the respective GCC economies have provided the impetus for increased financial investment and expansion. One of the major changes in these economies was the increasing marketization of economic activity. Economic reforms, privatizations, and a gradual liberalization of economic activity have increased the role of markets in generating and distributing wealth within the GCC economies. Thus, the domestic and global context of high oil prices was much different in the 1970s than it was in 2003. In the 1970s, GCC economies were primarily public sector based, with limited absorptive capacity, very limited intermediary capacity to circulate oil revenues, and a high dependence on oil production.

The Post-2003 Oil Boom

Structural Shifts in Financial Markets

Historically, in periods of oil booms, intermediaries such as international financial centers (IFCs) played a large role in circulating oil revenues. However, GCC countries have been successful in developing multiple investment vehicles to circulate oil revenues throughout the global economy. Indeed, as a 2008 Chatham House publication argues, GCC states have 'collectively decided that the financial services sector is an attractive one for their economies to specialize in: it offers an enticing range of high-income, high-value-added activities with much growth potential that complements well the resource extraction industries' (Nugée and Subacchi 2008, 2). More importantly, Nugée and Subacchi argue that this collective decision entails a transformation of GCC economies from users to providers of financial services (Nugée and Subacchi 2008, 3). This transition from users-to-providers of financial services highlights the role of finance in generating structural change.

Central to arguments about the rise of finance in GCC economies is the role that oil revenues (and hydrocarbon revenues in general) play in the financial services sector. Clearly, the claim that GCC countries are transitioning from users to providers of financial services is grounded in the assumption that oil revenue surpluses will be circulated through financial systems. Generally, there are two main channels for the circulation of oil revenues: The trade absorption channel gives states the chance to use revenues to support the import of goods and services, whereas the capital account channel allows countries to acquire foreign assets in international capital markets. Central banks, monetary authorities, institutional funds, companies, or individuals, all of whom have direct or indirect access to oil revenues, hold these assets. Central banks and monetary authorities typically hold these assets in bank-based instruments such as short- and long-term debt, US treasury bills, and foreign exchange reserves, while other vehicles typically hold assets in market-based financial instruments.

There are two broader patterns that suggest that oil revenues have been circulated primarily through the capital account channel. The first pattern is the decline in oil revenues used to finance imports in the GCC. In the 1970s, GCC countries mobilized a significant portion of oil revenues to finance imports from oil-importing countries, mainly in the United States and Europe. These imports served to adjust global imbalances produced by the transfer of money from oil importing to oil-exporting countries. However, since 2003, the percentage of oil revenues spent on imports has actually decreased to 15 percent from a high of 34 percent in 1973–75 and 25 percent in 1978–81.

Furthermore, GCC imports from the main oil-importing countries in Europe and the United States have decreased when compared to imports from the rest of the world, particularly Asia (see Davidson in this volume). The International Monetary Fund (IMF) estimates that between 1981 and 2004 the percentage of imports from the United States and other Western economies to all oil exporters *decreased* by around 15 percent, while imports from China and the rest of the non-Western world *increased* by the same amount (International Monetary Fund 2006). In a study on the relationship between petrodollars and imports in oil-exporting countries, Beck and Kamps concluded that the reduction in imports can be attributed to the accumulation of foreign assets (Beck and Kamps 2009) since revenues normally allocated to trade absorption are diverted to the capital account channel.

The second pattern is the decline in the percentage of oil revenues circulated into Bank of International Settlements (BIS) reporting assets. BIS data across different oil boom periods show the composition of oil exporters' invested funds.

The BIS does not track investments in a range of financial transactions, including: cross-border investments in regional capital markets, construction, real estate, private equity, hedge funds, and other forms of financial investment. The lack of verifiable data on these market-based financial investments makes

Table 6.1 Marginal propensity to import: GCC

	1973–74	1973–75	1978–80	1978–81	2003–2005
GCC	0.08	0.34	0.18	0.25	0.15

Source: International Monetary Fund 2006, 80.

Table 6.2 Composition of oil exporters' investable funds (%)

	1978–82	1999–2005
Portfolio Investment	28	28
Deposits and other investments	58	47
Foreign Exchange Reserves	Negligible	19
Other	4	6

Source: Magnus 2006, 13.

rendering conclusions about their direction dependent on anecdotal information. During the 1978–82 period, it is estimated that 50 percent of all oil revenues were channelled through BIS reporting instruments, however, the 1999–2005 period data only account for 30 percent of oil revenues. The decrease in BIS reporting instruments reflects a shift away from bank-based towards market-based financial instruments. According to one estimate, between 2000 and 2005, GCC countries had accumulated $542 billion in international financial assets through global capital markets (Bahgat 2008, 1193). Moreover, McKinsey Global Institute estimates that the total foreign financial assets of GCC-based economic agents is between $3.4 and $3.8 trillion (International Institute of Finance 2008).

GCC-Based Economic Agents

Although GCC central banks remain a major vehicle for the circulation of oil revenues, particularly since they hold savings, bonds and foreign exchange reserves, there have been a number of investment vehicles that have been created by GCC states to manage oil revenues. The large volume of acquired financial assets has led to the creation of various investment vehicles to manage these assets. These economic agents are the main vehicles for the circulation of oil revenues into financial markets. In particular, SWFs have been major beneficiaries of oil revenues. In contrast to central banks, SWFs invest in a wider range of assets and seek to support national developmental goals through long-term, high-return investments (see Ziemba and Malkin in this volume). All SWFs have three characteristics in common: they are publicly owned, they have limited or no liabilities, and they are managed separately from official state foreign exchange reserves (Beck and

Fidora 2008, 349). According to the IMF, SWFs can be distinguished based on five differing objectives (International Monetary Fund 2008, 5): *stabilization funds* are aimed at insulating the budget against commodity price fluctuations; *savings funds* facilitate the exchange of nonrenewable assets for more diversified assets; *reserve investment corporations* aim to increase returns on reserve funds; *development funds* finance economic projects and facilitate the realization of industrial policies; and *contingent pension reserve funds* support the state's pension obligations.

SWFs essentially follow an oil-to-equities strategy whereby oil revenues are translated into long-term financial assets. These agents are thus central to understanding the structural shift towards finance in the GCC. As investment vehicles, their objective is to provide profits and revenues within GCC economies, particularly in the long-term as oil prices decline (as they have since 2008), oil resources deplete, and GCC economies need to generate economic activity. This is especially true in countries such as the United Arab Emirates that have reduced their reliance on hydrocarbon revenues for their budgetary and overall economic expenditures. Thus, GCC-based SWFs serve a variety of economic functions. Principally, they provide an investment vehicle for the circulation of oil revenues. Because official reserves are sound and government debt is generally low, excess surpluses can be channelled to SWFs, which can pursue investment strategies in more complex and high-returning assets than central banks and monetary authorities. Thus, a second function of SWFs is to support diversification policies. Baghat's claim that SWFs have followed an oil-to-equities strategy that supports domestic diversification policies supports this point (Bahgat 2008, 1198). For example, Mumtalakat Holdings (Bahrain) acquired a 30 percent stake in the McLaren Group to help develop Bahrain's aluminum industry. Similarly, Mubadala (Abu Dhabi) acquired a 5 percent stake in Ferarri to support plans for a Ferrari Theme Park aimed at attracting global tourists (Farrell and Lund 2008, 33).

Indeed, Jen argues that for GCC states to maximize investment returns made with oil revenues, they 'should aggressively accumulate financial wealth through their SWFs' (Jen 2008, 164). For Jen the translation of oil revenues into financial assets offers public and private sector firms profits and revenues that far exceed the returns on investments in other sectors. Although exact data do not exist, Jen estimates that the asset composition of GCC-based SWFs is 25:45:30 in bonds/equities/alternative investments (Jen 2008, 165). Bond assets provide SWF asset managers with less volatile and more traditional assets. Equities and alternative investments (infrastructure, private equity, commodity and hedge funds), on the other hand, reflect a long-term investment strategy in which SWF profits and revenues accrue from financial assets, rather than through oil revenues. Because SWFs are not burdened with liabilities and have a dependable revenue stream through oil revenues, their investments can be spread across different asset classes and across differing levels of short-, medium – and long-term risk and returns. The ultimate strategic orientation of GCC-based SWFs is to provide for the long-term development, growth and budgetary needs of their economies.

For Beck and Fidora, SWFs operate in similar ways to private mutual funds in allocating foreign assets according to risk/return, rather than liquidity considerations (Beck and Fidora 2008, 353). This investment orientation reduces the bias that central banks and monetary authorities typically have towards the reserve currencies. As a result, SWFs only hold around 40–50 percent of their assets in US dollars, while the central banks of GCC countries hold between 85 and 95 percent of their reserves in dollars (Setser and Ziemba 2007, 11). Moreover, Beck and Fidora suggest that among the major SWFs in the GCC – the Abu Dhabi Investment Council, the Kuwait Investment Authority, the Investment Corporation of Dubai, and the Qatar Investment Authority – more than 2/3 of their total assets are held in the financial sector (Beck and Fidora 2008, 351), and the Institute of International Finance estimates that half of invested oil revenues were channelled towards financial assets (International Institute of Finance 2008, 18).

The majority of GCC foreign financial assets are held by SWFs. Of the $3.4–3.8 trillion in assets held by GCC investment vehicles, SWFs manage around $1.5 trillion in assets. GCC countries have also established government investment corporations (GICs), which function differently than SWFs. Whereas SWFs typically adopt a portfolio approach to acquire assets for long-term returns, GICs concentrate on acquiring and managing corporate assets, thus operating similarly to private equity firms. There are a number of established GICs in the region, including Dubai International Capital (DIC) and Istithmar. One of the main differences between GIC and other investment vehicles pertains to the management of acquired assets.

A more traditional investment vehicle in the GCC is high net worth individuals (HNWIs) and families with access to oil revenues. Approximately 40 percent of all invested oil revenues are channelled through these individuals and families (McKinsey & Company 2008, 17). In 2006, high net worth individuals held foreign assets valued at around $600 billion, with the top ten wealthiest families controlling $124 billion in these foreign assets (Farrell and Lund 2008, 17). While HNWIs are strongly committed to US and European capital markets, anecdotal evidence points to an increasing shift towards Asian, African and Middle Eastern markets (see Momani in this volume). The growth of Islamic financial instruments has also been supported by investments from HNWIs. Since 2000, HNWIs have sought to expand and diversify their assets, a process which was prompted in part by September 11, 2001 and the war on terrorism and was accelerated after the 2008 international financial crisis, as GCC investors sought to channel cash and assets towards more local investments.

During the second oil boom, then, HNWIs have diversified into Arab regional financial assets. In 2006, approximately 25 percent of total HNWI assets were in regional markets. Because of this increased circulation of oil revenues into Gulf Arab markets, the total value of Gulf Arab financial assets at the end of 2006 was estimated at $1.2 trillion. This represented a threefold increase from five years prior (Farrel and Lund 2008, 32). In Syria, for example, the liberalization of financial services has attracted GCC-based investments and partnerships that are drawn to the nascent banking and insurance sectors in that country. The majority of foreign investment in the Syrian banking and insurance sectors is GCC-based. These investments in Syrian services are consistent with overall inter-Arab investment patterns. In 2007, 44 percent of all inter-Arab investments were in services (The Arab Investment and Export Credit Guarantee Corporation 2007). The rapid growth of investment in services and a generally hospitable investment climate throughout the Arab World contributed to the *doubling* of the value of all Arab stock markets between 2006 and 2007. This over-valuation of Gulf stock markets was largely representative of GCC-based HNWIs and other investors acquiring assets in liberalizing Gulf Arab markets.

The Domestic Financial Services Sector

The previous section described how GCC-based economic agents have acquired, and in some cases managed, foreign assets. The majority of these assets are held in global financial markets. Thus, quantitatively at least, the circulation of oil revenues into these investment vehicles has contributed to a rise in the number and value of financial assets held by GCC economies. Equally important as investments abroad, are investments made in GCC markets. Unlike during the first oil boom period, in the second boom, GCC economies have developed an absorptive capacity that has facilitated the circulation of oil revenues into domestic economies. Public investment and spending has increased dramatically since 2003, and government debt has been reduced in all GCC countries. Oil revenues have also been circulated into domestic financial sectors, contributing to the growth of the banking and finance sectors, the proliferation of new market-based financial instruments based in the GCC, and the spread of Islamic finance instruments. While the banking and finance sectors remain immature and nascent in the GCC relative to other advanced economies, the current levels of investment, the growth of banking and finance institutions, and the increasing percentage of banking and finance *vis-à-vis* growth in other sectors of the economy reflects the growing financialization of domestic GCC economies.

Local banking and financial institutions have been primary beneficiaries of the oil boom. Between 2001 and 2006, GCC-based bank assets doubled to $500 billion (Hanna 2008, 107). Furthermore, the banking sector's return on equity rose from 16 percent in 2002 to around 30 percent in 2006 (ibid.). Profits of GCC-based banks rose 64 percent from 2004 to 2005 and another 20 percent from 2005 to 2006 (National Bank of Kuwait 2007, 24). The total net profits of GCC-based banks are represented in Table 6.3.

One explanation for the growth in the banking sector is a series of region-wide liberalizations that have created investment opportunities, including real estate, privatization, stock market, and infrastructural opportunities. As investment projects became available and high oil prices accelerated domestic spending and circulation of money within the regional economy, banking and financial institutions were positioned to offer more dynamic services. Thus, rapidly growing

Table 6.3 Total net profits, GCC banks by country 2006

Country	Total net profits (in billion USD)
Kingdom of Saudi Arabia	$8.84
United Arab Emirates	$4.09
Kuwait	$2.71
Bahrain	$1.50
Qatar	$1.34
Oman	$.356

Source: Ibid.

economies, in addition to region-wide liberalizations, provided the impetus for banking and financial sector growth. All major banking services in the region – credit, personal and private sector loans, and mortgages – were expanded.

In addition to these liberalizations, a favorable regulatory environment has opened a channel for GCC-based banks to insulate themselves from foreign competition, thus allowing them to overwhelmingly dominate the banking sector in the region. In the UAE, for example, over 60 percent of total bank assets are held by public banks, while in Saudi Arabia the figure is at 23 percent, and in Bahrain and Kuwait it is less than 5 percent (Sturm et al. 2008, 33). Despite their small size relative to public sector banks, private sector banking in the GCC contributes 44 percent of total private sector earnings in the region (Global Investment House 2009, 19). Indeed, private sector banking is one of the major growth sectors for the regional private sector.

The commitment to banking and financial services expansion is further reflected in projects to establish IFCs in the GCC. These IFCs are a response to a regional demand for greater financial intermediation and the desire of some GCC states to develop these intermediary services for regional and global markets. These centers focus on a wide range of financial services, including banking and brokerage, wealth management, insurance, and capital markets. In the GCC, Bahrain was the first country to establish an offshore IFC in the 1970s. However, Bahrain recently developed the Bahrain Financial Harbour (BFH) project. Similarly, in 2004 Dubai established the Dubai International Financial Center (DIFC) and in 2005 Qatar established the Qatar Financial Center (QFC). Saudi Arabia is also in the process of constructing the King Abdullah Financial District in Riyadh.

The creation of IFCs within the region is partly a response to the increased demand for Islamic banking and financial services. In general, Islamic financial services are one of the growing areas of regional and global financial markets. In 2007, Islamic financial assets held in the GCC were valued at $178 billion (35 percent of global Islamic financial assets). The Islamic financial sector represents 18 percent of the total value of the GCC's regional financial system. Furthermore, Islamic bonds, known as *sukuks*, represent more than half of all bonds issued in

GCC countries. Islamic financial services thus represent a significant portion of emerging financial services in the GCC. This growth in Islamic finance has led to the creation of a host of related regulatory institutions aimed at establishing standards and specifications for these financial instruments, and the expansion of this market has led to the creation of several public and private sector companies, management enterprises and even mutual funds that are compatible with the standards of Islamic finance (see Baker in this volume).

The growth and expansion of banking and financial services within the GCC that followed the second oil boom was preceded by liberalization policies that expanded the scope of private sector activity and increased the intermediary capacities of regional institutions. After 2003, regional demand for banking services, excess liquidity, and growing foreign investment accelerated these processes and encouraged the further expansion of banking and financial services. Evidence of this expansion lies in the increasing availability of these services, measured by the proliferation of banking services, IFCs, and Islamic banking instruments. This expansion was also propelled by the increased agency of domestic economic actors and their growing demands for financial services.

Diversification through Financialization

The structural dependence of GCC economies on hydrocarbons has meant that economic diversification is a key challenge for policy-makers. In boom periods, hydrocarbon revenues have placed enormous financial resources at the disposal of GCC countries. Around 49 percent of GCC economies' GDP is from hydrocarbons, which employ around 1 percent of the total population. Since economic growth in the GCC countries is overwhelmingly dependent on hydrocarbons, GCC economies have had to develop circulation and intermediation vehicles for the absorption of revenues into local economies, with the ultimate aim of supporting the growth of non-hydrocarbon sectors.

As resource-dependent economies, the GCC member states have collectively undertaken the shift away from resource dependence towards more diversified economies. Unlike many Western countries that are increasingly financialized economies, the GCC economic shift towards finance has not necessarily come at the expense of the productive sectors of the economy. For these countries, the challenge of diversification is multiple: providing employment, generating economic activity beyond hydrocarbons, providing private sector support, balancing social and economic interests, and providing long-term revenue streams to maintain social welfare programs and government budgets. The main question here is: how does the financial services sector fit into this transition towards more diversified economies?

Clearly, as this chapter has argued, there is a clear shift in the structure of regional financial markets. The mere growth of financial services suggests a shift towards developing finance as a key engine of growth and diversification.

Growth in financial services is also important to satisfy domestic financial needs. Indeed, 'encouraging growth and diversification in the financial sector is a logical development based on local needs for banking and insurance, property and project finance, wealth management and other financial services' (Chatham House 2008, 21). Sturm et al. have evaluated diversification of GCC economies and found a general trend towards diversification into finance. This research measured the direction and degree of diversification in terms of four sectors: commodities, tourism, finance, and manufacturing (Sturm et al. 2008, 15–18). Their measurements are based on calculating the share of each sector in national GDP. The Bahraini and the UAE economies display the highest diversification into finance, with both countries exhibiting low levels of dependence on hydrocarbons and increasing reliance on finance as a percentage of GDP. In Kuwait, finance is the second leading sector behind commodities. The only country in the GCC that does not exhibit significant diversification into finance is Oman.

The structural shifts towards finance have not reduced the GCC's dependence on the hydrocarbon sectors as a percentage of GDP. Despite diversification efforts, the share of hydrocarbons to overall GDP rose from 39 percent in 2000 to 49 percent in 2006 (Toksov 2008, 89). However, there is an acute awareness in the region of the finiteness of hydrocarbon revenues. The large share of hydrocarbons relative to other sectors is reflective of both the abundance of available resources and the high prices that generated the boom. The GCC countries have been relatively successful in staying the diversification course and not returning to previous patterns of petrodollar circulation that privileged domestic consumption and spending at the expense of economic growth. Rather, in the second oil boom, the GCC economies have begun to translate hydrocarbon revenues into long-term revenue streams, and the financial services sector is essential to this strategy.

There are a number of factors that explain the relationship between diversification and financialization. First, financial services offer GCC economies a sector through which to circulate hydrocarbon revenues and support other sectors of the economy through credit, project financing, and fund management. Thus, financial services are central to supporting growth throughout the economy. Second, because of the large influx of hydrocarbon revenues, the GCC economies are positioned to serve as financial service providers to regional economies and private sector actors. Furthermore, the GCC's provision of Islamic financial services is at the forefront of this growing niche of global finance (see Baker in this volume). This represents a huge potential for future growth, and in all likelihood, the GCC will continue to be the center of Islamic financial services. Fourth, growth in financial services can potentially provide widespread, high-wage employment for GCC nationals.

Conclusion

Drawing on the financialization literature to understand structural economic change in the GCC, this chapter has argued that the growth and expansion of financial services has been an important facet of diversification away from hydrocarbon dependence. Although the member economies of the GCC remain heavily dependent on hydrocarbon revenues, the increasing financialization of their economies, in addition to investments in the productive sectors of the economy, reflect a deliberate strategy of diversification in which finance-led growth is central to economic policy and strategy. While structural change is not entirely evident at the moment of writing because of the continued high oil prices and the long-term nature of many GCC-based investments, there are clear indications that financial services are playing an important role in the structure and operation of GCC economies.

Financialization was defined broadly as government attempts to support market-based, finance-led growth. Three conduits of financialization were highlighted: the changing structure of the economy, economic policy, and corporate behavior. In order to make the case that financialization is occurring within the GCC, considerable attention was given to the interrelationship between economic policy, the activity of GCC-based economic agents, and the growth of financial services markets. It was argued that the proliferation of market-based financial services was not an accident of the times but rather the outcome of deliberate government policies to encourage financial services growth. In particular, the mandates of GCC-based economic agents to provide long-term growth through investments in financial services, highlights the importance placed on finance in the long-term diversification plans of member economies. Similarly, the circulation of hydrocarbon revenues into domestic and regional financial markets has positioned the region as a provider of financial services. In this way, the GCC is emerging as a major financial hub. In the long-term, these patterns in financial services will have significant structural impacts on GCC economies.

PART II
Gulf Arab Investments and Trade

Chapter 7

The GCC's International Investment Dynamics: The Role of Sovereign Wealth Funds

Rachel Ziemba and Anton Malkin

Introduction

Over the course of the last decade governments of the Gulf Cooperation Council (GCC), fuelled by the second oil boom, have become major players in international capital markets and significant players in key sectors. This was accompanied by an expansion of activity of their investment management arm – the sovereign wealth funds (SWFs). While GCC governments and the countries' ruling elite have made substantial investments abroad in past oil booms, the recent uptake in GCC investment activity has taken on some novel characteristics. The scale of investments, the changes in asset allocation and the proliferation of investment vehicles, as well as the growth in the scope of sovereign wealth portfolios since 2002 has gained widespread attention in policy circles. The foreign asset holdings of the region's central banks and sovereign wealth funds has risen almost fourfold from around US$300 billion at the end of 1999, to an estimated US$1.2 trillion by the end of 2009.[1] However, as these assets have piled up, and as demands to reallocate these investments have risen, the mandates for these funds have undergone a transformation. The savings accumulated through the expanded activity of foreign asset managers in the GCC helped to improve the economic prospects for their sponsor governments during the recent financial crisis.

Certainly, the evolution of GCC sovereign wealth has both economic and political implications. As sovereign investors go global – no longer satisfied with being passive actors in international financial markets – they strike partnerships with foreign companies and governments to maximize their financial and commercial returns. Often, these partnerships not only provide capital to a foreign company but are also intended to meet a GCC government's domestic economic needs. But despite the present and potential importance of Gulf SWFs, the existing literature on the subject has inadequately explained their significance for the political economy of the Gulf Arab region and for the global political economy more broadly.

---

1   The methodology on which these estimates were based is explained below and draws heavily on Setser and Ziemba 2009.

Due to the institutional opaqueness of Gulf Arab investments the backlash that Gulf SWFs have experienced in recent years is perhaps not surprising. Their lack of transparency, especially relative to other significant SWFs (see Behrendt this volume) raises the political uncertainty around their motivations. Some observers have been quick to conclude that the very existence of these financial entities is indicative of the decline of American financial and, by extension, geopolitical power (see, for example, Anderson 2009). Others posit that the fears around SWFs are either exaggerated (Drezner 2008) or, on the whole, economically misguided and unwarranted (Seznac 2010). In this chapter, we survey the data surrounding the recent developments in SWF activities, with the aim of illuminating the motivations behind their international asset acquisitions. To be specific, in light of concerns raised about the investment activities of Gulf SWFs, and given the funds' role in the GCC's international investment dynamics, what can be said about the political and economic motivations of these funds and their broader global significance?

In this chapter, we argue that while SWF activities are certainly indicative of a domestic economic policy shift in the region, especially with respect to domestic economic diversification, there is still no clear sign of a deliberate challenge to the US-centered global financial system or of a move to gain leverage *vis-à-vis* US economic interests. This is largely due to the funds' firm dependence on the GCC's oil-related fortunes and the specific needs of the local economies, which are at the moment quite pressing and seem to overshadow any global strategic considerations. On the whole, the pattern of SWF investment points to a strategy of domestic diversification and domestic economic reform as a priority and precondition to any active assertion of financial power. These limitations, however, do not detract from their global significance, which reflects a broader shift in the role of the state in global financial affairs.

While the collective and individual domestic roles of Gulf Arab SWFs are indeed noteworthy, their international significance remains, to a great extent, uncertain. However, to shed some light on the issue, we explore the definition of a SWF and its significance for GCC states. We show how SWF activity is, in many respects, a response to oil boom and bust cycles. We also outline the factors surrounding the growth of the funds and the limits to such growth, especially in lieu of the global financial crisis, projected into the near future. We then explore the extent to which Gulf SWFs have directed their savings away from traditional dollar assets and describe the implications of this diversification. We conclude by drawing out some broader causes and implications of the GCC's international investment dynamics.

An Evolving Definition of Sovereign Wealth

Sovereign wealth funds (SWFs) are broadly defined as dedicated investment funds managed by governments, across a range of asset classes. Although there is no widely accepted definition of a sovereign wealth fund yet, much of the literature on the subject accepts that these funds are managed separately from a country's foreign exchange reserves – usually by a dedicated asset management team – and that they have no significant liabilities (see, for example, Cohen 2009, 715). Political representatives, including those from national ministries of finance, tend to be involved in setting the asset allocation and determining the funding for SWFs.

In part, the establishment of sovereign wealth funds aimed to save oil revenues outside the GCC economies rather than have them invested domestically, where they might swamp the regional economy, driving up prices and crowding out other investment trends. To this day, two essential factors determine the growth of sovereign wealth funds in the region: the size of a state's oil surplus (based on the size of oil revenues and the growth of domestic spending) and the rate of return on the funds' investments. From 2003–08, both factors supported rapid growth of Gulf SWFs.

The funds are commonly largely portfolio investors, taking relatively small shares in a variety of companies and asset classes. Funds like the Abu Dhabi Investment Authority and the Kuwait Investment Authority are prime examples of this trend.[2] However, in the search for higher yield, other, newer funds like the Qatar Investment authority (QIA) have opted for a more assertive investment strategy, taking substantial equity stakes in high profile companies, including 10.58 percent in the London Stock Exchange and a 24.97 percent share in the British grocer Sainsbury Plc (Seznac 2009). As SWFs take on new roles at home and abroad, our understanding of their defining characteristics is evolving as well.

However, the lack of clear boundaries between personal sovereign wealth and public sovereign wealth in the Gulf muddies the neat picture of Gulf SWFs as simple portfolio investment vehicles. The lines between the wealth of the ruling families and the wealth of the nation have long been murky in the GCC states. SWFs in the region are widely thought to be the treasurers of national wealth and some, like Kuwait's fund, seem to hint that the public might some day have a claim to its resources (judging at least by its name, the 'Kuwaiti Fund for Future Generations'). However, unlike sovereign funds belonging to democratically elected national and sub-national governments, the prospect of exercising such de-facto ownership rights in the GCC is uncertain. In Norway, for example, the performance, asset allocation and social responsibility of the US$450 billion pension fund, is often a major theme in public discourse. However, factors such

---

2 For example, the Abu Dhabi Investment Authority (ADIA) typically holds small equity stakes (below disclosure requirements) and has used derivatives and other financial instruments in its trading to avoid detection. It entrusts as much as 80 percent to external asset managers, with the bulk of equity holdings in index funds. Although it rarely takes significant stakes in companies, there were some exceptions in 2007 and 2008, as ADIA launched a strategic equities division. It took larger stakes in Citi, EFG-Hermes, and Apollo. Although these stakes are significant, the shares remain below 10 percent and account for only a small part of ADIA's total holdings.

as the opacity of the size, portfolio allocation and motivation of Gulf investments have made SWF in the Gulf region to occupy an entirely different category in global policy discourse. A further complication is the tendency of some member of Gulf royal families to co-invest personal 'private funds' alongside the sovereign wealth fund that they personally oversee. This trend has been most visible in Qatar, where the Emir of Qatar invested in Barclays at the same time as the Qatar investment Authority (QIA). Needless to say, this alarms many Western observers, who are used to a more clear separation between public and private finance.

Lessons from the Last Oil Boom

Nonetheless, the opacity of Gulf Arab SWFs as well as their lack of transparency should not obscure the more discernible characteristics of their purposes and intentions. One way to understand the purpose of the funds is to look at the shifts in their international operations, which – not incidentally – mirror the change in fortunes seen in the various oil booms and busts over the last several decades. Although their foray into widespread controversy is recent, GCC foreign investments and sovereign funds are not new. For example, the investment funds of Abu Dhabi and Kuwait were launched several decades ago and Saudi Arabia is known to have made high profile trophy purchases in the 1970s. Moreover, SWFs have not always been entirely passive investors. While a large fraction of the region's revenues throughout the 1970s has found a way into US dollar deposits, which were subsequently loaned out by global banks to other emerging economies, high profile investments in global companies and purchases of property were also part of the GCC portfolios then.

Losses on some of these assets, as well as the difficulty in extracting the funds when it was deemed necessary during the 1980s, led some GCC investors like Saudi Arabia and Kuwait to boost the liquidity of their foreign assets. For instance, Kuwait has used this liquidity to help in financing government spending and reconstruction after the first Gulf War (see Seznac 2008). However, by the end of the 1990s, when oil prices crashed, the total assets of GCC government investors had fallen to under $300 billion, with Abu Dhabi accounting for over half of the regional total.[3] In addition, soon after the oil price boom of the 1970s, which had given GCC states (especially major oil producers like Saudi Arabia) considerable political and economic power via the ability to influence international oil prices, the leverage of GCC oil producers in petroleum markets began to wane. OPEC, and much of the GCC by extension, ceded considerable price-making power to global financial markets. Russia's and Norway's introduction into world oil markets, along with

---

3   The size of Abu Dhabi's portfolio is a closely guarded secret. However several news reports from the beginning of the decade suggest a portfolio size of around $150 billion, a number that is consistent with the UAE's cumulative current account surplus from the late 1970s onward.

UK offshore drilling, wrested market power away from OPEC members, relegating most of the influence to oil futures markets (Momani 2008).

Probably the most important lesson learned following this dwindling of fortunes was the GCC states' vulnerability to the price of oil and the need to create alternative streams of incomes. The need to balance domestic employment and social welfare concerns with ensuring an equitable share of oil wealth for future generations has persuaded GCC governments that mechanisms must be created to ameliorate the impact of oil boom and bust cycles (see IMF 2008b). The idea of relying on direct governments revenues via portfolio investments, rather than depending on wealth generated in the private sector, was not an unpredictable one for the GCC governments, given their rent-reliant economies. To be sure, this trend may be gradually changing (see Hvidt in this volume), and the proliferation of SWF activities may be part and parcel of the strategy leading toward a restructuring of domestic economic incentives. Nonetheless, the public sector remains the chief source of economic rents for Gulf Arab citizens.

On the whole, both domestic and international political economy concerns were the main drivers of the recent uptake in SWF activity. The Gulf states' desire to actively diversify their streams of revenue away from oil have led them to move away from passive investments and to take on more risks in their portfolios. And while national security concerns, along with worries about the politicization of financial markets, have dominated discussions in the financial media (for an overview see, for example, Drezner 2008) there are reasons to believe that SWFs are behaving quite similarly to their private-sector counterparts like pension and endowment funds (Ziemba 2008). To be sure, Gulf Arab SWFs tend to have a higher appetite for equity, and notably private equity (Smith-Diwan 2009). But this characteristic is not, by itself, sufficient to suggest the existence of an ulterior motive.

Perceptions and Realities

Many concerns color the landscape of fears surrounding the activities of SWF, and much of these fears are related to the purported economic power and political influence objectives of Gulf Arab SWF activities. Given the lack of evidence about the funds' intentions it is perhaps important to keep in mind that, while their role in the GCC's overall investment patterns has certainly grown, the more prominent SWFs, like the Abu Dhabi Investment Authority (ADIA) have existed for decades. Moreover, some have argued that the capital under the purview of each individual SWF, while large, is not large enough at the individual fund level to cause a significant disruption in trade, commercial activity, or financial markets. As Seznac (2009) notes,

> ... Gulf funds are not large enough to even think of taking controlling interest in large Western firms. Citibank's market capitalization at a very depressed price

today is over $120 billion. Major financial and industrial concerns like General Electric have market caps of $320 billion. The net profits after tax of ExxonMobil are twice the GNP of Bahrain [2008 estimates]. Hence, the Gulf SWFs by their size cannot present any strategic danger to the United States. They have learned from experiences such as the Dubai Ports World debacle in the United States and the BP divestment under Margaret Thatcher that such use of their money can backfire and that, ultimately, they cannot create hostile takeovers.

Nevertheless, it is worth noting that the aggregate total of assets held by all GCC sovereign wealth funds leading up the global financial crisis was considerable – close to $1 trillion by the end of 2007. More importantly, the combined 'sovereign wealth' of the GCC, which includes central bank reserve assets, rivals the total foreign exchange reserves of China (and perhaps even exceeds it if the estimated private assets of members of the respective Emirates' royal families is included) (Setser and Ziemba 2007). Herein lie the roots of the controversy surrounding the activities of Gulf SWFs.

One reason for the attention directed at these funds is the SWFs' role in a broader trend of a growing capital account deficit in the US and the perceived American vulnerability to emerging market creditors. During the early stages of the credit crunch in the wider global financial crisis, prominent members of the US political establishment echoed this notion directly. In March 2008, US Senator Charles Schumer, for example, called SWFs, 'the most available form of capital right now', lamenting that 'we import more than we export; we consume more than we save. The best choice would be that financial institutions could raise capital within the US. But we don't have that choice' (CRS 2008, 12). Directly tied to this anxiety regarding US macroeconomic vulnerability to SWFs is the fear that, because they are government-run investment funds, they cannot be expected to follow the logic of private market actors. As Senator Evan Bayh summarized the view during a congressional hearing, 'just as the United States has geopolitical interests in addition to financial ones, so do other countries. Just as we value some things more than money, so do they. Why should we assume that other nations are driven purely by financial interests when we are not?' (CRS 2008, 12).

There is little doubt that the global financial architecture has shifted in the 2000s, that financial globalization is taking on a new shape whereby financial assets are increasingly concentrated in emerging markets economies. As such, in addition to the opaqueness of SWF operations, the anxiety and hostility in Washington toward GCC investments is also an outgrowth of the popular fear of growing US indebtedness and its perceived consequences for US sovereignty. Moreover, given the nature of Gulf investment patterns such attention surrounding SWF activity is not unexpected. After all, unlike East Asia's central bank reserve managers and SWF investors, GCC states invest their respective petrodollar earnings and not money channelled from its domestic financial institutions – that is to say, Gulf Arab SWFs invest tangible and not borrowed money. This allows them to invest more actively in equities and, perhaps more importantly, to diversify their investments into more varied portfolios than those centered on US assets. In short, it gives them potential leverage *vis-à-vis* the US financial system.

Another aspect of the widespread anxiety surrounding the funds stems less from the worry that exceeding sums of money will be borrowed from the GCC, but the notion that the Gulf SWFs will increasingly take their money elsewhere, investing in emerging market assets and in their own domestic financial markets, thus lessening their dependence on US markets and making future financing of US deficits a precarious affair (Anderson 2009).

Indeed, the purported mystery surrounding the intentions of authoritarian governments dabbling in the global financial system has caused much alarm among Western observers. The diversification away from the US market undertaken by the GCC may be a natural choice for Gulf Arab states looking to avoid the mistakes of the oil boom of the 1970s, and so the prospect of GCC governments using such diversification as economic leverage *vis-à-vis* the West, and the US in particular, is not entirely specious. But while diversification has indeed taken place, as we will discuss further below, it is not so clearly detrimental to the current global financial status quo, nor to the financial interests of the US.[4]

To illustrate this point, the rest of this chapter will focus on the nature of SWF growth and investment dynamics (recent and projected future dynamics), and outline the extent have GCC economies directed their savings away from dollar-based assets, as well as the nature of this diversification (i.e. where is it leading the GCC). It will also explore the broader implications of SWF investment dynamics for the evolution of the global financial system.

The Limits of Growth Among Gulf Sovereign Wealth Funds

One way to unravel the controversy surrounding the funds' intended purposes (since it is infamously difficult to discern the motivations of GCC authorities) is to look at what spurred the growth of the funds in the first place. Three concurrent trends added to the prominence of GCC investors after 2005: (1) a significant increase in the revenue of GCC governments through the increase in the price of oil; (2) a repayment of domestic and external debt incurred into the late 1990s; (3) and a desire for higher returns on the savings tied to oil revenue. These developments have been matched by a greater tendency to accumulate foreign exchange reserves elsewhere in the recent decade, especially in many key emerging markets economies. Accordingly, other governments, particularly those in Asia, also sought higher returns on their investments. China and Russia both moved to establish sovereign wealth funds of their own.

---

4   Meanwhile, it is even less clear whether a shift away from US assets, causing depreciation in the value of the dollar is detrimental to a sluggish US domestic economy marred by American current account deficits.

Table 7.1 Assets of selected sovereign wealth funds (all US$ billion at end of period)

	Dec–99	Dec–07	Jun–08	Dec–08	Jun–09	Dec–09
ADIA/ADIC	150	453	476	337	358	415
Mubadala, other UAE	–	30	40	45	50	55
Kuwait Investment Authority	55	259	286	226	234	267
Qatar Investment Authority	–	65	82	59	61	77
Total GCC	205	807	883	667	704	813
Norway Government Fund–Global	28	371	391	323	367	450
Kazakhstan Stabilization Fund	–	21	26	27	22	24
Libyan Investment Authority	–	40	45	50	52	60
Chile stabilization fund	3	14	19	20	16	11
Commodity Funds	*236*	*1253*	*1364*	*1087*	*1161*	*1358*
China Investment Corp	–	100	100	95	100	100
Government Investment Corporation (Singapore)	100	245	242	165	179	206
Temasek (Singapore)	10	75	85	55	65	70
Korea Investment Corporation	–	18	25	25	28	28
Asia	*110*	*438*	*452*	*340*	*372*	*404*
Total Major Sovereign Funds	*346*	*1692*	*1816*	*1428*	*1533*	*1763*
Reserve-like						
SAMA non-reserve + pensions	47	335	414	475	423	410
Russian Reserve and wealth funds	–	157	163	225	184	167
Total Reserve-like Funds	*47*	*492*	*577*	*700*	*607*	*577*
GCC share of total	0.59	0.48	0.49	0.47	0.46	0.46
Commodity %	0.68	0.74	0.75	0.76	0.757	0.77

Source: National Central Banks, Author estimates.

As illustrated in Table 7.1, GCC funds account for about half of global sovereign wealth fund assets under management. Norway's fund accounts for another US$450 billion, bringing the commodity funds share of the global total to almost 80 percent. In contrast, the combined foreign holdings of the Chinese, Singaporean and South Korean funds account for about US$500. As such, the asset allocations of the GCC are quite significant for the overall picture of the management of sovereign assets.

The foreign holdings of GCC sovereign funds and central banks rose by more than a factor of four from their 2000–03 levels by mid-2008 (IMF 2008b). Saudi Arabia and Abu Dhabi each managed over US$400 billion and Kuwait managed close to US$280 billion. Qatar shifted from a net external debt position in the year 2000 to having a sovereign fund managing well over $70 billion. The significant savings rate, at least through 2008, and the high returns on the sovereign funds of Abu Dhabi, contributed to the rapid growth of these collective assets. It is also noteworthy that many of these assets were not concentrated in the US financial system. Unlike their private sector counterparts, Gulf SWFs have a greater tolerance for emerging market risk (also see Momani in this volume). For example, ADIA placed some 14 percent of its portfolio investments in emerging markets, while US pensions funds have only allocated some 5 percent of their portfolio there (Smith-Diwan 2009, 349). By the end of 2007 it is estimated that GCC funds had 53 percent of their assets in non-US dollar currencies (Setser and Ziemba 2007). These funds also developed significant clusters of holdings in property (tourism and others), health care, automotive and aerospace, as well as with the GCC traditional strength in the resource sector. However, the bulk of the GCC portfolio (including assets beyond SWFs) remained in bonds and equity, an allocation largely reflecting the composition of the funds of Abu Dhabi and Saudi Arabia's central bank, the two largest pools of capital in the region.

In the early stages of the global financial crisis some had concluded that the SWF shift to emerging market equities, as part of a broader ambivalence about investing in US assets, foreshadowed a gloomy future for US public finances and marked the decline of the dollar-based international monetary system (see, for example, Anderson 2009). Some official rhetoric throughout the crisis fanned the flames of these suspicions, as several political figures in emerging markets suggested that dollar asset holders were looking for alternatives to the greenback and refusing to offer US Treasury and Wall Street definitive support.[5] But SWF activity at the outset of the crisis also included propping up US financial institutions via asset purchases to stem the global financial contagion. This included capital injections of $60 billion starting in early 2007 and around an additional $40 billion from November to January (2009), to recapitalize distressed financial institutions. Such investments contributed to making the financial sector dominant among the sectors of investment of Gulf SWFs and gave the Gulf funds an aura of power that

---

5　China had made repeated warnings that the US should not feel complacent about its debt (see, for example Bloomberg 2009).

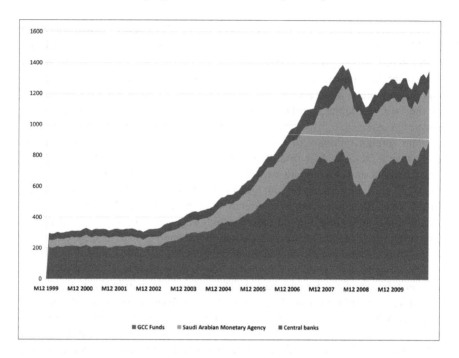

Figure 7.1 GCC, estimated stocks by fund

quickly captured the popular imagination in the US (Senator Schumer's comments were, in fact, referring to some of those very purchases).

The crisis had eventually altered these dynamics. The significant allocation of funds to risky assets worldwide led to an equally significant fall in market value in late 2008. Accordingly, GCC governments faced a decrease in investment revenue as oil revenue also collapsed. Many of these funds were forced to turn inward and invest more domestically in 2008–09 – a trend that is likely to continue even if the price of oil remains relatively high. If past trends ring true in the near future, and if we assume relatively modest investment returns, it would take many years for GCC portfolios to reach their 2007–08 levels. As such, the issue of diversification of the funds' international investments may have recently lost its immediate relevance. The pressing question for GCC governments is how much ought to be allocated to domestic markets as opposed to international ones, rather than how much should go to the US as opposed to other foreign assets.

Gulf SWFs need to be seen as a part of the GCC states' broader national asset allocation strategy, which means that some sovereign funds have both an investment and a savings motive. As the 2008 international financial crisis had dawned, the savings that the funds incurred throughout the years were a key resource that various GCC government could draw on to shore up their domestic financial systems; to offset revenue shortfalls and to continue with economic development

Table 7.2 Estimated assets of GCC governments and their domestic investments

Country	Fund (all estimates end 2008 unless specified)	Estimated losses/net gains in 2008	Support of financial sector/fiscal stimulus
Saudi Arabia	$423 billion in of central bank non-reserve assets (including those managed for other government institutions)	Limited losses given bond heavy portfolio.	GOSI (retirement fund) increased its holdings of domestic assets. Expansionary fiscal policy funded by savings. New investment vehicles will provide capital for Saudi government investors.
UAE	$400 billion – ADIA, ADIC, Mubadala (foreign assets only)	An estimated over $100 billion in investment losses in 2008, which exceeded record revenues.	Central bank provided funds to UAE banks and funds to Dubai ($10 billion bond issue).
Kuwait	$235 billion	As much as $80 billion in investment losses. Boosted cash allocation.	Increased exposure to domestic equities. Participated in gulf bank capital raising. Guaranteed bank deposits.
Qatar	$70 billion (QIA)	Losses of as much as $30 billion on equity/alt heavy portfolio including leveraged UK real estate. Had gains on stakes in foreign banks.	Took stakes in state banks of up to 20% of deposit base. Facilitated purchase of property and investment holdings of domestic financial institutions.

goals. This domestic stabilization motive has, in fact, long been an essential element of the SWFs' function in the GCC, and as the financial crisis unravelled further, this motive quickly subsumed the former emphasis on investment. Accordingly, not only has domestic spending increased through greater transfer payments and infrastructure but new, domestically focused, asset managers have sprung up to lay claim to some of the Gulf governments' revenues, drawing down the current and potential source of funds for SWFs. Table 7.2 illustrates some of the vehicles through which these funds supported domestic asset markets and their domestic economies. Such capital needs at home certainly increase the incentive to have liquid assets available to channel funds for domestic purposes – channel to increase market share in key domestic sectors including automotive/aerospace, energy, property and the financial sector. In other words, the international assets of Gulf SWFs are, in the near future, likely to be liquid and short term, rather than strategic and long term.

How likely are such projections? Recent events, especially the sudden decline in the price of oil in 2008, have shown that the growth of SWF international investments is still heavily constrained by the needs of their domestic economies. The problem of adjustment to the future movements in the price of oil still remains. As such, the growth of GCC foreign assets projected into the future depends on two essential dynamics: the size of the oil revenues of GCC governments and the size of domestic spending in their respective economies. With oil above $100 a barrel, GCC investments will grow, with oil below $50 a barrel they will shrink (Setser and Ziemba 2007).

Most GCC countries have currently at least one fund that invests in sectors supportive of domestic goals. Not only have government funds increased their domestic investments but they are also being used to make up for fiscal deficits. A return to the $70 oil price, allows most GCC governments to balance their budgets on current revenues (despite a drop in oil production, which increases the break-even level). To be sure, even Saudi Arabia, the country that bore the brunt of the OPEC production cuts (followed by the UAE and Qatar), should at most be able to balance its budget at current levels. Not surprisingly, the region has largely shifted from having a large current account surplus to a small deficit for some countries and small surpluses for the rest. As a result of the recent financial crisis and of the decline in oil revenues, and given the political necessity of supporting domestic job growth, domestically-oriented foreign investment vehicles are likely to continue to be among the most significant investors even if oil prices remain at current levels or climb.

To summarize, given the current domestic needs of GCC economies, and absent a significant spike in the price of oil well above the US$98/barrel average for 2008, the growth of the funds' international assets is likely to slow. This means that 2008 is likely to have been a watershed year for the injection of new capital and investment vitality into these funds. In GCC countries, as with many other oil exporting economies in the emerging world, what is left after oil and gas production costs as well as domestic spending needs are accounted for remains precarious (see, for example, the discussion on labour nationalization in Hertog in this volume). The increase in domestic spending throughout the region as well as the incentive to increase liquid assets to meet domestic liquidity needs could certainly restrain the Gulf SWFs' future role in global asset markets, especially when compared with their acquisitions in 2007 and 2008, when the funds were in the global spotlight. In short, for the GCC, any considerations of flexing their financial muscle – of projecting their economic power abroad – remain subject to future movements in the price of oil.

Sovereign Wealth Funds and Global Capital Markets

This section examines the Gulf SWFs' broader pattern of international investment and looks at where current trends seem to be leading the GCC and their sovereign funds. Because the fortunes of Gulf Arab SWFs are, as discussed above, still dependent on the oil incomes of GCC governments and the domestic needs of their respective economies, the trajectory of SWF investments is highly uncertain. But this uncertainty is unlikely to quell the political anxieties surrounding the funds' activity in global capital markets – in particular, the anxieties over weather sovereign wealth managers can be said to be in support of a US-centered global financial system or whether they stand in opposition to it. Therefore, it is useful to unravel the logic behind the SWFs' global investment dynamics.

To better understand the role of SWFs in the GCC's international investment dynamics – specifically, the extent to which they are activists or defenders of the status quo in the global financial system – it is useful to see sovereign investors on a broad spectrum of risk appetite and asset allocation. At one extreme we find central banks, which have the most liquid assets and have a goal of preserving price stability – in the case of the GCC, also exchange rate stability. On the other end of the spectrum we find state owned enterprises, national oil companies and other such direct investors owned by the government. In between there is a category that includes stabilization or reserve funds, which have predominately liquid assets and are similar to central banks (pension funds in the Gulf region tend to have a similar, and mostly liquid asset allocation but tend to be undercapitalized). In this category we can locate 'sovereign wealth funds', which resemble other institutional investors like pension and endowment funds (ADIA, KIA) or in some cases hedge funds (QIA). Other hybrid funds or holding companies such as Mubadala and Aabar are more similar in their activities to state-owned corporations.[6]

While each of these actors has a different, if sometimes shifting, investment strategy they all play a part in the national investment strategy. Therefore, it is difficult to paint all Gulf Arab funds with a broad stroke and to determine precisely how they contribute to, or erode, the influence of the US-centered global financial system. Most significantly, the recent inward turn on the part of many Gulf SWF activities seems to suggest an inward-, rather than outward-looking imperative of their collective and individual activities. On the other hand, this does not imply that GCC sovereign wealth has become completely inept in global financial markets. The case of Saudi Arabia, for example, illustrates the GCC's international investment potential particularly well. Whatever one makes of the GCC's role in the dollar-centered global monetary system, Saudi Arabia's place – at least as visible through the holdings of its central bank (SAMA) – has been one of support. Saudi Arabia's official dollar assets occupy a far higher share of official reserve assets than that of other GCC states (see Setser and Ziemba 2007). In addition to important strategic military ties between the Saudi government and the US, financial ties between the two are no less significant. Nevertheless, the country maintains a large number of 'privately-held' foreign assets, especially those assets held privately by Saudi princes, many of which are denominated in currencies other than the dollar. As Smith-Diwan notes, once the private investment of Saudi royals is taken into account, the composition of Saudi 'sovereign' wealth does not look so different from the other Gulf Arab states (2009, 353). The recent creation of a Saudi SWF matches this dual objective of maintaining support for the US

---

6   The IMF's 2008 Regional Economic Outlook for Middle East and Central Asia region provides a brief but detailed list of the different types of SWFs in the region (see IMF 2008b, 35).

while allowing for a real degree of diversification, especially domestically, where reform schemes and economic diversification have been undertaken in recent years (Smith-Diwan 2009).

Diversification away from the dollar-denominated assets might gradually be taking place, but only within the broader context of the GCC states' national investment strategies, which is currently subordinated to more pressing domestic needs. Indeed, even before the global financial crisis and the most recent fall in the price of oil hit GCC revenues, Gulf governments were most concerned with domestic diversification (see, for example, Smith-Diwan 2009). As such, the focus on global financial diversification obscures the more important issue at hand. Rather than asking, for example, how Gulf SWFs are being used to challenge the US financial interests, it is more appropriate to ask what role do SWFs international investments play in the GCC's domestic diversification strategy? It is easy to overstate the impact of sovereign wealth, firstly because of the uncertain nature of their activities, but also because their role is only one part of broader Gulf Arab international investment dynamics and is not meaningful when viewed in a vacuum. Therefore, we need to place the SWFs' investment dynamics within the broader role of public investors in the global financial system.

Sovereign Wealth Funds and Financial Globalization

In this final section we explore the broader global significance of Gulf Arab SWF investment dynamics. Many of the uncertainties surrounding the growth of SWFs, and Gulf Arab sovereign fund activity in particular, have been at least somewhat assuaged by the decline of economic activity brought about by the fallout of the global financial crisis. As external surpluses diminished and as the accumulation of foreign currency reserves slowed throughout the GCC countries, the availability of resources at the disposal of SWF managers dwindled. In part, this is attributable to, as we have argued in this chapter, the fact that evidence has not substantiated the perceived threat surrounding SWFs: the threat of the execution of political or economic objectives – beyond market-based rationales – on behalf of the governments to which they answer. But does this mean that the crisis diminishes, if not removes, the significance of Gulf SWFs' global investment activities?

Given the recent trajectory of financial globalization, one would be hard-pressed to reach such a conclusion. Many of the issues surrounding the significance of SWFs' investment activities are unlikely to disappear just because the vitality of the GCC's sovereign funds has cooled. To paraphrase Daniel Drezner's summary of the collective uncertainty surrounding the role of sovereign wealth in global financial markets,

> State-led development societies, in which governments use SWFs to buy off dissent and promote development and technology transfer, could emerge as a viable challenger to the accepted political economy of the advanced

industrialized states. This would have corrosive effects on the West's soft power. It would be an open question of whether the rest of the world would look at the Western development model as one to emulate. Crudely put, far fewer counties would want what the United States and European Union want. (Drezner 2008, 119–120)

The global financial crisis could exacerbate this uncertainty, especially if one of the consequences from the crisis is a decline in confidence in the role of the free market. In other words, the threat to the United Sates and other advanced industrialized countries is not direct. Rather the issue at hand is the broader appeal of the economic model that may be implied in the role played by sovereign investors in the global financial system.

Much in the same way that the financial crisis has shaken the foundations upon which SWFs have grown and prospered, so too can it be said to have shaken the faith in the promises of US-led financial globalization and of the benefits of integrated global financial markets. Could the controversy surrounding the recent growth of SWFs a part, or perhaps a symbolic sign, of a countertrend to market-led financial globalization? Contrary to such a perspective, it is useful to conceive of sovereign wealth funds as a symbol of the obsolescence of a simple 'state-versus-market' dichotomy. In short, the inherent tension between the logic of internationalized financial markets and the domestic prerogatives of states are not mutually exclusive.

Brad Setser (2008) has argued that in the past decade the global financial system has taken on an increasingly 'Neo-Westphalian' character. State actors, alongside market actors, have come to play a key role in the movement of global financial markets rather than standing in opposition to the latter's impact on domestic sovereignty. In other words, the state is increasingly an active participant in global finance. In other words, 'financial globalization has not proved to be the same as financial Americanization': the earlier proclamation of the victory of neoliberal models of international finance – of the reduction in the role of the state – had effectively jumped the gun (Setser 2008). While the immediate global role of SWFs may have been reduced during the recent global financial crisis – or rather, retreated to abide by a more domestically-focused prerogative – the broader global economic role of sovereign asset holders, such as those in East Asia as well as oil exporters like the GCC states, has anything but diminished. While the immediate political implications of SWF investments are currently less pressing for host countries, the implications for the emerging markets, where the funds are located, remains significant, as sovereign funds persist in their roles of managing economic activity.

Edwin Truman, for example, has concluded that 'the philosophical, political, and economic contest between the traditional model of mature industrial democracies, with their reliance on markets, and state capitalism, with its appeal to power and nationalism, is far from settled in many emerging market economies' (Truman 2010, 162). Indeed, because of the status of SWFs as investment arms of authoritarians and, in many aspects, reactionary social regimes, one may even be tempted to conclude that they represent Polanyi's 'regressive movements for social protection' – a nationalist backlash against the advancement of market-driven globalization. Indeed, perhaps this recent reassertion of the role of the state in global finance represents a rise of nationalist authoritarian elements that 'confront the arrogance of the neoliberal order with their own version of certainty' (Evans 2008, 285). Nonetheless, such a point is perhaps difficult to assert, as nationals in the respective GCC emirates both prosper from the 'material well-being promised by markets' and benefit 'from the security supposedly delivered by the state' (Evans 2008, 285). In other words, they remain isolated from many of the socio-economic pressures of the market. Nor can it be said that they offer a global counter-hegemonic alternative to market capitalism, as they are, in fact, quite dependent thereon.

In short, the rise of SWFs and the greater prominence in the role of the state in the global financial system offers no neat convergences with our existing understanding of financial globalization. SWF investment dynamics, as part of their broader role in the investment strategy of the GCC broadly reflect a greater role for the state in future evolution of the global financial system. However, given their current domestic orientation, it is still unclear precisely what that role will be.

Conclusion

This chapter has examined the role of sovereign wealth funds in the GCC's international investment dynamics. To be specific, we have examined the significance of the growth in SWF activity leading up to the 2008 international financial crisis and the role of this activity to relative to the GCC states' investment goals. Our goal has been to discern, given the available data, the political and economic motivations of Gulf SWFs. In doing so, we have attempted to elucidate the significance of these government owned-investment vehicles and their role in the global financial system and the global economy more broadly.

We have argued that the fears surrounding the unknown political and economic motives of SWF asset acquisitions are not substantiated by the pattern of SWF growth and investment behavior. Given the multitude of obligations and constraints faced by SWF managers, the rise in the activity of sovereign-managed investment cannot be viewed in a vacuum. Most significantly, the scale and composition of SWF activity is highly dependent on the price of oil and the domestic needs of the GCC economies. The main lesson to take away from recent developments is that the GCC's aggressive appetite for risk and international diversification is not an end in itself. If there is a particular strategy, on the part of GCC states collectively or individually, to mount a challenge to the prevailing global financial architecture, it certainly seems to have taken a backseat to domestic prerogatives, which included domestic fiscal rescue packages to stem the tide of deteriorating profits caused by a sharp contraction in world oil prices.

GCC funds must undergo a tight balancing act between international asset allocations and the needs of the domestic economies. The strain on the capital from other government sources undoubtedly reduces the money available to SWFs. Moreover, the pressures to assume the debt of the private sector, including domestic financial sector and corporate debt, and the increasing demand for safe and liquid assets further restricts the kind of ambitious international investment dynamics witnessed leading up to the crisis. But just as the global financial crisis has highlighted the limitations of the perceived global aspirations of SWFs, it has not diminished the significance of the funds themselves. To say that the recent dwindling in the fortunes of the various GCC government diminishes the relevance of these funds is to miss a broader shift in the significance of sovereign wealth in the global financial system. At the very least, the international significance of Gulf Arab SWFs is only one part of a potentially broader shift in the significance of the state in global financial markets.

Chapter 8

Arab Sovereign Wealth Funds: The Challenge of Transparency

Sara Bazoobandi and Tim Niblock

Introduction

Sovereign wealth funds (SWFs) have been actively operating for decades. It has, however, only been recently that some have seen them as problematic to the international financial system. The term itself was coined in 2005 by a financial analyst from the City of London (Rozanov 2005) and it was not until 4 May 2007, when Morgan Stanley published its report 'How Big Could Sovereign Wealth Funds be by 2015?', that the issue became controversial. The Morgan Stanley report predicted that by 2015 the value of the funds held by SWFs could have grown from the estimated 2007 figure of $2.5 trillion to double that size before 2010, 'and rise to around the $10 trillion mark before 2010, before reaching around $12 trillion by 2015' (Jen 2007). The assets of the SWFs would, in this perspective, surpass the official reserves of governments by 2011.

Much of the initial debate in the Western world focused on the lack of transparency of many SWFs. This was considered central to the 'threat' which they posed to the international financial system: their actions were unpredictable, their objectives unclear, and the probity of their operations impossible to investigate or verify. A number of surveys suggested that Gulf Arab SWFs were particularly opaque in their activities. The demand for transparency has, in fact, constituted a major element in the response of Western governments and institutions to the supposed threat (in addition to the introduction of some protectionist measures). The assumption underpinning the demand for transparency was that greater openness would make the activities of the SWFs more comparable to those of the investment banks of the Western world, and would turn them into acceptable investors in Western business. The various dimensions of supposed threat would be reduced, and Western economies would be able to benefit from new sources of investment funding. At the same time, this was seen as a big task – requiring a substantial transformation in culture and approach to be taken by the SWFs. It is worth noting that practical experience provides little evidence of deviant behavior occurring under the cloak of SWF lack of transparency – at least as regards the supposed political interests of regimes. Nor is their evidence of SWFs acting unethically in their financial transactions. Most investments can be clearly shown to be geared to the maximization of long-term economic gain for the fund concerned

This chapter takes a different line to that just outlined. It will contend that SWFs may be able to adapt to greater transparency relatively easily. Should this be achieved, however, the scale of the problems which SWFs pose for Western economies will not necessarily be lessened, and may in fact be intensified. Greater transparency is likely to mean that the SWFs will become more open to criticism by public opinion within their home countries. Home public opinions are already questioning why so much money is being invested abroad while the domestic economies are (sometimes) suffering from a lack of investment. Such questions are likely to be raised more insistently when the public has access to more information about the activities of the funds. Issues over the direction of investments may also arise, with suggestions that Gulf Arab SWF assets would be safer and more productive in the Middle East and Asia than in the Western world. Middle East and Asian countries are less likely to take punitive action in the case of intergovernmental political conflict (see Momani; Davidson in this volume). Public opinion may even contest the appropriateness of certain fields of investment.

In short, an increase in transparency will probably reduce the flow of investment from the SWFs to the Western world. This will intensify the more fundamental problem for Western economies posed by the rapid growth of the SWFs: the shift of global financial and economic power away from the Western world. Transparency is in itself valuable and must be pursued, but at the same time Western governmental institutions and the private sector need to focus attention on the longer-term structural change in international investments that is now under way. The issue here is how they can adapt best to that structural change.

The chapter will first review the development of the debate on the transparency of SWFs. The procedures and operations of the Norwegian SWFs will be given attention, as these are often regarded as forming a model of best practice on transparency (which other SWFs would be advised to copy). We will then look at a counterpart dimension of the transparency debate: the perception on the part of SWFs (and their home governments) that Western governments themselves lack transparency in dealing with SWFs. The allegation here is that Western governments proclaim the need for free movement of capital but in practice restrict it when it is perceived as running counter to national interest writ large. SWFs have, it is claimed, been a prime target of protectionist measures. Some of the arguments lying behind this claim will be given attention. Attention will then be given to the procedures and operations of the Gulf Arab SWFs, with a view to assessing the extent to which these particular funds are transparent. The chapter will end with discussing possible outcomes of more transparent operation of the Gulf Arab SWFs on the region and on the world economy.

The Transparency Debate

The image which was created by the Morgan Stanley report, then, was of a massive transformation taking place in the global political economy, with a substantial shift in economic power away from the established centers of financial power in the West. The fact that the financial institutions which would control these vast resources were government-owned was seen as significant, marking a retreat from the neoliberal-led dominance of private sector institutions. The governments controlling the new investment resources, moreover, were ones whose political traditions were seen as different from (and perhaps alien to) those of the Western world. SWF investment decisions might, it was said, be motivated more by political considerations than by profit driven objectives, and funds could target security-sensitive and other 'strategic' assets. The investment flows between the developing world and the industrialized world would, it seemed, be inverted: part of the developing world (if that term could still be applied) would be in a position to buy up key economic assets in the developed industrial world. Banks, leading industries, and critical infrastructural facilities in the West could all come under the ownership and control of SWFs based in the Gulf and the Far East. Overall, there was the danger of financial-market turmoil and conflicts of interest between political and economic pressures (Truman 2008, 3)

The character of Western concerns needs, moreover, to be placed in the context of the events of September 11, when there was a rapid deterioration in US perceptions of Gulf Arab investments. These perceptions were now heavily shaped by fears over US national security. Public as well as governmental attitudes towards Arab money came to be moulded by suspicion and apprehension. Saudi institutions and corporations were blamed for the rise of terrorist networks, whether through encouraging attitudes which were prejudicial to the West or by channelling money to organizations which supported terrorism (directly or indirectly). Members of US Congress resented Saudi Arabia's refusal to allow the US air force to launch a strike against Afghanistan from Saudi territory (Congressional Research Service 2006), and there was further unhappiness when the Saudi government chose to distance itself from the US-British military campaign against Iraq in 2003. Gulf Arab investment in strategic sectors of the US economy (and to a lesser extent other Western economies) had, therefore, begun to raise concern even before the rapid rise in SWF resources had attracted public attention.

Inevitably, the comments in Western circles following the publication of the Morgan Stanley report in 2007 created a climate of uncertainty and concern for the SWFs themselves. It was unclear how their activities might be affected. More widely, the host governments of the Gulf Arab SWFs became concerned that Western governments would react to the growing financial strength of the GCC states by adopting protectionist measures in the financial sector (OECD 2008, 1).

The intergovernmental debate on the transparency of SWFs has been conducted most articulately within the context of the International Working Group of

Sovereign Wealth Funds (IWG). This was established in May 2008, as a platform for dialogue, ultimately enabling the countries with sovereign wealth funds to design and introduce best practices for their funds (see Behrendt in this volume). Both host and home governments of SWFs participated in the meetings of the IWG. Although it was the countries with SWFs which were taking the initiative forward, formally constituting the membership of the IWG, there was no doubt that it was the concerns of the host governments which constituted the motivating factor.

The outcome of the deliberations of the IWG was the adoption of 24 principles and recommended practices. These were compiled as the Generally Accepted Principles and Practices of Sovereign Wealth Funds (GAPP), and are now widely known as the 'Santiago Principles'. They can be regarded as the core of the global endeavor to create a mutual understanding of SWFs through greater transparency of operations and disclosure of information by the funds. The SWFs clearly hoped that the adoption of these principles and practices would deter host governments from protectionist measures. The 24 principles and practices, most of which refer to information being 'clearly defined', 'reported on' or 'publicly disclosed', reflect most of the key demands which host governments had been making with regard to SWF transparency (IWG 2008, 22; see Behrendt in this volume). The IWG also provided explanations and commentaries of what each of the 24 principles and practices entailed. Considerable emphasis is placed on the objectives and investment strategy of the funds being clearly stated and frequently modified to reflect changing conditions. For example, Information about portfolio and risk management should be made available, how the funds are incorporated into the investment mechanism, and how changes can be effected (IWG 2008, 22). The governance of the funds should be set out clearly so as to define the relationship with government, with a provision that a SWF's management should be operationally independent from the owner (normally the government). SWFs should not take advantage of privileged information coming from government sources. There was also the intention that ethical standards should be defined and made known, in addition to maintaining the usual commercial requirements for auditing of accounts, setting out procedures on risk-exposure, having established reporting systems, defining the role of internal/external investment managers, publication of annual reports etc. The strategy pursued should be consistent with sound assessment management principles. Where investment decisions were subject to economic and non-economic considerations, the latter had to be clearly set out and publicly disclosed.

In addition to the intergovernmental debate there has also been a debate among analysts of international finance and investment. The starting point here was also the view that an international standard on government cross-border investments by SWFs needed to be developed, covering the investment objectives, governance and transparency of behavior of the funds (Truman 2007b, 19). Considerable emphasis was placed on the dangers inherent in a system where there was insufficient information about SWF activities. Transparency, it was said, would promote intra-organizational 'horizontal accountability', at both domestic and international levels, and would strengthen the relationship between the investor and the host economy. It would also create 'vertical accountability' between the investment decision-makers and the home country. Crucial to this would be the publication of annual reports and the institution of regular auditing processes (Truman 2008, 17). The analysts' debate went beyond the intergovernmental debate in one important respect: it developed systems for the measurement of transparency so that the record of different SWFs could be assessed and compared. There were different approaches in developing such systems, but the most common one involved score-boards, using a binary score counting method to quantify the record in each aspect of operations, with the conclusion based on the overall score.

This method of evaluation was used in the Transparency Index and was applied by Edwin Truman of the Peterson Institute in 2007 to SWFs. He created 24 questions which cover the structure, governance, accountability and behavior of the SWFs. The given weight to each question is either 0 or 1 and the total score of each fund is an indicator for the level of transparency of that fund (Truman 2007b, 19). The Sovereign Wealth Fund Institute has also introduced an index based on the same methodology but with a rather succinct list of questions (Sovereign Wealth Fund Institute 2009, 18).

Norwegian SWFs: A Model of 'Best Practices'

Debates about the transparency of SWFs often make reference to one experience which is sometimes seen as an ideal model for SWFs to emulate. This is the Norwegian experience. Given that the Norwegian SWFs is used as benchmark of 'best practices', it is worth noting some information about the Norwegian SWFs, especially with regard to the dimension of transparency. The Norwegian Government Pension Fund–Global (GPFG) was established in 1990. The fund is managed by the Central Bank of Norway. It has a well-defined system of regulations, named the Ethical Guideline, which was proposed by the Ministry of Finance in 2005. The Ministry of Finance decides, on the basis of this code, whether specific companies should be excluded from investment. In order to monitor application of the regulations the Council on Ethics, which is an organization responsible for observing the funds' operation, provides its own evaluation of whether potential investments in financial instruments issued by specified issuers are consistent with the ethical guidelines.

The GPFG's ethical guidelines are based on two premises. First, the fund is an instrument for ensuring that a reasonable portion of the country's petroleum wealth is saved for future generations. To achieve this objective, the GPFG's investment strategy should promote long-term financial returns. The ownership rights in any investment needs to be based on the investment guidelines developed by the UN and the OECD (OECD 2009). Second, the GPFG should not make investments which carry the risk of violating fundamental humanitarian principles, serious violations of human rights, gross corruption or severe environmental damage.

The Council on Ethics is required to report on its exercise of ownership rights in its annual reports to the Ministry of Finance (Siddiqi 2005; Norway Ministry of Finance 2005).

Norges Bank is the organization in charge of managing the GPFG, and it receives immediate notification of all relevant decisions issued by the Ministry of Finance – stemming from the recommendations made by the Council on Ethics. Norges Bank informs companies in which an investment is planned, or has been made. Moreover, the recommendations and decisions are all subject to public disclosure (Ministry of Finance 2005, 5).

Norges Bank is required to prepare accounts in keeping with the provisions of the Norwegian Accounting Act. Under current practice, the bank's Supervisory Council establishes the bank's accounting rules in accordance with the law and chooses an external auditor. The Office of the Auditor General then audits the Ministry of Finance's management of the GPFG on the basis of the bank's audited accounts. There is, then, a well-defined and detailed auditing procedure, bringing in the Office of the Auditor General, Norges Bank and the Supervisory Council on all of the GPFG decisions.

Transparency, in the case of Norway's main SWF, therefore, is enforced and overseen by a variety of different institutions and regulations. Norges Bank, the Ethical Council, the Ministry of Finance, and the Accountancy Act are all parts of the network of interacting institutions and regulations which ensure that the GPFG follows best practice. This is a model which presumably Gulf Arab SWFs would be wise to emulate and follow. The Gulf Arab SWFs, however, are created by governments which are themselves not transparent. In general, transparency in the operation of SWFs is more feasible in democratic systems, which already have in place the institutions with a duty to enhance transparency and the procedures in place to enforce it.

The Protectionist Threat: Lack of Transparency in the West?

To the home countries of SWFs, the issue of transparency is regarded in a different manner than in Western policy circles. States that own SWFs are concerned that Western policies geared towards protecting strategic assets may be used, more generally, to restrict SWF activity. Without clear definitions of what constitutes a 'strategic asset', Western governments may exploit enacted legislation to restrict SWF activity with political discrimination. Western policy-makers may also misuse protectionism as an instrument of retaliation for SWFs non-compliance with transparency requirements. Both the US and the EU have both threatened the use of protectionist policies as a direct way of responding to the SWF's growing financial strength (see Committee on Foreign Affairs House of Representatives 2008, 7). The insistence on SWF transparency, however, could also be used as an excuse to impose protectionism.

Throughout US financial history, foreign investors have traditionally been instrumental in financing the country's large current account deficit. Foreign investment in the US has, therefore, been seen by economists and US policy-makers as a stable and beneficial source of long-term capital. As noted, after the events of September 11, American public debate over national security started to spill into debates on the source and home countries' of foreign investment. In 2005, the China National Offshore Oil Corporation felt obliged to withdraw its purchase offer for UNOCAL, in the face of Congressional comments that the deal posed a threat to 'the US's oil lifelines' (Rubinoff and Savio, 2008). The UNOCAL accepted, instead, a less valuable purchase offer from Chevron. In 2006, Dubai Ports World was forced, again by Congressional allegations of a threat to national security, to sell its newly-acquired (from P&O) US ports operations to the US-owned Global Investment Group (Rubinoff and Savio 2008). This was despite the fact that P&O itself was also not an American company, but a British one.

Just over a year after the Dubai Ports episode the US Congress sanctioned the 2007 Foreign Investment and National Security Act (FINSA). This adjusted the 1950 Exon-Florio Amendment to the Defence Production Act relating to the notification of foreign investments in the United States. The new law recalibrated the role of the Committee on Foreign Investment in the United States (CFIUS), expanding the CFIUS' scope of national security reviews. The CFIUS now had the authority to review 'any merger, acquisition or takeover ... which could result in foreign control of any person engaged in interstate commerce in the United States'. All firms acquiring 'critical infrastructure' and 'foreign government-controlled transactions' were required to proceed to a 45-day investigation. There was, then, an implicit presumption that purchasing transactions involving critical infrastructure were likely to raise national security concerns. Included in the FINSA parameters of critical infrastructure is major energy assets; how far it extends beyond that (and whether it includes assets which relate to economic security, public health or public safety), remains unclear (Rubinoff and Savio 2008). To the home governments of some SWFs, the phrasing of the FINSA law seemed to open the possibility of selective and discriminate action against specific SWF investments, and where the considerations influencing the CFIUS' decisions would not be made transparent.

In the EU, as well, there has been debate about sovereign investments. On the one hand, leading European politicians have promised to keep their economies open to all investors, sovereign or otherwise. They have welcomed SWF investments as vehicles for channelling some of the emerging market economies' oil wealth and capital savings into European economies. Some European governments have, moreover, argued that SWF investments will promote global balancing of capital by linking oil-producing countries and emerging Asian markets more closely to the West. EU regulations on multi-lateral investment are entrenched in EU commitments to international treaties and agreements. Individual EU members cannot easily impose restrictions on foreign investment without violating those regulations. To elaborate: Article 63 of the Treaty on the Functioning of the

European Union states that 'all restrictions on the movement of capital between Member States and between Member States and third countries shall be prohibited' (Official Journal of the European Communities 2008). At first reading, it would appear the individual EU countries were required to accept the EU treaty on providing a liberalized investment environment.

The EU Treaty, however, leaves individual member governments with some room for manoeuvre. The above-mentioned prohibition of restrictions on the movement of capital is preceded by the words 'within the framework of the provisions set out in this Chapter'. Article 64 allows the Council of Ministers to limit direct investments from non-EU countries, while stipulating that such a measure would require a unanimous vote in the Council. It recognizes that the measure would constitute 'a step back in Community law'. Article 65 affirms the right of individual member-states to restrict capital flows 'on the grounds of public policy or public security', while stressing that such measures shall not constitute a means of arbitrary discrimination or a disguised restriction on the movement of capital' (ibid.).

Although the EU's legal framework provides recipient countries some room for restrictive manoeuvre against the foreign investors, in practice the law has been rather strictly upheld. In some cases, the European Commission has taken EU governments to the European Court of Justice (ECJ) for limiting the free movement of capital.

Nonetheless, a number of EU countries have reacted in different ways to the growing strength of SWFs. Both Germany and the UK restated their commitment to providing an open business climate to foreign investors. Notwithstanding these claims, in 2008, Germany reacted to public pressure when Temasek-owned Neptune Orient Lines attempted to buy Hapag-Lloyd and workers went into the streets to demonstrate against feared job-losses. Reacting to this pressure, Hapag-Lloyd was then instead sold to a German consortium (Barysch 2008, 12). Spain actively encouraged SWFs from the Gulf to buy Spanish government bonds, but made no mention of investment in its Spanish private companies. The Italian government, in a more explicitly negative reaction, established a 'national interests committee' to establish rules about SWF investment, proposing that SWFs should not be allowed to own more than 5 percent of shares in any individual Italian company (Dinmore 2008). French President Sarkozy stated that 'I will not be the French president who wakes up in 6 months time to see that French industrial groups have passed into other hands', and he went further to propose that EU countries should themselves create SWFs to 'protect national companies from predators' (Hall 2008).

Among the many other policy proposals suggested for limiting SWF activity in the European Union, it has been proposed that EU governments acquire 'golden shares' in particular industries with veto rights to prevent foreign takeovers. Others have suggested the introduction of a 'reciprocity principle', where foreign investment would be permitted when the SWF's home country offered the same liberal foreign ownership rules as found in the EU host country. The latter proposal was made in a 2008 report commissioned by the French government (Demarolle 2008, 14). Observers pointed out that France itself would fail such a test if it were applied within the EU; French energy companies have made acquisitions in other EU countries, but have made it difficult or impossible for foreign energy firms to acquire their counterparts in France.

Gulf Arab Sovereign Wealth Funds

With the rapid increase in oil revenue in the second oil boom, Gulf Arab governments increased both domestic and foreign investments (McKinsey Global Institute 2009, 21). Interestingly, 61 percent of total SWF assets in 2008 were composed of commodity-based (as opposed to trade-based) funds. Specifically, approximately 44 percent of total assets were managed by Gulf Arab SWFs (Sovereign Wealth Fund Institute 2009, 18).

The contribution of Gulf Arab funds in total under management assets of SWFs globally is about 10 percent more than the non-commodity funds of Asia. The noticeable growth and size of these funds' assets has put them in a powerful position in the global financial system. The emerging market economies of the Gulf are owners of large pools of assets, a fact that only further heightens European and American anxieties over how this wealth might be strategically utilized and whether Gulf Arab investment decisions may be politically-driven. While the controversy regarding SWFs has intensified after 2007, the SWFs been also been the focus of some concern in the United States since September 2001.

Controversy aside, the question is how transparent are the Gulf Arab SWFs. Two sets of transparency ratings were compiled by Edwin Truman and the SWF Institute generally known as the Linaburg-Maduell (LM) Transparency Index. Both indexes use two different calculation methods and consequently the gap between the two indexes' transparency scores is striking. Gulf Arab SWFs which do well in one index in some cases do poorly in the other. Most of the SWFs have gained a lower overall score with the Truman method than with the LM model. There are a number of possible explanations to this. One is that there is inevitably a large element of subjectivity in the rankings, with different degrees of weight given to different dimensions of transparency. Another possible explanation, however, is that the transparency of the Gulf Arab SWFs has been improving rapidly, due to the international pressure exerted on them. The Truman scoreboard was prepared in 2007, while the LM model was updated in 2009.

The main focus in what follows in this section will be on three of the largest Gulf Arab funds: the Kuwait Investment Authority, the oldest SWF in the Gulf; the Abu Dhabi Investment Authority (ADIA), estimated as the world's largest SWF; and the Saudi Arabian Monetary Agency (SAMA), from the country with the world's largest oil reserves. It should be noted that SAMA is not formally a SWF, given that it functions as Saudi Arabia's central bank. It does not, therefore, have the characteristic of being a 'special purpose investment fund', which is the

Table 8.1 Gulf Arab SWFs: History, size, and transparency levels

Country	Fund name	Assets $ billion[1]	Establishment	Source of finance	Linaburg-Maduell transparency index (max: 10)*	Truman scoreboard (max: 24)**
Kuwait[2]	Kuwait Investment Authority	240	1953	Oil	6	12
UAE–Abu Dhabi	Abu Dhabi Investment Authority	470–740	1976	Oil	3	0.5
UAE–Abu Dhabi	Mubadala Development Company	14.7	2002	Oil	7	3.5
UAE–Abu Dhabi	International Petroleum Investment	14	1984	Oil	n/a	n/a
UAE–Federal	Emirates Investment Authority	n/a	2007	Oil	2	n/a
UAE–Dubai	Investment Corporation of Dubai	82	2006	Oil	4	n/a
UAE–Dubai	Dubai World	n/a	2006	Oil	n/a	n/a
UAE–Ras Al Khaima	RAK Investment Authority	1.2	2005	Oil	3	n/a
Saudi Arabia	SAMA Foreign Holdings	390	1952***	Oil	2	n/a
Saudi Arabia	Sanabil El Saudi	5.3	2008	Oil	3	n/a
Saudi Arabia	Hassana	n/a	2009	Oil	n/a	n/a
Qatar	Qatar Investment Authority	50	2003	Oil & Gas	5	2
Oman	State General Reserve Fund	8.2	1980	Oil & Gas	1	5
Oman	Oman Investment Fund	n/a	2006	oil	n/a	n/a

Note: [1] The estimated under management assets are from Sovereign Wealth Fund Institute at www.swfinstitute.org; [2] KIA is managing two separate funds of Kuwait, General Reserve Fund (GRF) and Future Generation Fund (FGF). The figure is the sum of the total value of both funds; * Latest update April 2009; ** Latest update October 2007; *** The establishment of Saudi Arabian Monetary Agency took place in 1952, and the foreign reserve holdings were created after the founding of the agency. There is no available information on the exact date when SAMA gained its foreign reserve holdings.

Source: Sovereign wealth fund institute and McKinsey Global Institute.

critical element in the definition used by the International Working Group on SWF. Nonetheless, it is frequently included in information on SWFs, in so far as its investment activities operate in similar ways to those of SWFs, and often faces the same kinds of Western scrutiny. Some of the relatively smaller and newer funds of the region include: Abu Dhabi's investment vehicle, Mubadala and the newly-established investment institutions of Saudi Arabia, Sanabil el Saudia and Hassana.

Commodity-based funds share many similarities such as having a long term objective of providing inter-generation savings, nonetheless based on the nature of their activities they can be divided into three different categories,. First, there are the conservative and passive portfolio investors, with unadventurous but stable and risk-averse strategies. These focus primarily on fixed incomes. SAMA and KIA-GRF fall into this category.

Second, there are the multi-asset portfolio type funds which are yield-seeking yet passive SWF investors. They have more diversified portfolios than the conservative investors, with higher expected returns and risks and so they are largely invested in equities. Many of these SWFs combine safe income assets and higher risk alternative investments: included in their portfolios, they carry hedge funds, leverage funds and real estate. The main examples of this type of funds in the Gulf Arab states are ADIA and KIA-FGF Fund (McKinsey Global Institute 2009, 21).

Finally, the last group of funds are the private equity investor-type funds. These are strategic investors and they are smaller than the first two groups in terms of the total amount of assets under their management. They hold more direct and active stakes in companies with higher investment risks. Among these are Dubai Istithmar, and Mubadala (McKinsey Global Institute 2009, 21; Smith-Diwan, 2009). The two new Saudi investment funds, Sanabil el Saudi and Hassana, also appear to fit into this grouping. The rationale behind the establishment of these smaller funds is that they may be able to make substantial gains if they are given as much freedom to operate as possible, independent of central bank or ministry of finance controls. However, they also pursue a more risky strategy and so they are given a smaller share of funds to invest (Oxford Analytica 2009, 4).

In the financial world there is often a correlation between the character of the investment strategy and the transparency of financial institutions. In other words, a conservative investment strategy usually coincides with higher transparency. However, this is not the case when it comes to the Gulf Arab SWFs. In the above-mentioned classification of funds into conservative, semi-conservative, and non-conservative, the more conservative investment strategies are, surprisingly, the least transparent. For example, KIA-GRF fits into the conservative category but it is not transparent, and ADIA is semi-conservative yet is also not transparent. Promotion of greater transparency within the Gulf Arab region has achieved some success. Previously secretive funds have started to open up to the public and disclose internal information which they had been highly sensitive about for the past few decades. Mubadala, for example, has pursued a relatively open policy,

Table 8.2 Planned investment projects in the GCC (2009–2015)*

Country	Construction	Petrochemicals	Oil & Gas	Power	Bahrain, Qatar, and Oman
Saudi Arabia	306	36	49	44	14
Kuwait	171	2	49	9	4
United Arab Emirates	396	17	57	29	9
The rest of GCC	121	7	36	16	7

Note: * All the figures are in $ billion.
Source: McKinsey Global Institute.

publishing its first annual report in 2009. ADIA, the main state-owned investment vehicle of government of Abu Dhabi, was also previously regarded as a highly secretive regional SWF, but it hired a public relations firm in early 2008 to disclose new information on its operations. Other sources of self-disclosure can be found in the IWF's explanations and commentaries, such as the 'Discussion of the GAPP' paper issued in October 2008.

The Gulf Arab funds are investing in companies which are not only commercially attractive but also can bring new skills, technology and business opportunity to their domestic economies. They have invested $1.4 trillion in the domestic sectors of the GCC economies over the past five years in the GCC, and new projects have been announced (see Table 8.2). While several SWFs lost in the immediate aftermath of the international financial crisis, the Gulf Arab SWFs are expected to continue an upward income trend and further invest in their domestic economies and bring social economic development to their home countries.

Gulf Arab funds have recently been noticeably more aggressive in their appetite for risk, holding higher percentages of equities and investing with greater frequency in emerging markets than many other SWFs. Moreover, funds such as Mubadala in Abu Dhabi, Istithmar and DIC in Dubai, and the Qatar Investment Authority in Qatar act more as government-owned investment firms than sovereign savings funds. Their mandate to diversify and develop their domestic economies has led them to form partnerships and to take direct equity stakes in firms which offer technology or expertise needed in certain strategic industries. Similarly, they have not shied away from high profile projects (Smith-Diwan 2009, 20).

As some of the smaller Gulf Arab states have made news headlines with their bold investments, the largest and most strategically important of the Gulf Arab states, the Kingdom of Saudi Arabia, has seemingly played it safe. Until the announcement in April 2008 that Saudi Arabia will be launching a sovereign wealth fund, no dedicated oil investment fund existed in the Kingdom. Instead, as noted above, its foreign assets have been managed by the Saudi central bank – the Saudi Arabian Monetary Agency (SAMA) – which has taken a conservative approach to investing the nearly $300 billion in Saudi non-reserve foreign holdings. While neighboring funds moved into private equities, SAMA investments remained predominantly in low-yielding bonds. For this reason, SAMA's assets were little affected by the international financial crisis. While neighboring countries sent more of their holdings further afield, SAMA remained overwhelmingly dollar-denominated, continuing to be heavily invested in US Treasury bills.

Transparency and the Record of Gulf Arab Sovereign Wealth Funds

As noted above, Western governments and opinion-formers have generally taken a pessimistic view of the ability of Gulf Arab SWFs to operate in a more open and transparent fashion – and therefore of the likelihood of their being able to do so. This chapter contests this view. There is already some evidence that a more optimistic view is appropriate. Reference has already been made to the speed with which some Gulf Arab SWFs have sought to change their practices and operate in a more public and transparent fashion. Besides the instances given here, consideration must also be given to the central role played by the SWFs in the International Working Group on Sovereign Wealth Funds. The IWG was convened under joint chairmanship, that of Jaime Carauna (director of the monetary and capital department of the IMF) and Hamad al-Hurr al-Suwaidi (undersecretary of the Abu Dhabi Finance Department, which holds overall responsibility for the activities of ADIA). All of the major Gulf Arab SWFs, as defined by the IWG, were members of the Group, and SAMA attended as an observer. All participated in discussion of the Generally Accepted Principles and Practices (GAPP) and, once they were adopted, bound themselves to implement them. The pressures which brought the IWG into existence may have come from Western governments and institutions, but the Santiago Principles were as much the achievement of the SWFs as they were of the other bodies involved.

While the enunciation of principles does not necessarily lead on to the implementation of the latter, the follow-through from the announcement of the Santiago Principles suggests a seriousness of intent. In April 2009, six months after the Santiago Principles were agreed, the International Working Group on Sovereign Wealth Funds reconvened, in Kuwait. The meeting ended with the adoption of the Kuwait Declaration, on 6 April, which created an International Forum of Sovereign Wealth Funds. This body would monitor and encourage the implementation of the Santiago Principles. The declaration lists the Forum's purposes as follows:

1. exchanging ideas and views among SWFs and with other relevant parties. These will cover, *inter alia*, issues such as trends and developments pertaining to SWF activities, risk management, investment regimes, market and institutional conditions affecting investment operations, and interactions with the economic and financial stability framework;

2. sharing views on the application of the Santiago Principles including operational and technical matters; and

3. encouraging cooperation with investment recipient countries, relevant international organizations, and capital market functionaries to identify potential risks that may affect cross-border investments, and to foster a non-discriminatory, constructive and mutually beneficial investment environment.

The mandate of the new body is:

1. to help maintain a stable global financial system and free flow of capital and investment;

2. to comply with all applicable regulatory and disclosure requirements in the countries in which they invest;

3. to invest on the basis of economic and financial risk and return-related considerations; and

4. to have in place a transparent and sound governance structure that provides for adequate operational controls, risk management, and accountability.

The regular meetings which the Forum intends to convene will clearly ensure that there will be a continuing focus on effective implementation.

It is worth, too, addressing the political dynamics which affect the transparency dimension of Gulf Arab SWFs. Critics of the Gulf Arab SWFs tend to link their erstwhile secretiveness to the political objectives, manipulative practices and perhaps corruption of the regimes. The assumption is often that these funds must suffer from the blurring of the borderline between state and ruling family which has sometimes been present in the home countries. As such, their activities on the international financial market will be unpredictable and moulded by other considerations than those of effective asset-management.

Yet there is little evidence to support such a view. The secretiveness of the major Gulf Arab SWFs, far from being a cover for malign intentions or corrupt practices, is no more than a reflection and perhaps enhancement of the general administrative practices in the countries concerned. There is a widespread attitude within administrations that information can be dangerous. The less which is made available, the less criticism there will be – and the less opportunity people will have to oppose government policies. This is magnified in the case of institutions which are central to a state's resources or resource base. SWFs clearly fall into this category. A similar degree of secretiveness can be found in national oil companies and central banks. In the case of SWFs there is an added factor. Commodity-based SWFs, in particular, are intended to be insulated from domestic political pressures and intrigues. They are, mostly, geared towards providing the state with income once commodity-based revenues decline. The more information is made available to the public, the more scope there is for politicians or pressure groups to campaign for money to be used for short-term gains and objectives. Secretiveness, therefore, serves the cause of insulation and helps protect the funds for the benefit of future generations. It has been seen as necessary to protect against domestic pressures, not to pursue devious strategies in international markets.

The concept of Gulf-based organizations that maintain a degree of separation from the normal operations of the state (and the interference of local elites) may seem surprising. Yet it is a characteristic of some of the Gulf Arab states that 'islands of efficiency', where decisions are taken solely according to technocratic criteria, have often survived and thrived within a wider sea of administrative weakness and political interference. Institutions which are necessary to the long-term survival of the state are, sometimes, protected from the manipulation which may occur elsewhere in the system. The SWFs have generally fallen into that category. The managers of the funds (as opposed to the systems of which they are part) have no particular reason to restrict information – apart from that which any investment institution would regard as being commercially sensitive. Indeed, their interests may well lie in greater openness: they are pursuing effective investment strategies, and their success deserves recognition. Despite serious issues arising over the KIA in the 1990s, cases of corruption have been relatively rare.

Nor is it true that the investments of the Gulf Arab SWFs have been heavily influenced by non-economic factors. As indicated above, the major Gulf Arab SWFs all fall into the conservative and semi-conservative categories. Their focus has been on effective asset-management, avoiding undue risks. Where situations have become, or seemed likely to become, politically complicated they have generally withdrawn quickly. From what is known, few of their investment decisions are ones which a Western investment institution might not also have taken.

Conclusion: Likely Future Directions

It seems probable that the investment strategies of Arab SWFs of the Gulf will undergo some change in the future. To some extent, this is already happening. Since 2007 they have begun to shift away from investing in Western markets, particularly the financial sector. They have substantially increased their investment in local businesses and banks, and have decreased the dollar ratio in their investment portfolios. They have also begun to be more transparent (Oxford Analytica 2009, 4). The shift has been brought about in part by their consciousness of political and economic risks facing their investments in the West. The 2008 international financial crisis and the political commentary has shaken their confidence. But in part the shift reflects new western trends of thinking in their home countries. There is now a wider tendency for home political elites and public opinion to question whether a strategy based mainly on investment in international markets is wise. Domestic investment would not only benefit the home economies but could also be more profitable and secure for the long-term. It is not suggested that investment might be directed entirely towards domestic markets but that the balance between international and domestic may change.

The move towards greater transparency, which is already under way, is likely to strengthen the trend towards domestic investment. With more information being made public, the SWFs will be forced to become more accountable to the citizens of their home countries. The populations will demand this (as they are already beginning to do). This is not to say that the SWFs will suffer from political interference, but rather that they will need to think and act skillfully in making the right balance between local and international investment.

The scale of the problem which SWFs pose to the Western economies may well be increased by this development. Investment flows to the West will be reduced. Paradoxically, then, transparency could require the Western economies to undergo more substantial structural changes than would have been necessary without it. This is the challenge which needs to be faced.

Chapter 9

Gulf Arab Sovereign Wealth Funds: Governance and Institution Building

Sven Behrendt

Introduction

Sovereign wealth funds (SWFs), sovereign-owned asset pools that are neither traditional public-pension funds nor reserve assets supporting national currencies from around the world (Rozanov 2005), have turned into an important investor class. Many SWFs have also developed increasingly diversified investment portfolios, branching out into equity and alternative investments, thereby increasing their public visibility.

The Gulf Arab economies have been very much at the center of the SWF growth story due to their increasing visibility in global financial markets and in the public eye. The emergence of SWFs has caused an initial political backlash among the economies of the industrialized world. Policy-makers and the public perceived SWFs, in particular those from emerging economies, as opaque financial powerhouses which threatened the security and competitiveness interests of their countries and national economies. In response to this backlash, a group of SWFs, the International Working Group of Sovereign Wealth Funds (IWG), signed and published a voluntary code of principles in September 2008, also known as the 'Santiago Principles', codifying a set of best practices seeking to increase the commitment across SWFs to higher accountability, transparency and governance standards. The Gulf Arab countries have also been central actors in designing and implementing policy responses to the backlash, most notably through the creation of the IWG. Are the Gulf Arab SWFs demonstrating commitment to the 'Santiago Principles'? Can this further provide an indication for their broader commitment to governance, transparency and accountability standards? This chapter seeks to answer these questions.

The emergence of SWFs from the Gulf region, their investment behavior, their role in the global financial architecture, and not least their political preferences and associated policies in recent years has turned into one of the most curious phenomena in international affairs. It is also a newly prominent item on the policy agenda of the US, Europe and the Arab world. A region that has been viewed by much of Europe and the US mainly as a source for oil and natural gas – also as a source of considerable geopolitical instability with low governance standards and little implementation of democratic principles – is beginning to leave increasingly large footprints in global financial markets. As Gulf Arab sovereign investors are seeking to diversify their national economies, they are also strengthening their role as powerful strategic investors, and may over time substantially impact the ownership structures in established industrialized economies. While on a larger scale the investments of Gulf Arab SWFs might still appear to be marginal, scenarios that assume an important role for Gulf Arab sovereign investors in the future design of the industrial landscape of Europe and the US appear to be plausible (McKinsey 2007).

This chapter is organized in three sections. The first section provides a brief overview of the emergence of SWFs as a relevant global investor class, focusing on Gulf Arab SWFs. A short overview of the emergence of the 'Santiago Principles' in the second section provides the context for a subsequent assessment of the governance and transparency standards of Gulf Arab SWFs, which in turn is compared with the compliance performance of SWFs from other countries. The third section tests several hypotheses that could possibly be used to explain the strikingly low commitment of Gulf Arab SWFs to the 'Santiago Principles'.

The Rise of Gulf Arab Sovereign Investors: A Brief Introduction

In the past years, SWFs have made an entry as a new relevant investor class in global finance, as well as a relevant actor in global political affairs. One could argue that the first SWFs were created back in the 1950s and therefore their very existence is nothing but an old feature in the world of global finance. However, the high monetary surpluses of commodity-based economies and of those economies that benefited from considerable trade surpluses – most notably China – which in turn channeled excess reserves into SWFs, have moved SWFs from the periphery to the center of the global economy and financial markets; in turn, they became an increasingly relevant item on the global public policy agenda.

GCC countries have been right at the center of these developments. Many Gulf Arab countries have set up SWFs and mandated them to manage excess revenues accrued from high oil incomes and from modest government spending to ensure the just distribution of oil wealth across generations (Saidi 2009). The investment authorities of Abu Dhabi, Kuwait and Qatar rank amongst the largest global sovereign financial institutions. They are complemented by a host of smaller, more specialized government investment agencies and government holding entities from Dubai, Saudi Arabia, Bahrain and Oman.

The *Saudi Arabian Monetary Agency* (SAMA) was established in 1952 as the Kingdom's monetary agency (Wilson 2009). Although not a formally dedicated SWF, SAMA has been managing the Kingdom's foreign financial assets since its establishment. The origins of the Kuwaiti SWF go back to 1953, when the Kuwait Investment Board was established in London eight years before Kuwait's independence in 1961. Its mandate was subsequently taken over by the *Kuwait Investment Authority* (KIA) in 1982. These two entities were joined by two Abu

Dhabi-based entities, the *Abu Dhabi Investment Authority* (ADIA) in 1976, a long-term oriented portfolio investor; and the *International Petroleum Investment Company* (IPIC) in 1984, a strategic investment entity mandated to engage in hydrocarbons and related sectors outside the emirate of Abu Dhabi.

Towards the middle of the past decade, due to exorbitant price levels in commodity markets, the assets of existing SWFs swelled, and new ones were established to absorb the liquidity glut. In Abu Dhabi, ADIA and IPIC were joined in 2002 by the *Mubadala Development Corporation* (Mubadala) with a mandate to diversify Abu Dhabi's national economy into non-hydrocarbons related sectors. The *Qatar Investment Authority* (QIA) was created in 2005 to help the Qatari government diversify its holdings. The Bahraini *Mumtalakat Holding Company* was established by Royal Decree in June 2006 as the investment arm of the Kingdom of Bahrain. Dubai too became more active in managing its external wealth through dedicated investment vehicles, run mostly by Dubai World.

Although Gulf Arab SWFs played an ever increasing role in global financial markets, they were hesitant to provide the public with concise information about the value of their assets, their investment policies, or governance arrangements. Trying to fill this void, a growing 'epistemic community' (Behrendt 2009b) of independent institutions, think tanks, financial services providers, and academia, offered their own estimates about the asset values of Gulf Arab SWFs based on ever more sophisticated financial models and speculated about their investment policies (see Table 9.1).

To be sure, SWFs from different parts of the world became as prominent as their Gulf Arab brethren. Norway's Government Pension Fund–Global has developed a portfolio that includes stakes in almost 2,700 companies. The value of its equity holdings represents an estimated 0.8 percent of global equities. It has become one of the biggest shareholders of Royal Dutch Shell Nestlé SA, and BP. In the second half of 2009 alone, the Chinese Investment Corporation placed or planned investments in the global mining industry around the world valued at just below US$5 billion, including stakes in the Canadian Teck Resources, Indonesian or the Australian, Fortescue Metals Group, supposedly to satisfy the immense Chinese demand for natural resources. By late 2009, the investment volume of Singapore's Government Investment Corporation amounted to just under US$250 billion; the holdings of Singapore's Temasek Holding were worth just under US$120 billion.

The rise of SWFs was accompanied by an increasingly extrovert investment policy. Rather than focusing their investments in traditionally safe assets such as US treasury bills and other prominent debt securities, Gulf Arab SWFs increasingly engaged in equity acquisitions. The motivation for this policy shift has either been to diversify their asset base and arrive at more beneficial risk/return positions, or to position them as strategic investors taking direct stakes in lucrative industrial assets, also with the intent to diversify the industrial base of their own national economies. QIA, for example, in December 2009 announced to have become the third largest shareholder of Volkswagen, the German car manufacturer, with a

Table 9.1 Estimated Values of Selected Gulf Arab SWFs and Central Banks, in US$ (billion)

	Truman April 2008	Setser/Ziemba January 2009	McKinsey GI May 2009	Institute of Int. Finance November 2009
ADIA	500 to 875	328*	470-740	395
KIA	213	228	240	295
QIA	60	58	50	70
SAMA	330	501	390	447**

Note: * Including the Abu Dhabi Investment Council; ** Official reserves of Saudi Arabia, mostly held by SAMA, included for reference.

concentrated stake of 17 percent. Aabar, a smaller government investment agency from Abu Dhabi is, at the time of writing this chapter, set to increase its stake in Daimler, another German car manufacturer, from 9.1 percent to 15 percent, thereby becoming the second largest Gulf Arab Investor besides the KIA, which holds a 6.9 percent stake in Daimler. During the early phase of the 2008 international financial crisis, KIA and ADIA have played significant roles in providing liquidity to faltering financial institutions in the US and the UK (Table 9.2 presents an overview of the largest global SWFs).

Table 9.2 includes only SWFs that are members to the International Working Group of Sovereign Wealth Funds (IWG) and that signed the 'Santiago Principles,' which were drafted by the IWG and will be discussed further below. There has been an intense debate about the conditions that a government investment or holding company is required to meet in order to qualify as a SWF. This, in turn, has considerable ramifications for what constitutes the definition of SWFs. It can be plausibly argued that SWFs that signed the 'Santiago Principles' are widely perceived as SWFs, and clearly perceive themselves as such. This table therefore does not include the IPIC or Mubadala from Abu Dhabi; SAMA and the Public Investment Fund from Saudi Arabia, or the government or 'quasi' government investment and government holding companies of Dubai. All of these institutions might or might not qualify as SWFs, depending on the definition of a SWF.

Emergence of and Commitment to the 'Santiago Principles'

Having developed a sense for these new actors in financial and broader global affairs, we turn to a short assessment of the political exposure that SWFs faced in 2007 and 2008 and examine how they collectively reacted to this pressure.

The increasing prominence of SWFs in international financial markets and the associated increase of their influence in the global economy, as perceived by the global and in particular Western *body politic*, has exposed SWFs to considerable

Table 9.2 Size of selected Sovereign Wealth Funds which signed the Santiago Principles (partly estimates) as of March 2010

Country	Fund	Volume (US$ bn)
Norway	Government Pension Fund	399.3
UAE	*Abu Dhabi Investment Authority*	*395.0**
China	China Investment Corporation	297.5
Kuwait	*Kuwait Investment Authority*	*295.0**
Singapore	Gov. of Singapore Investment Corporation Pte. Ltd.	247.5
Singapore	Temasek Holdings Pte. Ltd.	119.0
Korea	Korea Investment Corporation	92.6
Russia	National Wealth Fund	91.9
Russia	Reserve Fund	76.4
Qatar	*Qatar Investment Authority*	*70.0**
Libya	*Libyan Investment Authority*	*65.0*
Australia	Australian Future Fund	58.3
United States	Alaska Permanent Fund	33.7
Ireland	National Pension Reserve Fund	23.8
Chile	Economic and Social Stabilization Fund	20.2
Azerbaijan	State Oil Fund	13.3
Canada	Alberta Heritage Savings Trust Fund	13.3
Iran	Oil Stabilization Fund	13.0
New Zealand	Superannuation Fund	9.8
Botswana	Pula Fund	6.9
Timor-Leste	Petroleum Fund of Timor-Leste	4.9
Trinidad & Tobago	Heritage and Stabilization Fund	2.9
Chile	Pension Reserve Fund	2.5
Bahrain	*Future Generations Reserve Fund*	*NA*
Equatorial Guinea	Fund for Future Generations	NA
Mexico	Oil Revenues Stabilization Fund	NA
Total (estimate)		2,351.8

Note: * Estimates provided by the Institute of International Finance (2009).
Source: Author's compilation from annual reports, latest web-based information provided by SWFs and owners of SWFs as of December 2009.

public attention. Policy-makers, in particular in the US and Europe, have been watching SWFs' move from the periphery to the center of global financial markets with considerable unease, if not outright confusion. On the one hand, the stabilizing role that some SWFs played during the initial stages of the global financial crisis indicated how important SWFs had become as provider of liquidity. On the other hand, geopolitical arguments prevented them from fully embracing SWFs as constructive partners. 'How do you get tough on your banker?' US Secretary of

State (then Senator) Hillary Clinton once pointedly remarked, referring to China as one of the world's most important creditors, and as a competitor for global political influence (Clinton 2008). Secretary Clinton's thoughts are indicative of a host of arguments about the trade-offs and political risks associated with the engagement of sovereign investors in the US and European economies.

The lack of confidence, on the part of policy-makers and the broader public, in global and national institutions' ability to check the increasing power of SWFs in 2007, had transformed debate into a significant political backlash. SWFs across the board, admittedly because of the opaqueness that many of their principals chose to surround them with, were portrayed as sinister financial powerhouses and associated with a hidden political agenda that their owners were assumed to pursue (Summers 2007; Kissinger and Feldstein 2008; Ferguson 2009; Kimmit 2008; Bergsten 2009).

Gulf Arab Reactions and the IWG

From late January 2008 onwards, owners and fund managers of Gulf Arab SWFs began to position their case more proactively. Attempting to alleviate Western concerns, the leadership of Abu Dhabi sent a letter to Western financial officials affirming that the emirate's SWFs exclusively sought to maximize risk-adjusted returns (al Otaiba 2008). Others reconfirmed their commitment to national and international regulations in addition to their support for the international economy.[1] In a move to pre-empt tighter legislation, the US Treasury reached an agreement with Singapore and Abu Dhabi on principles for sovereign wealth fund investment (US Treasury 2008).

The concerns of Gulf Arab policy-makers and those from other emerging economies were subsequently directed into an initiative that would result in a voluntary 'code of principles' for SWFs. Already in October 2007, the International Monetary and Financial Committee (IMFC) had expressed the need for further analysis of key issues for investors and recipients of SWF investment flows. When the policy process advanced in spring 2008, the IMF assumed a more active role in mediating a joint position amongst SWFs. The idea of a voluntary set of best practices or a code of conduct for SWFs was then floated. David Murray, Chair of the Australian Future Fund's Board of Guardians, who would become one of the protagonists of self-directed work by SWFs, suggested that the initial impulse for SWFs to take collective action was the pressure from the US Congress through the IMF for increased regulation of foreign investment of various kinds from SWFs and state owned enterprises.[2] Yet, Gulf Arab leaders, and those of other countries

---

1   Sultan bin Sulayem, Head of Dubai World, and Seikh Hamad bin Jassem, Prime Minister of Qatar and Head of the Qatari Investment Authority, quoted in: Gulf Investor Warns of EU Over-Regulation (Financial Times 2008).

2   David Murray, Chair, Future Fund Board of Guardians, Proof Committee Hansard, Economics References Committee (Foreign Investment by States Owned Entities 2009).

with SWFs, initially rejected an active IMF role. In April 2008, the Governor of the Central Bank for the United Arab Emirates issued a statement on behalf of thirteen countries, arguing that the IMF did not have the requisite expertise to produce a set of best practices for SWFs (*Al-Suwaidi* 2008).

The Gulf Arab SWFs' position changed substantially some weeks later. The International Working Group of Sovereign Wealth Funds (IWG) was established at a meeting of countries with SWFs on 30 April–1 May 2008, in Washington D.C., with the IMF playing a facilitation and coordination role. Hamad Al Hurr Al Suwaidi, Undersecretary of Abu Dhabi Finance Department, and Jaime Caruana, Director of the Monetary and Capital Markets Department of the IMF, were selected to co-chair the IWG. After a series of working meeting throughout summer 2008, the IWG agreed to develop a voluntary 'Code of Principles', or 'Generally Accepted Principles and Practices' (GAAP), for SWFs. The GAAP became also known as 'Santiago Principles' (the venue of the final drafting session of the principles) and was published on 11 October 2008, during the IMFC meeting in Washington (IWG 2008).

From a purely technical point of view, analysts have concluded that the 'Santiago Principles' were a 'solid piece of work that should help dispel some of the mystery and suspicion surrounding SWFs' (Truman 2008a/b). Formally, the 'Santiago Principles' (see Annex), comprising 24 individual principles, were designed to meet four objectives: to help maintain a stable global financial system and the free flow of capital and investment; to ensure that SWFs would comply with regulatory and disclosure requirements of the countries in which they invest; to ensure that they invested on the basis of economic and financial risk and return-related considerations; and to reconfirm that SWFs should have in place a transparent and sound governance structure that provided for adequate operational control, risk management, and accountability (IWG 2008).

The IWG convened again on 5 and 6 April 2009 in Kuwait City. Recognizing that the reasoning behind the principles could benefit from a continuing exchange of views and study of activities, the IWG reached a consensus to establish the International Forum of Sovereign Wealth Funds (IFSWF), as part of the so-called 'Kuwait Declaration.' The declaration noted that the Forum would comprise a 'voluntary group of sovereign wealth funds', seeking to encourage an exchange of views on issues of common interest and to facilitate the understanding of the 'Santiago Principles' and SWF investment behavior in general. It was important for the authors of the declaration to state that the Forum was not a supranational authority, and that its work would not carry any legal force. The Forum was designed to operate in an inclusive manner and facilitate communication among SWFs, recipient country officials, representatives of multi-lateral organizations and the private sector (IWG 2009).

The IFSWF held its inaugural meeting in Baku, Azerbaijan on 8–9 October 2009. A declaration issued by the IFSWF confirmed a continued commitment to assess the application of the 'Santiago Principles', but also voiced their expectation towards recipient economies which were encouraged to make 'investment regimes more transparent and non-discriminatory, avoid protectionism, and foster a constructive and mutually beneficial investment environment' (IFSWF 2009).

The 'Santiago Principles' and the associated process nurtured by the IFSWF provided an incentive for many SWFs to more proactively increase their governance, accountability and transparency commitments and provide information about their raison d'être and investment philosophies.

Nearly a year after the Santiago Principles were published we have assessed the progress that its signatories, i.e. 26 SWFs from around the world, have made towards implementation. From September to December 2009 we have analyzed information available in the public domain as provided through official publications of SWFs themselves, including Annual Reports, other reports prepared by SWFs, as well as official websites maintained by SWFs. The data sources also include material gathered from publications of the IWG and the work of the IMF. We excluded information provided by other information sources, such as business journals and newspapers, since the data points offered by these sources often cannot be verified. We examined these data sources with reference to each of the 24 commitments contained in the 'Santiago Principles'. By referencing compliance and non-compliance for each principle, including sub-principles, we created a rudimentary 'Santiago Compliance Index', which in a numerical form documents each SWF's compliance with the 'Santiago Principles'.

The purpose of the exercise in the context of this chapter has been to evaluate the commitment of Gulf Arab SWFs to the 'Santiago Principles', providing an indication for their broader commitment to governance, transparency and accountability standards. Gathering data from non-Arab peers allows for a comparative perspective and the evaluation of the Gulf Arab SWFs' performance relative to that of SWFs in other parts of the world. It also helps to reach some tentative generalizations on possible drivers of compliance.

Evidently, any assessment of the compliance of SWFs with the 'Santiago Principles' needs to acknowledge a number of factors that might affect data accuracy. First, SWFs might have implemented processes and practices that correspond to the provisions of the 'Santiago Principles' but that may not be documented in the public domain. However, because transparency constitutes an important element of the Santiago principles, the availability of information in the public domain is an important indicator in itself. Second, the assessment might further be affected by suboptimal data accessibility, meaning that although data might exist in the public domain these data might be presented in a way that requires disproportionate resources to access them. Finally, given the complexity of the matter, compliance might also be affected by shortcomings of data applicability, i.e. the semantic discrepancy between the language used in the provisions of the 'Santiago Principles' and the language used in the information sources we used for this analysis.

Compliance with the Santiago Principles

It is beyond the scope of this chapter to discuss the content of the 24 principles that collectively constitute the body of the 'Santiago Principles' in full detail. Technically, their provisions cover SWFs' mandates, objectives, and coordination with macroeconomic policies; SWF institutional framework and governance structures; and the SWF investment and risk management framework. These provisions constitute the institutional 'checks and balances' that ensure that SWFs operate strictly according to financial risk/return parameters and ensure a degree of predictability of the non-financial motivations of their operations.

Figure 9.1 presents the findings of our evaluation in a summary form on the basis of my 'Santiago Compliance Index'. The first observation is that the performance of SWFs across the 'Santiago Compliance Index' varies tremendously. The top performers are close to full compliance with the 'Santiago Principles'. On the bottom of the table are those funds that have difficulties fulfilling a mere 40 percent of the 24 principles.

Three clusters of SWFs can be identified from the index: The group of highly 'Santiago-compliant' SWFs, which includes the Superannuation Fund from New Zealand, the Government Pension Fund–Global from Norway, the Australian Future Fund, the Irish National Pension Reserve Fund, and the China Investment Corporation. All of these funds display a 'Santiago-compliance' ratio of around 80 percent or more.

The midfield is populated by the two SWFs from Singapore, GIC and Temasek, Chile's Economic and Social Stabilisation Fund and the its Pension Reserve Fund, Russia's National Wealth and Reserve Funds, the Korea Investment Corporation and the smaller funds from Timor-Leste, Trinidad and Tobago and Azerbaijan, as well as the sub-national funds from the province of Alberta in Canada and the state of Alaska, in the US.

The group of low performers includes the Kuwait Investment Authority, the Qatar Investment Authority, the Abu Dhabi Investment Authority, the Mexican Oil Revenues Stabilization Fund, the Pula Fund from Botswana, Bahrain's Future Generations Reserve Fund, the Libyan Investment Authority, and the funds from Equatorial Guinea and Iran, for which no public data points are available.

Given the low commitment of Gulf Arab SWFs to the 'Santiago Principles' as of 2010, we are left with two guiding questions: which principles do Gulf Arab SWFs comply with and what additional information can be extracted using the framework of the 'Santiago Principles'?

Principle 1, amongst others, commits SWFs to ensuring the legal soundness of their operations and requires signatories to report on their legal basis and structure. All four Gulf Arab SWFs comply with this principle. ADIA's constitutive document is Law No. 5 of 1981, which also concerns itself with the ADIA's governance architecture. It is wholly owned and subject to the supervision by the Abu Dhabi Government. In Kuwait, Law No. 47 of 1982 established the Public Investment Authority, known as Kuwait Investment Authority. The QIA was founded based

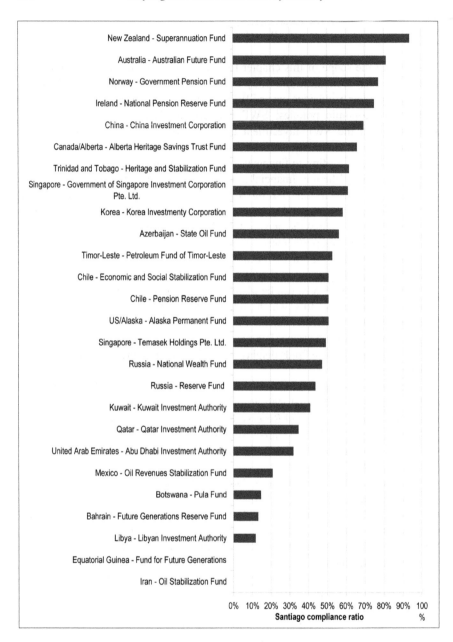

Figure 9.1 Overall degree of compliance with Santiago Principles (Santiago Compliance Ratio, SCR)

Source: Author's compilation from annual reports, latest web-based information provided by SWFs and owners SWFs as of December 2009.

on Article 5 of Emiri Decision No (22) of 2005 as an independent government investment institution. The Future Generations Reserve Fund (FGRF) of Bahrain was established with a Royal Decree issued on 17 July 2006.[3]

Principle 2 covers the policy purpose of SWFs. There are marked distinctions between the various purposes SWFs with which have been set up. Das et al. (2009) suggest five types: (i) reserve investment corporations aim to enhance returns on reserves; (ii) pension-reserve funds; (iii) fiscal stabilization funds; (iv) fiscal savings funds; (v) development funds that use returns to invest for development purposes. Broadly speaking, three of the four Gulf Arab SWFs can be categorized as serving a reserve investment function. ADIA's mission is to secure and maintain the current and future prosperity of the Emirate of Abu Dhabi through the prudent management of the Emirate's investment assets. KIA's mission is to achieve a long – term investment return on the financial reserves entrusted by the State of Kuwait, with the goal of eventually providing an alternative to oil reserves. The FGRF's purpose is to strengthen Bahrain's long-term fiscal management and help preserve the state's hydrocarbon wealth. QIA's mission is somewhat different from its three peers. Its investment mandate also covers the diversification of Qatar's real economy and its financial resources. Though it states, like its three peers, that future generations should benefit from its financial investments, the diversification of Qatar's national economy is a legitimate purpose for QIA's investment policies.

Principle 4 commits SWFs to develop clear and publicly disclosed policies, rules, procedures, or arrangements guiding the SWF's general approach to funding, withdrawal, and spending operations. Though this principle appears to be a central one, as it addresses the allocation process of public funds as well as the distribution of generated public wealth (these are important elements in the SWFs' overall fiscal policies), Gulf Arab SWFs only report on these activities to a very limited extent. Some rudimentary references are made towards the funding of SWFs. For example, the FGRF receives, in monthly payments, part of the oil income accruing from higher than budgeted oil prices. ADIA receives funds from the Government of Abu Dhabi to be allocated for investments. QIA states that its funds come from the State of Qatar. These, of course, are fairly trivial divulgences and do not suffice to meet the standards set out in Principle 4. Though SWFs played a very active role in shielding their national economies from the global financial crisis by providing liquidity to domestic financial markets and institutions, there is no official communication of withdrawal and spending policies.[4]

---

3   Please note that there is considerable data uncertainty about the FGRF. The only public information about the FGRF can be found in the International Working Group of Sovereign Wealth Funds (2008).

4   In a rare occasion, Sheikh Ahmed Bin Zayed Al Nehayan, Managing Director of the Abu Dhabi Investment Authority, gave some hints about withdrawal policies in Abu Dhabi,

Principle 18.3 asks SWFs for a description of their investment policies. This description should include qualitative statements on the investment style or investment themes, the investment objectives, the investment horizon, and the strategic asset allocation. Gulf Arab SWFs provide some very rudimentary information about these aspects. The FGRF invests only in liquid instruments with the aim of preserving its capital. KIA seeks to diversify investments across various geographic locations and asset classes, as well as within asset classes. QIA suggests taking a flexible approach to its investment strategy and has interests across a wide range of geographies and in different asset classes including listed securities, property, alternative assets and private equity. It also mentions the beneficial effect of a portfolio company having synergies with the Qatari national economy as it seeks to diversify.

ADIA has been somewhat more forthcoming than its peers providing more information about its asset allocation. In a rare interview given to *Business Week* in 2008, ADIA's managing director, Sheikh Ahmed Bin Zayed Al Nehayan had given some very broad indication about ADIA's strategic asset allocation: stocks in developed markets of 45–55 percent, stocks in emerging markets of 8–12 percent, small-cap stocks of 1–4 percent, government bonds of 12–18 percent, corporate and other bonds of 4–8 percent, alternative investments of 5–10 percent, real estate of 5–10 percent, private equity of 2–8 percent, infrastructure of 0–4 percent, cash of 0–5 percent (*Business Week* 2008). In the interview given to the *Handelsblatt*, a German economics daily newspaper, in early 2010, Sheikh Ahmad disclosed that ADIA has 35–50 percent of its assets in the US., 25–35 percent in Europe, 15–25 percent in emerging markets and 10–20 percent in Asia. He also disclosed ADIA's asset allocation average between 40–60 percent in global equities, 15–30 percent in fixed income and the remainder is divided between other asset classes including real estate, private equity, alternative investments and infrastructure (Handelsblatt 2010).[5]

Principle 21 requires SWFs to report on their approach to executing ownership rights, including key factors guiding the exercise of ownership rights. FGRF and QIA do not provide formal information about their policy on executing ownership rights.[6] KIA states that it exercises its voting rights in the manner that it believes will protect its financial interests. Sheikh Ahmad confirmed in the interview given to the *Handelsblatt* that ADIA acquires more than a minority stake in companies, but stated that the SWF does not seek control or active management of the companies in which it invests.

---

confirming that the Abu Dhabi government can, at any time, request funds from ADIA to meet its short-term needs (*Handelsblatt* 2010).

5   Note that there is some discrepancy between the asset allocations suggested in June 2008 and January 2010.

6   It should be noted that QIA, after having acquired a 17 percent stake in the German automotive company Volkswagen and obtaining a seat on the supervisory board of Porsche, a subsidiary of Volkswagen, will probably execute ownership rights, at least in this very case.

One of the key features of the 'Santiago Principles' is ensuring that the operational management of the funds is pursued in an independent manner (Principles 9, 16). Gulf Arab SWFs provide some rudimentary information about their governance arrangements. However, there is only sparse disclosure about the manner in which the SWF's management is operationally independent from the owner. All four Gulf Arab SWFs that have been assessed in the context of this study fail to provide publicly accessible data that covers the remaining principles. Again, we should note that this statement is subject to the availability, accessibility, and applicability of data.

Towards an Explanation of 'Santiago' – Compliance Patterns

What, then, can possibly explain the uneven commitment to the 'Santiago Principles' across SWFs? In the following section, I test a number of explanatory or 'independent' variables against the 'Santiago Compliance Index'. Can the degree of compliance be related to the maturity of the SWF, or the country's level of economic development? Can the country's institutional context, as reflected in governance or democracy indices provide any indication about the deeper rationale for the uneven performance of SWFs?

Maturity of the Fund

One could assume that SWFs that are more mature, i.e. were established some time ago, such as the KIA or the ADIA, have over time established more robust governance frameworks, which made them more compatible with the 'best practice' requirements of the 'Santiago Principles' than their younger peers. Conversely, one could also argue that younger and therefore institutionally less mature SWFs were in the position to react more flexibly to the regulatory provisions of the 'Santiago Principles' and therefore reach higher compliance levels.

Can we identify any correlation between the ages of SWFs against their respective performances on the 'Santiago Compliance Index'?

The analysis here suggests that neither of these two contradicting hypotheses can be confirmed. Figure 9.2 identifies no correlation between the age of a SWF and its performance in the 'Santiago Compliance Index'. The age of a SWF does not provide an indication of a fund's performance in the 'Santiago Compliance Index'. The performance of Gulf Arab SWFs makes this very clear. KIA's and ADIA's, both of whom represent comparatively mature institutions, perform worse than the average of SWFs. These SWFs' low commitment to the 'Santiago Principles' is matched by their younger peers, QIA, the Bahraini FGRF and, further afield, the Libyan Investment Authority.

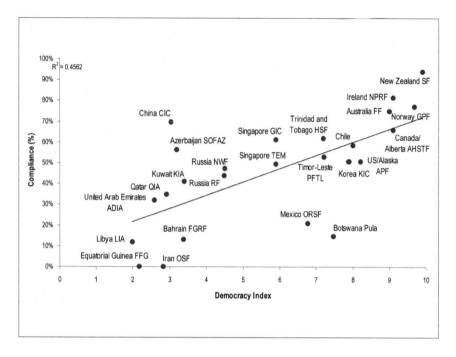

**Figure 9.2 Santiago compliance by maturity of the fund
(based on year of establishment)**

Source: Author's compilation from annual reports, latest web-based information provided by SWFs and owners SWFs as of December 2009.

Level of Economic Development

Alternatively, an argument could be made that those economies that display higher levels of development can be assumed to have established a more robust appreciation for the value of transparency, good governance and accountable institutions, underpinning the viability of markets and providing the backdrop for more transparent and well-governed SWFs. Accordingly, Figure 9.3 is modelled on the assumption that the ranking of individual SWFs in the 'Santiago Compliance Index' might be explained by the level of economic development of their home countries, as measured by GDP per capita.

As Figure 9.3 indicates, this hypothesis cannot be confirmed either. SWFs from countries with relatively low GDP per capita, such as China, Azerbaijan or Timor-Leste are among the better performing SWFs. Those from the GCC states, whose GDP per capita ranks at similar levels as those of mature industrialized economies, display low compliance ratios.

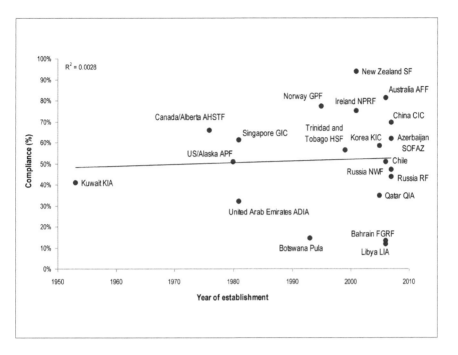

**Figure 9.3 Santiago compliance by level of economic development
(as measured by GDP per capita)**
Source: IMF 2009, World Economic Outlook.

Governance and Government Effectiveness

We can also assess the explanatory power of a country's institutional characteristics. To do so we can use an indicator provided by the World Bank's 'Worldwide Governance Indicators' (WGI), which reflects government effectiveness.[7] One could argue that those SWFs that are owned and operated by a country with high overall government effectiveness perform better on the 'Santiago Compliance Index' than those SWFs originating from countries with lower government effectiveness.

My analysis suggests a fairly strong correlation between SWFs' performance on the 'Santiago Compliance Index' and the government effectiveness indicators.

---

7   The WGI project reports governance indicators for 212 countries and territories over the period 1996–2008 and assesses the global quality of governance along six dimensions: voice and accountability, political stability and absence of violence, government effectiveness, regulatory quality, rule of law, and control of corruption (World Bank 2009b).

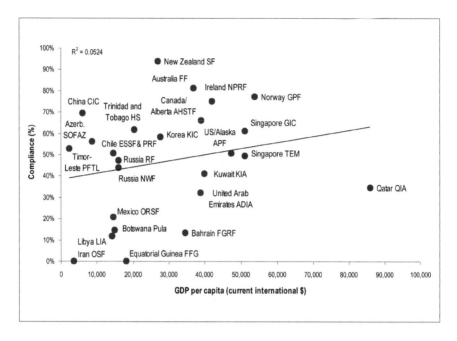

**Figure 9.4 Santiago compliance by governance standards of the home
countries (as measured by the World Bank governance indicators)**
Source: World Bank 2009, Governance Matters.

Figure 9.4 illustrates that countries with high government effectiveness also tend
to display a high degree of commitment to the 'Santiago Principles'. Conversely,
countries with low government effectiveness also rank low on the index. This
finding also holds for the group of Gulf Arab SWFs. The World Bank indicator
suggests low government effectiveness throughout the Arab world – which may be
a useful explanation for the under-performance of Gulf Arab SWFs on the index.

Democratic Institutions

Lastly, we can test a hypothesis that assumes political factors to play a more important
role in SWFs transparency, accountability and governance arrangements. Despite
plausible and convincing macro-economic arguments that provide the backdrop
for the creation of a SWF, they are the result of a deliberate political calculation of
governments. One could therefore expect them to reflect the political governance
arrangements that prevail in their countries.

To see if there is indeed a relationship between the state of political institutions
of countries with SWFs and the commitment of their SWFs to the 'Santiago
Principles', we use the 'Democracy Index' of the Economist Intelligence Unit

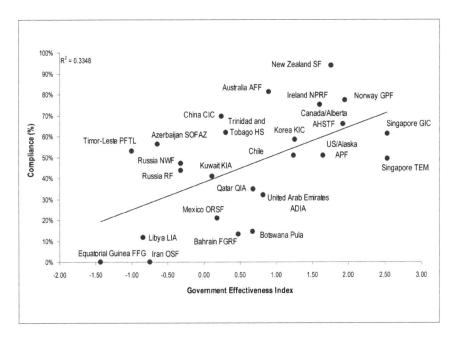

**Figure 9.5 Santiago compliance by level of democratization
(as measured by the Economist Democracy Index)**
Source: Economist Intelligence Unit 2009, The Economist Intelligence Unit's Index of Democracy 2008.

(2009). The Index provides a snapshot of the current state of democracy worldwide for 165 independent states. The index is based on five categories: electoral process and pluralism; civil liberties; the functioning of government; political participation; and political culture. Countries are placed within one of four types of regimes: full democracies; flawed democracies; hybrid regimes; and authoritarian regimes.

My analysis suggests a surprisingly close correlation between the 'Santiago Compliance Index' and the 'Democracy Index'. SWFs of democracies that are based on stable institutions, pluralism, political participation and a liberal political culture do feature a higher ranking in the 'Santiago Compliance Index'. Conversely, SWFs of countries that are governed by authoritarian regimes generally perform worse in the 'Santiago Compliance Index' than average. In fact, the correlation suggests three distinct clusters of SWFs: (i) well governed, accountable and transparent SWFs from full democracies; (ii) moderately accountable, transparent and governed SWFs from flawed democracies and hybrid regimes; (iii) and underperforming SWFs from countries with authoritarian regimes.

The Gulf Arab SWFs are part of group (iii), suggesting that the authoritarian political structures in the Gulf Arab region reflect on the commitment of its SWFs to display accountability, governance, and transparency standards.

Conclusion

This study has identified a relatively low commitment of Gulf Arab SWFs to the 'Santiago Principles' that were voluntarily agreed upon as a minimum set of general governance, transparency and accountability standards for SWFs.

Looking at possible explanations for SWF's compliance with the 'Santiago Principles', neither the level of economic development nor the fund's maturity were found to be systematically related to the SWF's performance. Instead, this chapter suggests that there is a link between governance and democratic standards prevailing in Gulf Arab domestic polities and compliance with the 'Santiago Principles'. There is a clear correlation between the compliance of individual SWFs and the governance and democratic standards of the countries that own them. Consequently, it is argued that SWFs from countries that are governed by authoritarian regimes tend to be less transparent, feature lower governance standards, and exhibit less accountability toward their countries' citizens. There are notable exceptions, though, for example the cases of China and Azerbaijan, whose relatively good compliance with the 'Santiago Principles' would warrant further analysis.

The effect of the exposure of SWF managers and principals on the global discourse about accountability, transparency, and governance standards of SWFs and other financial institutions- or norm socialization in the words of constructivists (see Barnett and Finnemore, 2004) remains to be explored. An argument could be made that integrating Gulf Arab SWFs into the international discourse could have a positive spill-over effect on individual SWFs' standards. This, in turn, could have a moderating effect on the overall governance and accountability arrangements of the political institutions of Gulf Arab countries, and could even contribute to increasing their overall commitment to democratic principles. If this should be the case, an increasing commitment to the 'Santiago Principles' across Gulf Arab SWFs could be an indicator for – and possibly a catalyst of – deeper reforms of the political institutions across the Gulf Arab states.

Annex: General Accepted Principles and Practices (GAPP), 'Santiago Principles'

	Principle	Text
1	Principle	The legal framework for the SWF should be sound and support its effective operation and the achievement of its stated objective(s).
1.1	Subprinciple	The legal framework for the SWF should ensure legal soundness of the SWF and its transactions.
1.2	Subprinciple	The key features of the SWF's legal basis and structure, as well as the legal relationship between the SWF and other state bodies, should be publicly disclosed.
2.	Principle	The policy purpose of the SWF should be clearly defined and publicly disclosed.
3.	Principle	Where the SWF's activities have significant direct domestic macroeconomic implications, those activities should be closely coordinated with the domestic fiscal and monetary authorities, so as to ensure consistency with the overall macroeconomic policies.
4.	Principle	There should be clear and publicly disclosed policies, rules, procedures, or arrangements in relation to the SWF's general approach to funding, withdrawal, and spending operations.
4.1	Subprinciple	The source of SWF funding should be publicly disclosed.
4.2	Subprinciple	The general approach to withdrawals from the SWF and spending on behalf of the government should be publicly disclosed.
5.	Principle	The relevant statistical data pertaining to the SWF should be reported on a timely basis to the owner, or as otherwise required, for inclusion where appropriate in macroeconomic data sets.
6.	Principle	The governance framework for the SWF should be sound and establish a clear and effective division of roles and responsibilities in order to facilitate accountability and operational independence in the management of the SWF to pursue its objectives.
7.	Principle	The owner should set the objectives of the SWF, appoint the members of its governing body(ies) in accordance with clearly defined procedures, and exercise oversight over the SWF's operations.
8.	Principle	The governing body(ies) should act in the best interests of the SWF, and have a clear mandate and adequate authority and competency to carry out its functions.
9.	Principle	The operational management of the SWF should implement the SWF's strategies in an independent manner and in accordance with clearly defined responsibilities.
10.	Principle	The accountability framework for the SWF's operations should be clearly defined in the relevant legislation, charter, other constitutive documents, or management agreement.
11.	Principle	An annual report and accompanying financial statements on the SWF's operations and performance should be prepared in a timely fashion and in accordance with recognized international or national accounting standards in a consistent manner.
12.	Principle	The SWF's operations and financial statements should be audited annually in accordance with recognized international or national auditing standards in a consistent manner.
13.	Principle	Professional and ethical standards should be clearly defined and made known to the members of the SWF's governing body(ies), management, and staff.
14.	Principle	Dealing with third parties for the purpose of the SWF's operational management should be based on economic and financial grounds, and follow clear rules and procedures.

15.	Principle	SWF operations and activities in host countries should be conducted in compliance with all applicable regulatory and disclosure requirements of the countries in which they operate.
16.	Principle	The governance framework and objectives, as well as the manner in which the SWF's management is operationally independent from the owner, should be publicly disclosed.
17.	Principle	Relevant financial information regarding the SWF should be publicly disclosed to demonstrate its economic and financial orientation, so as to contribute to stability in international financial markets and enhance trust in recipient countries.
18.	Principle	The SWF's investment policy should be clear and consistent with its defined objectives, risk tolerance, and investment strategy, as set by the owner or the governing body(ies), and be based on sound portfolio management principles.
18.1	Subprinciple	The investment policy should guide the SWF's financial risk exposures and the possible use of leverage.
18.2	Subprinciple	The investment policy should address the extent to which internal and/or external investment managers are used, the range of their activities and authority, and the process by which they are selected and performance monitored.
18.3	Subprinciple	A description of the investment policy of the SWF should be publicly disclosed.
19.	Principle	The SWF's investment decisions should aim to maximize risk-adjusted financial returns in a manner consistent with its investment policy, and based on economic and financial grounds.
19.1	Subprinciple	If investment decisions are subject to other than economic and financial considerations, these should be clearly set out in the investment policy and be publicly disclosed.
19.2	Subprinciple	The management of an SWF's assets should be consistent with what is generally accepted as sound asset management principles.
20.	Principle	The SWF should not seek or take advantage of privileged information or inappropriate influence by the broader government in competing with private entities.
21.	Principle	SWFs view shareholder ownership rights as a fundamental element of their equity investments' value. If an SWF chooses to exercise its ownership rights, it should do so in a manner that is consistent with its investment policy and protects the financial value of its investments. The SWF should publicly disclose its general approach to voting securities of listed entities, including the key factors guiding its exercise of ownership rights.
22.	Principle	The SWF should have a framework that identifies, assesses, and manages the risks of its operations.
22.1	Subprinciple	The risk management framework should include reliable information and timely reporting systems, which should enable the adequate monitoring and management of relevant risks within acceptable parameters and levels, control and incentive mechanisms, codes of conduct, business continuity planning, and an independent audit function.
22.2	Subprinciple	The general approach to the SWF's risk management framework should be publicly disclosed.
23.	Principle	The assets and investment performance (absolute and relative to benchmarks, if any) of the SWF should be measured and reported to the owner according to clearly defined principles or standards.
24.	Principle	A process of regular review of the implementation of the GAPP should be engaged in by or on behalf of the SWF.

Source: International Working Group of Sovereign Wealth Funds, 2008. Sovereign Wealth Funds: Generally Accepted Principles and Practices. Washington DC: IWG.

Chapter 10

Shifting Gulf Arab Investments into the Mashreq: Underlying Political Economy Rationales?

Bessma Momani

Introduction

This chapter discusses the growing economic integration between the Gulf Arab states and the Mashreq (Egypt, Lebanon, and Jordan) region – specifically, the former's growing investments in the latter. It surveys the present strengths and future potential of the financial sector among GCC states and outlines the changing patterns and composition of GCC investments. This chapter, moreover, briefly traces the pattern of petrodollar recycling from the 1970 onward, which has begun to shift GCC investments from the US financial sector – US Treasury bills, US banks, and US direct investment – to an increasingly diversified portfolio. Throughout the 2000s, Gulf Arab investments have increasingly moved into Asia and the broader Middle East, with notable capital flows to the Mashreq region in recent years. The chapter outlines the underlying rationales for this shift in Gulf Arab investment.

Two major push factors driving a shift in the composition of Gulf Arab investment include the deterioration in US-Gulf relations after September 11 2001 and the shock to the global financial system brought on by the 2008 US-led, international financial crisis. These push factors, however, do not explain why we have seen a shift in Gulf Arab investments toward both the Middle East and Asia. As this chapter will show, those same economic forces that induce states to liberalize their economy (in particular, the need to move away from oil dependence in the Gulf, and a corresponding need to attract foreign investment in the Mashreq) cause the structure of trade and investment to take on a more regionalized form, as states seek regional arrangements to participate in globalization rather than to avoid it. This, 'new regionalism' approach suggests that states voluntarily choose to deepen integration, not because of top-down agent pressure, but because within the state there are bottom-up distributional coalitions pushing for regionalism. This is further evidenced in an emboldened business class as it divorces itself from rentier politics (see Hvidt and Hertog this volume)

To explain how these structural processes take place, this chapter suggests three key political economy variables to explain the increasing investment ties between the two regions. These variables include economic reforms in the Mashreq (specifically, the gradual move toward liberalization and opening of the economies of Lebanon, Egypt and Jordan in the 1980s and 1990s); the drive to diversify Gulf Arab investments, driven by various factors not limited to economic welfare-driven incentives; and the existence of 'horizontal networks' that bind the citizens of both regions closer together, and economic diplomacy prompted by an abundance of skilled Mashreqi labor in the Gulf. All three factors can be understood within the context of increasing economic liberalization, and the role of regionalization in minimizing its costs and maximizing its benefits.

Growth in GCC Investments

The GCC members – Bahrain, Kuwait, Oman, Qatar, the United Arab Emirates, and (lead by) Saudi Arabia – have the largest proven oil reserves in the world, are among the world's largest oil-exporting states, and have throughout the 2000s become undeniably dynamic international investors. With record high oil prices from 2004 to mid-2008, the GCC oil-exporters had experienced impressive economic growth. For example, GCC oil earnings averaged $146 billion/year in the 1997–2002 period, which more than doubled to $327 billion/year in the 2002–2006 period. Oil prices had also risen from $20/barrel in 2001, to $60/barrel in 2006, to $140/barrel by mid-2008. These oil earnings translated into positive economic indicators for the GCC states. The GCC's real GDP growth rates increased on average by 3.2 percent/year from 1999–2002 and on average by 7.1 percent/year from 2003–2007 (IMF 2008a, 44). The GCC's gross official reserves also increased substantially: $53.5 billion (2003); $67.8 billion (2005); $388.4 billion (2007); and $514.3 billion (IMF 2008a, 61). Enhanced oil-earnings have also meant that the six GCC states attained burgeoning current account surpluses – numbering at $50 billion in 2003–2004 to approximately $400 billion in 2007–2008 (Samba 2008, 4). As a note of comparison, the GCC states had a $200 billion current account surplus in 2006, compared with China's $250 billion in the same year (GCC 2007). This burgeoning current account surplus is the product of a number of years of record high oil prices, whereby Gulf Arab states have accumulated large foreign exchange reserves and have recycled this mainly dollar wealth through purchasing foreign debt and assets.

The IMF had once projected that, over time, oil-exporters (including non-GCC states) will accumulate more foreign exchange reserves and Asia will acquire less (Magnus 2006, 5). Some have even argued that the scale of GCC foreign exchange reserves actually underestimated its foreign savings because investment agencies outside the Central Banks, like the Abu Dhabi Investment Authority and the Saudi Arabian Monetary Agency, professionally manage a large portion of their states' unreported foreign reserves (Moin 2006). It is estimated that the GCC had $1.6 trillion (or 225 percent of its GDP) to $2 trillion in foreign assets at the end of 2006; of these foreign assets 67 percent were owned by GCC governments and 33 percent by private individuals (McKinsey & Co. 2007). In comparison, China held $1.1 trillion in foreign reserves (or 42 percent of its GDP) and much of that wealth is also public owned (GCC 2007). Moreover, investment firm Samba estimates that only a small part of the GCC's current account is held in foreign exchange reserves and the majority has been directed into a diverse asset class and a diverse geographical distribution (Samba 2008, 4).

Although the 2008–10 international financial crisis has impacted the Gulf Arab states (particularly Dubai), the GCC states remain key players in international investment. Nevertheless, because much of the GCC states' economic gains were made because of the second oil boom, the sharp decline of oil prices from a mid-2008 high of nearly $140/barrel to a low of nearly $40/barrel in 2009, had a temporary negative effect on GCC economic growth. There are estimates, for example, that the GCC stock markets dropped in value by more than 50 percent in 2008/2009. The once fledgling finance sector in the Gulf had also suffered from credit shortages and overall decline in global activity as well. The foreign reserves position of the GCC states has also decreased but it remains sizeable by relative standards. As oil prices levelled off at $70/barrel by 2010, most Gulf Arab states returned to reporting, albeit less dramatic, economic growth.

It is estimated that GCC central banks and sovereign wealth funds hold $1.1 trillion, and that both the UAE and Saudi Arabia own $400 billion of these assets. Samba financial group also predicted that between June 2008 and June 2010, GCC capital outflows still amounted to $430 billion. More importantly perhaps, the future of the GCC states arguably remains a bright one (Samba 2008, 14). The EIU estimates, for example, that the GCC economy will be valued at nearly $2 trillion by 2020; while much of this growth will be based on oil exports, petrochemicals, and plastics, the EIU also predicts that Gulf Arab states will internally diversify its economies with manufacturing and finance and diversify its outward investments in the Middle East, Africa and Asia (EIU 2009). For a number of years, the GCC has shifted investments from the United States and Europe to the emerging market economies of the Middle East and Asia. The question this chapter seeks to explore is related to the latter phenomena: the key pull and push factors that explain increased Gulf Arab investments in the Mashreq, specifically the countries of Jordan, Lebanon, and Egypt.

Changing Patterns in GCC Foreign Investments

The GCC is keenly interested in foreign investment because the six GCC states have relatively small populations: only 38 million people in total in 2009, of which 25 million live in Saudi Arabia. Relative to other capital-surplus countries, the GCC's small population has meant that many Gulf Arab states have had limited 'absorption channels' to reinvest oil earnings domestically. By comparison, China has more than a billion people, a large number of rural poor, a real need for improved infrastructure in its large countryside and a need for greater social development;

China can therefore choose to absorb much of its current account surplus into domestic investments. While the GCC has poured money into domestic real estate, capital markets, tourism, and banking to promote domestic investment and consumption, there remains considerable current account surplus to be invested. Despite the massive construction boom in the Gulf – the most notable example being Dubai – 'only the GCC states came to enjoy the status of higher-rated sovereigns' (Siddiqi 2006). Out of necessity, the GCC needed to resort to using the 'capital account channel' by augmenting their central bank reserves, purchasing foreign assets – through vehicles such as sovereign wealth funds (such as that used by overwhelmingly by the UAE) and through official liabilities such as US government treasury bills – and by investing in international financial institutions such as the IMF (Nsouli 2006). With an abundance of petrodollar wealth generated by states with a relatively small number of people that have high socio-economic indicators, the question of where and how will the Gulf Arab states continue to recycle their oil earnings is an important one for the study of shifts in foreign investment.

During the 1970s oil boom, Gulf Arab states had recycled their petrodollars in dollar-based assets and securities, particularly in US Treasury Bills. Attempts to track the whereabouts of petrodollar investments have always run into difficulties, as many Western governments had guaranteed GCC states a certain degree of anonymity. By drawing in a bulk of all oil-exporters' dollar holdings and investments in the United States, Washington had avoided breaking down holdings on an individual country basis (GAO 1979). With oil earnings in dollars and the US promise of anonymity, GCC states have invested heavily into US Treasury bills, US banks, and US direct investment. During the first oil boom of the 1970s, the US government and the Gulf Arab states managed to mute the debate on disclosing their holdings. After 9/11, however, there has been renewed domestic pressure on the US government to limit, disclose, and scrutinize Gulf investments in the United States.

Since September 11, further compounded by the 2006 Dubai Ports controversy, there have been renewed anxieties over the activities of Sovereign Wealth Funds (SWF), and especially over Gulf Arab investments in the United States (see Bazoobandi and Niblock in this volume). Morgan Stanley's President of the Middle East division, for example, had stated '[with] the Dubai ports fiasco, they're [Gulf investors] saying "we don't need the hassle"' (quoted in Timmons 2006). American critics of the SWF warned that these government-owned investment funds would be guises for geopolitical influence in US corporate governance and US economic policy (Summers 2007). Without doubt, there was increased Gulf Arab worry about the rising tide of US protectionist sentiment that threatened their existing and future investments- a point raised directly by US Secretary Paulson's 2006 visit to the region (see Paulson 2008). Coupled with Gulf Arab fears that their US assets may be confiscated due to Congressional 'witch-hunts' on Arab investments, there is a general sentiment that the GCC has become less confident in investing in the United States. With added scrutiny on GCC investments in the

United States, shifts in GCC petrodollar recycling beyond the United States had begun to occur. In response to congressional and public anxieties over Gulf Arab investment in the United States, Gulf Arab states have diversified their petrodollar investments beyond US securities and investments by investing more at home and within the neighboring Middle East and Asia. This is explained, perhaps, by the depreciation of local currencies and reduced external purchasing power of GCC states that are pegged to the dollar (Menegatti and Setser 2006). Not to be underestimated, however, is that the GCC states have been undergoing a slow but significant shift in carving a new identity for themselves – a concerted process of political 'rebranding' (see Cooper and Momani 2009). Promoted by a young, entrepreneurial, and Western-educated class of individuals, Gulf Arab citizens have been demanding that their government invest more wisely and more broadly (Legrenzi 2008). Consequently, GCC states have diversified their US investments by purchasing less US securities and engaging in more corporate acquisitions. As Sheikha Lubna, UAE's Minister of Economy, noted:

> ... 9/11 was an economic turning point. Anxiety about traveling, freezing assets, and the extra scrutiny of people entering the United States made a lot of businessman here more inclined to invest at home. At the same time they gained confidence in themselves ... one result has been the emergence of companies like DP World and Emirates airlines, which are successfully exporting their homegrown competencies and developing branded services that are recognized and admired internationally. (Al-Shahrabani and de Boer 2007, 86–87)

The GCC states were not only investing more at home and less in the United States, but also in investments outside the United States. Based on market assessments, three trends in GCC petrodollar recycling had taken place from 2003–2008: 1) GCC capital surpluses were increasingly invested in regional and domestic projects; 2) the GCC states diversified their US investments with less US securities and more corporate acquisitions in the United States; 3) GCC capital outflows shifted into more investments *outside* the United States – in Asia and the Middle East.

Intra-regional investment in the Middle East is a growing phenomenon in Gulf Arab foreign investments. In recent years, the GCC have been recycling their petrodollars into the Middle East, specifically into Jordan, Egypt and Lebanon (known as the Mashreq). Most active investors from the Gulf are the Emiratis, the Saudis and to a lesser extent the Kuwaitis. As the IMF Middle East department chief noted 'We see a lot more investment with hedge funds in dollars or deposits in banks in Beirut or Egypt ... they haven't gone out of dollars but [are] not holding so much treasury bills and deposits in US banks' (Moin Siddiqi 2006). While it is difficult to obtain exact figures, some estimate that between 50 to 75 percent of the stocks in Egyptian and Jordanian stock exchanges, for example, are Gulf Arab owned (Siddiq 2009, 34–38). Moreover, in January 2008, it was estimated that 47 percent of direct foreign investment in Egypt was from GCC states; predominantly from the UAE and followed by Saudi Arabia (Khalaf and England 2008). Prior to the 2008 international financial crisis, increased FDI in the Mashreq had resulted in impressive growth in countries' economic growth (Ilahi and Shendy 2008). For example, Egypt boasted 7.2 percent, Lebanon 6.5 percent, and Jordan 5.5 percent GDP growth in 2008.[1] Based on June 2003–June 2008 estimates, 13 percent of GCC foreign assets or $120 billion went to the Middle East and North Africa (MENA), predominantly in Jordan, Egypt, and Lebanon (Samba 2008, 12). This represented a significant increase from previous years and a shift away from US based assets. Understanding why the GCC have focussed investments in the Mashreq merits further elaboration. But first, it is important to outline some of the caveats and limitation to analyzing investments coming from the GCC states.

Gulf Arab Investments in the Mashreq: Jordan, Egypt, and Lebanon

As noted above, GCC states are typically secretive about their capital outflows and it is difficult to obtain Gulf Arab data on the geographical distribution of their assets and their holdings. By one estimate, only 41 percent of all GCC assets can be traced and the overwhelming majority cannot (ibid., 7). The US treasury, Bank of International Settlements, UNCTAD, and the Bloomberg database of acquisitions and mergers have been the main sources of information used by firms and organizations (such as the IIF) attempting to estimate Gulf Arab capital flows. That said, even US Treasury figures have tended to greatly underestimate Gulf Arab deposits in US securities and investments. This is because the Treasury department does not track capital flowing through intermediaries and third party investment managers – something Gulf Arab states have been increasingly doing to bypass US and foreign government oversight.[2] Consequently, the exercise of determining Gulf Arab investments and holdings has been one of estimation that includes both known and untracked assets.

Two sets of estimates on GCC capital outflow data exist for comparison. Of the GCC's $542 billion of capital outflows from 2002 to 2006, the Institute of International Finance estimates the geographic breakdown noted in Table 5.1 below. Using similar data sets, Investment firm Samba updated the IIF estimates for 2004–2008 and estimated that the GCC's capital outflow increased by approximately 68 percent to $912 billion with a geographical breakdown also noted below.

Table 10.1 above confirms several trends that were noted by investment firms, officials, and analysts. Most notably, during the second oil boom, the GCC states shifted their investments away from the United States and into Europe, the MENA region, and Asia. Presumably, we could see further shifts away from the United

---

1   World Bank GDP based in constant 2000 US dollars.
2   See *The Economist*. 'The Petrodollar Puzzle', 9 June 2007, 86.

**Table 10.1 Estimated GCC capital outflows by region
(billions of dollars; percent of change)**

	2002–2006	2004–2008	Change (%)
United States	$300	$450	+50
Europe	100	200	+100
Middle East and North Africa	60	120	+100
Asia	60	120	+100
Other	22	22	0
Total	542	912	+68

Source: International Institute for Finance, Regional Briefing Gulf Cooperation Council, 31 May 2007, http://iif.com/emr/emr-af; Samba Chief Economist Office, 'Tracking GCC Foreign Investments: How the Strategies are Changing with Markets in Turmoil', December 2008, p. 12.

States and Europe following the international financial crisis and through the longer term. Gulf Arab investors may choose to direct their capital away from the epicentre of the financial crisis and seek opportune investments in this increasingly multi-polar world economy.

This chapter seeks to further explore what explains the Gulf Arab's added investments in the Mashreq. In particular, Jordan, Egypt and Lebanon are the key destinations for Gulf Arab investment in the Middle East. At a broader level of analysis, this chapter seeks to outline the broad structural trend in the global economy that underpins this new direction in Gulf Arab investment. This trend is defined by the proliferation of regionalism as a response to globalization – global economic integration, specifically. As this chapter will show, those same economic forces that induce states to liberalize their economy (in particular, the need to move away from oil dependence in the Gulf Arab states, and a corresponding need to attract foreign investment in the Mashreq) cause the structure of trade and investment to take on a more regionalized form, as states seek regional arrangements to participate in globalization rather than to avoid it. In this context, regionalism can be conceived as a vehicle for states and non-state actors alike, to participate in the process of global economic integration, and the constraints it imposes, on more advantageous terms. This, 'new regionalism' approach suggests that states voluntarily choose to deepen integration, not because of top-down super-power pressure, but because within the state there are distributional coalitions pushing for regionalism (see Hettne and Soderbaum 2008; Momani 2008a). To put it another way, 'new regionalism needs to be understood as a multi-dimensional and multi-level process, which is not based solely on or around states, but reflects the activities of states, firms, and social groups and networks' (Hurrell 2005, 42).

To be sure, the international political economic literature on intraregional investments is mixed on what are the key determinants to attract foreign investment. As one economist points out: 'the relation between FDI and many of the controversial variables (namely, tax, wages, openness, exchange rate, tariffs, growth and trade balance) are highly sensitive to small alterations in the conditioning information set' (Chakrabarti 2001). Similarly, identifying the key factors and disincentives to promoting foreign direct investment in the Middle East is also a subject of debate in the economic literature (see Moosa 2008; Aysan, Nabli and Veganzones-Varoudakis 2006). Instead, this chapter tries to suggest key political economy explanations, rather than test economic modelling and general theories. It is argued that there are three compelling factors that help to explain a growing shift in Gulf Arab investments towards the Mashreq: economic reforms in the Mashreq; drive to diversify Gulf Arab investments; and 'horizontal networks' and economic diplomacy. All three factors can be understood within the context of increasing economic liberalization, and the role of regionalization in minimizing its costs and maximizing its benefits.

Economic Reforms in the Mashreq

Despite the spread of economic liberalization throughout the developing world in the 1980s and 1990s, the Middle East remained one of the most protectionist and inward-looking economic regions in the world (Noland and Pack 2007). Characterized by high tariff and non-tariff barriers, government legislation that protected most state-owned industries and weak links to global financial markets, the Middle East was relatively inhospitable toward foreign direct investment and multi-national corporations (Abed and Davoodi 2003). Among the many factors that thwarted foreign investment included the stringently-regulated and inward-looking nature of local economies. Countries in the region remained classic rentier states, providing subsidized state goods and services in exchange for political complacency (see Hvidt in this volume). Non-oil exporting countries were heavily dependent on oil rents received through expatriate workers in the Gulf. After declining oil rents in the 1980s and rising commodity prices, many Middle East countries faced bloated government expenditures and declining incomes. Middle East governments came to the realization that they needed external financial support from foreign governments, international financial institutions, and foreign direct investment.

A number of countries sought the financial support of the IMF and World Bank and the international donor community for a way out of their fiscal woes. Specifically, Egypt, Jordan, Morocco and Algeria adopted IMF/World Bank structural adjustment policies in the late 1980s and 1990s. Deemed to be vital to geostrategic security, Western government support for Egypt, and to a lesser extent Syria and Jordan, also resulted in international creditors giving them unprecedented amounts of loan forgiveness through the Paris Club (Momani 2004). Moreover, international and US financial support for Jordan was linked to its 1994 peace treaty with Israel. Subsequently, many of the Middle East countries also undertook domestic reforms to join the World Trade Organization. Jordan, Morocco, and a number of Gulf Arab countries also undertook domestic regulatory reforms to sign free trade agreements with United States.

The GCC similarly reformed its domestic economies to prepare for an interregional free trade agreement with the European Union (see Antkiewicz and Momani 2009). Similarly, the Barcelona Process and the Algadir Agreement motivated many Arab Mediterranean countries to liberalize their economies for closer economic ties with the EU (see Momani, 2009). Despite these externally induced political and economic reforms throughout the 1990s and early 2000s, the Middle East continued to attract a relatively low share of global foreign investment during the late 1990s through to the 2000s compared to other emerging market economies. As figures 10.1, 10.2 and 10.3 demonstrate, the Arab region has historically attracted a low share of global foreign direct investment, a trend that changed dramatically during the oil boom years of 2003–2008. However, the perceived political risk associated with the regional instability of Iraq, Israel/ Palestine, Lebanon, and Iran, plus the continuation of bureaucratic difficulties to doing business in the Middle East, had continued to scare-off global investors (Laabas and Abdmoulah 2009, 4). The Gulf Arab countries, however, took advantage of Mashreq economic reforms and liberalization by investing their oil surpluses during the second oil boom years in a dramatic way.

After years of economic reforms, Jordan, Egypt and Lebanon had become more hospitable to foreign investment. They privatized state-owned assets and revitalized their domestic stock exchanges. The Mashreq is generally hungry for capital. It has a growing consumer base of young people and a highly educated and relatively inexpensive workforce. But it also has a difficult time attracting international investors because of the 'neighbourhood effect' of the tense regional security situation. In cross-country regression analysis, it was concluded that improvement in Middle East technology and knowledge were less valuable to attracting foreign direct investment than was improved political openness and civil rights and reducing bureaucratic red tape (Onyeiwu 2008). Keeping this in mind, it is argued that Gulf Arab investors are less spooked by geopolitical instability in the region, are familiar with the political and bureaucratic constraints of these countries, and view the Mashreq as a relatively safe investment climate. In fact, many of the Gulf Arab citizens vacation in the Mashreq during the unbearable summer heat of the Gulf. It is undeniable that for Gulf Arab citizens the Mashreq is viewed as a safe place to vacation; by extension, one could argue that this has a positive branding effect for the Mashreq as well, improving the outlook for investment in the region. The most popular Middle East destination for Gulf Arab tourists is Egypt and it is estimated that 60 percent of all tourists in Egypt come from the GCC states. The prices are right and the investment climate is viewed as relatively safe and culturally familiar one for Gulf Arab investors. These pull factors have made the Mashreq region an attractive and opportune site for Gulf Arab investments.

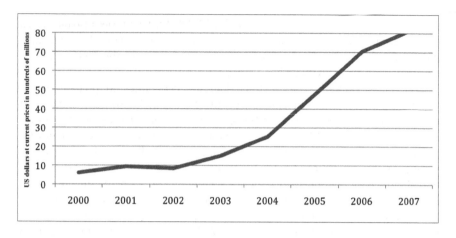

Figure 10.1 FDI inflows into Arab countries, 2000–2007
Source: Arab Investment & Export Credit Guarantee Corporation, 2009, http://www.iaigc.
net/?id=7&sid=21.

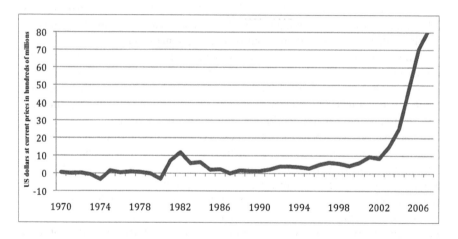

Figure 10.2 FDI inflows into Arab countries, 1970–2007
Source: Arab Investment & Export Credit Guarantee Corporation, 2009, http://www.iaigc.
net/?id=7&sid=21.

The GCC states are buying Middle East telecommunication companies, real estate, banking, construction, and tourism projects (Smith 2007) While it is difficult to determine exactly how much Gulf Arab investment makes its way to the Mashreq, the IMF estimates that from 2002–2007 the GCC states provided 60 percent of total FDI inflows into Lebanon and approximately 70–80 percent of FDI into Jordan from Arab sources (IMF 2009, 16). The relative size of Gulf Arab foreign

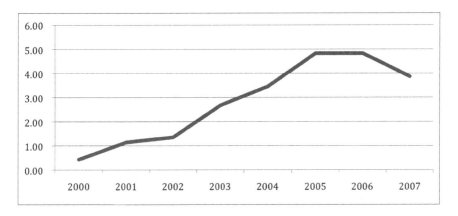

Figure 10.3 Arab countries share of global inward FDI (percent)
Source: Arab Investment & Export Credit Guarantee Corporation, 2009, http://www.iaigc.
net/?id=7&sid=21.

direct investment into the Mashreq is noteworthy. For example, compared to other major investors in the region, Gulf Arab states and MENA boasted by far the highest share of declared global FDI into the Mashreq between 2003 and 2008, amounting to 42.1 billion euros (ANIMA 2009, 30). Moreover, the IMF estimates that Arab investment, primarily from the GCC states, accounted for 50 percent of foreign ownership in Egypt and 75 percent in Jordan (IMF 2008a, 8).

As the Mashreq countries tried to integrate deeper into the global economy, they found regional investment from the GCC states to be the most logical source of FDI. Unable to fully realize the benefits of economic liberalization in the Mashreq, due to the political and regional security factors outlined above, intraregional investment became the Mashreq's stepping stone to participating in global economic integration. Likewise, for the Gulf Arab states, US markets once looked like the most logical place to invest oil revenue, but the demographic, as well as political makeup of the Arab monarchies of the Gulf is no longer satisfied with past trends in petrodollar recycling. The following section looks closer at these trends, and examines how domestic changes within the GCC are driving diversification of investments.

Diversification of Investments

The future of economic development in the Gulf is also an important factor that explains why the GCC states have increased investments in the Mashreq. Gulf Arab states today are undergoing a noteworthy change in its economic direction, as noted by Hvidt in this volume. While the Gulf remains dependent on oil incomes to stimulate its socio-economic development, GCC states are also attempting to become more diversified as the finite resource diminishes (Hanna 2006, 7). In

Table 10.2 Arab countries FDI compared

	Total FDI flows in US Dollars at current prices in millions (in percentage)							
	1998	2000	2001	2002	2004	2005	2006	2007
World	705543.62	1398182.82	824444.78	625167.88	717695.50	958697.47	1411018.20	1833324.05
Arab countries	5548.58	5956.87	9325.53	8360.28	24706.47	45723.96	67568.48	72368.62
	0.79	*0.43*	*1.13*	*1.34*	*3.44*	*4.77*	*4.79*	*3.95*
Africa	9609.82	9670.99	19904.64	14592.12	18019.71	29459.47	45753.90	52982.23
	1.36	*0.69*	*2.41*	*2.33*	*2.51*	*3.07*	*3.24*	*2.89*
America	282811.48	479126.58	268106.10	154393.14	230656.08	208195.07	392466.28	467795.59
	40.08	*34.27*	*32.52*	*24.70*	*32.14*	*21.72*	*27.81*	*25.52*
Asia	103376.28	163763.88	126743.12	114032.11	189532.42	222627.35	289694.83	361315.52
	14.65	*11.71*	*15.37*	*18.24*	*26.41*	*23.22*	*20.53*	*19.71*
Europe	301542.50	730022.57	401369.62	323261.66	239682.67	531498.51	647911.56	925032.03
	42.74	*52.21*	*48.68*	*51.71*	*33.40*	*55.44*	*45.92*	*50.46*
Oceania	8203.53	15598.79	8321.29	18888.86	39804.61	-33082.92	35191.63	26198.68
	1.16	*1.12*	*1.01*	*3.02*	*5.55*	*-3.45*	*2.49*	*1.43*

Bahrain, Oman and Qatar, for example, oil reserves may be no more within the next twenty years. Economic diversification in the Gulf does not necessarily imply moving completely away from oil production, but also involves 'downstream integration' and injecting value added into oil refining and petrochemical production (Luciani 2007, 166).

Nevertheless, Gulf Arab states are keen on diversifying their economies to move away from dependence on oil incomes. Dubai is a prime example of a transformation of an arid and sparsely populated emirate into a commercial, service, real estate, tourist, and banking hub that will act as a conduit between Asia and the West. In joining the World Trade Organization and supporting private sector investment, the Gulf Arab states aim to open their economies to alternative sources of income. The public sector remains the dominant engine of growth in Gulf Arab economies, but in many ways a new private economic class can attribute its rise to the successes of the region's economic liberalization (see Hertog this volume). Again, Dubai was exemplary of the region's novelty in creating economic growth – at times a fabricated one at that (Hvidt 2009). Consequently, this dynamic Gulf Arab private sector has ambitions to both promote Gulf Arab power in the greater Middle East and to promote economic diversification at home (Hertog 2007). While the ambitions of the GCC states will require more than significant rebranding to take hold, the desires and frustrations of a new class are gaining the attention of wary Gulf Arab leaders. While far from being revolutionary, this class is often young and makes up a substantial part of the population. For example, the median age is 30.1 years for the UAE, 21.6 for Saudi Arabia, and 18.8 in Oman (US 2009). Moreover, this demographic group is foreign-educated and increasingly sceptical of its governments' inefficient investments in the West.

Among the shift toward economic diversification at home, the GCC states are also trying to diversity their income streams away from oil and toward interest and profit gains made on foreign investments. Gulf Arab governments are mindful of the socio-economic and political challenges they have and will continue to face during oil busts (see Tétreault in this volume). The 1980s and 1990s brought enormous socio-political challenges to many Gulf Arab countries when citizen's high socio-economic expectations were unmet due to falling national incomes. During that time, Gulf Arab citizens blamed their governments for wasteful spending and poor investment choices in the first oil boom, which often were managed by US banks, ending up in US coffers. These 1970s and 1980s investments are often seen by Gulf Arab citizens as their governments' 'bailing out of Western economies' – an economic price that was exchanged for the comforts of the American security umbrella during regional insecurity in the Gulf (such as the Iranian Revolution, Iran-Iraq war, and the Soviet invasion of Afghanistan) (Momani 2008b). By the time of the second oil boom, Gulf Arab governments witnessed the dissatisfaction of their citizens, who have become more sceptical of their governments' spending, particularly abroad. Moreover after the US invasion of Iraq and US sabre-rattling with Iran, the Gulf Arab publics started to question the value of the US' role as military protectorate in the region.

As Gulf Arab citizens are increasingly more critical of their governments' investment choices abroad and at home, we see Gulf Arab investors no longer happy with both giving up management of their assets to foreign banks and with being idle investors in US securities. Instead, they are showing a greater willingness to play an active role as managers, partners and investors of their portfolios and companies (Abdelal et al. 2008). Part of this increased confidence in managing their own investments is attributable to the Gulf Arab's 'brain gain' of highly skilled international financial investors, analysts, and bankers. This has made them bolder and consequently they have taken on more risk than previous years, both within the Middle East and the wider world. Whereas in previous oil booms Gulf Arab investors had tried to stay out of the limelight of corporate acquisitions, in the second oil boom they are purchasing high profile companies, taking large stakes in visible entities, and funding megaprojects with high public profile (ibid.).

The added boldness of Gulf Arab investors is furthered by the realities of strong financial returns. It has been argued that the Gulf Arab's sovereign wealth funds and fund managers were taking advantage of 'excesses' in their portfolios to move beyond perceived safer 'liquid investments' to more riskier property investments in the Middle East and elsewhere (Samba 2008, 11). With strong gains made in the financial markets prior to the 2008 international financial crisis, Gulf Arab investors have added more risk to their portfolios. Moreover, as Gulf Arab investors involved in Islamic banking projects sought out fixed investment assets as part of the terms of contract, they turned to the Middle East market (ibid.). Islamic banking rules preclude investors earning interest on their assets as part of the *shariah* compliant terms of contract. As a result, Islamic bonds (or *sukuk*) have a higher content of fixed assets in their portfolios than traditional, Western investment banks.

Coupled with growing political assertiveness of its citizens, Gulf Arab states are increasingly shifting their investments away from US government debt and financial institutions and playing a more assertive role with their petrodollars. Certainly, the Dubai ports controversy, not to mention the diminution of the United States' image following the third Gulf War, has also played a role in this shift. But the broader picture reflects a gradual structural reorientation away from US markets and toward an increasingly regional, as well as global, focus. The driving force behind this shift is a domestic economic pressure to diversify Gulf Arab investments, to be more active and more globally involved. In this context, the Mashreq – a regional market that lacks investment from abroad – is a logical place for Gulf Arab investors to invest some of their capital. The next section explores these dynamics more closely.

Horizontal Networks and Economic Diplomacy

Two central trends bring Gulf Arab and Mashreq economies increasingly closer. The first trend is the proliferation of horizontal (dispersed) as opposed to vertical (top-down, hierarchical) economic networks in the two regions, whereby intraregional economic integration is increasingly driven by the reliance of Gulf Arab economic prosperity on the influx of skilled Mashreqi labor. As a consequence Mashreqi workers' long-standing non-permanent residence in the Gulf, as well as the Gulf's close proximity to the Mashreq, warrants Gulf Arab economic diplomacy – namely, the use of financial resources to ensure stability in the Mashreq. This forms an increasingly important aspect of the intraregional political dynamics and is the second defining trend that binds the two regions together.

The growing economies of the sparsely populated Gulf Arab states have been highly dependent on foreign labor. The local Gulf Arab population is often a minority in their countries and foreign workers with temporary residency and no citizenship rights are the majority. The Gulf's labor shortage is concentrated in both low-skilled markets in construction and oil extraction and in highly-skilled markets in engineering, education, finance, healthcare, and private sector management (see Hertog this volume). Through poor policy choices and distorted incentive structures, we have seen further segmentation of the Gulf Arab labor market. The local Gulf Arab labor is increasingly incompatible with the needs of the Gulf Arab economy. Gulf Arab labor tends to have low, non-technical education levels and have rising expectations for high wages. With feelings of self-entitlement, they also feel unobligated to compete with educated foreign workers. Consequently, they are often employed in the bloated and overpaid public sector. This is further aided by GCC governments' labor nationalization programmes where local Gulf Arab labor is preferred by the public sector and where quotas are put on specific industries. To fill the labor vacuum in the private sector, the GCC states relied on foreign workers. In the low-skilled category, Asian workers primarily from India, Pakistan, Bangladesh, and the Philippines have been employed; in the high-skilled category, non-Gulf Arabs from the Mashreq and Westerners have been employed. In the case of Kuwait, it was estimated that Arab workers occupy more technical, scientific, managerial, and clerical positions than their Asian counterparts (see Table 10.3).

One runs into considerable obstacles obtaining exact figures on the number and sectoral distribution of foreign workers throughout the Gulf. It is estimated, however, that 56 percent of the GCC's workforce, or 31 percent of the Gulf Arab population, are foreign expatriates (Sturm et al. 2008). In the UAE and Qatar, for example, 91 and 92 percent of the labor force is occupied by foreign workers (EIU 2008). Moreover, there is a stronger growth in, or demand for, foreign workers than national or local workers in the labor market (Girgis 2002). Unlike Asian workers, Arab workers in the Gulf speak the local language, tend to be relatively more educated than their local counterparts and occupy mid-to-high level management positions. Arab workers in the Gulf are primarily Egyptians (approximately 1.5 million), Yemenis (0.9 million), Palestinians/Jordanians (0.5 million), and Lebanese (0.4 million) (ANIMA 2009). The impact of the workers' remittances on Arab sender countries is also noteworthy. For example, one third of the Lebanese workforce is in the GCC, and Jordanians that work abroad (especially in the Gulf)

Table 10.3 Kuwait, Distribution of Arab and Asian foreign labor, 2000

Foreign Labor	Technical & Scientific	Managerial	Clerical & government	Sales & services	Agriculture	Production
			Occupation			
Total	87,716	19,710	68,251	376,650	15,227	427,581
% Arabs	57.6	61.1	65.2	16.8	26.6	32.2
% Asians	35.8	30.2	33.4	83.1	73.3	67.5

Source: Girgis, M. 2002, 'Would Nationals and Asians Replace Arab workers in the GCC?' http://www.eces.org.eg/Uploaded_Files/%7B3D6C8AB9-D53E-4D52-B195-1AA1F C8CA91F%7D_ECESWP74.pdf.

provide Jordan with an estimated $3 billion every year (EIU 2009). As a result, among the world's emerging market economies, Lebanon is the 'most remittance-dependent country' (Kapiszewski 2006, 6–7).

As Mashreqi workers play a key role in the Gulf Arab labor market, their presence is a necessity, but it is often perceived to be a threat to Gulf Arab rulers as well. In some respects, they have intimate knowledge and understand internal power relations. Those coming from the Mashreq have also tended to hold views of or have been influenced by pan-Arabism, an anti-colonial ideology of Egyptian leader Gamal Abdel Nasser in the 1950s and 1960s (ibid.). Pan-Arabism has tended to disregard the legitimacy of Gulf Arab monarchs, and views them as installations of British colonialism. Moreover, pan-Arab ideology posits that the oil riches of the Gulf Arab region ought to belong to the Arab people collectively. No doubt the 'betrayal' felt by Kuwaitis in the Iraqi invasion of 1990–91 and the siding of Palestinians, and to a lesser extent of Jordanians, with the Baathist regime had reinforced the Gulf Arab perception that Arab workers in the Gulf were not loyal to the Sheikdoms' sovereignty and legitimacy. Moreover, it has been pointed out that unlike some of their Asian and Western counterparts, Arab workers in the Gulf relocate their families and tend to stay for a long period of time, creating 'facts on the ground' that have been perceived as a threat to Gulf Arab nations (ibid.). Consequently, there has been a noticeable and relatively successful attempt by Gulf Arab rulers to reduce the number of Arab foreign workers and increase Asian workers over the years (see Figure 10.4). There are supply and demand rationales to this, but it argued here that the Arab workers were increasingly viewed as a threat: a potential 'fifth column' in Gulf Arab societies.

Taking the view that educated and professional Arab workers in the Gulf can also form 'horizontal networks' to influence Gulf Arab policy choices and investments, it is argued that the consequences of a strong representation of Arab workers in the

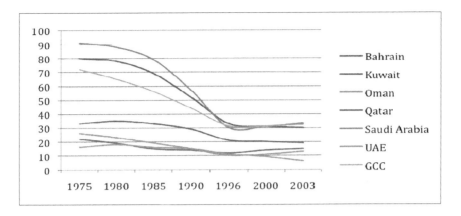

Figure 10.4 Percentage of Arabs among immigrant population in GCC, 1975–2003
Source: Based on Kapiszewski, A. 2006, 'Arab Versus Asian Migrant Workers in the GCC Countries', United Nations Expert Group Meeting on International Migration and Development in the Arab Region, Beirut 2006, http://www.un.org/esa/population/meetings/EGM_Ittmig_Arab/P02_Kapiszewski.pdf.

Gulf could be quite significant.[3] Two ideas are considered. First, as noted among the Arab nationals in the Gulf, there are Lebanese, Jordanian, Palestinian, and Egyptian professionals predominantly working in the private sector. Some have consequently argued that one of the reasons for increased investment into the Mashreq region, and these countries specifically, is the presence of a high number of Gulf Arab investors originating from the Mashreq who have strong network ties to their home countries and are more comfortable with increasing their financial portfolios there (Sfakianakis and Woertz 2007, 132). Not surprisingly, there is a shortage of local or national Gulf Arab investors and managers at the helm of investment portfolios even if their number is increasing (EIU 2009).

Second, Gulf Arab rulers are increasingly interested in preserving the geopolitical stability of its Arab Mashreq neighbours. Because of the large presence of foreign workers among GCC economies, and the resultant potential of these Arab workers to use their domestic political affiliations to link political movements across state divides and thereby influence political outcomes in the Gulf, GCC governments are becoming increasingly dependent on the economic prosperity and political stability of the Mashreq and are more willing to use their economic diplomacy to achieve stability in the region. As the case of Lebanon's 2009 elections most aptly demonstrated, the internal geopolitical dynamics of the country have regional consequences and benefactors. Gulf Arab states,

---

3   On 'horizontal networks', see Anne-Marie Slaughter, *A New World Order* (Princeton University Press, 2005)

Saudi Arabia in particular, shored up the Lebanese banking system by injecting $1 billion into the Lebanese economy after Israel's 2006 invasion and played a strong financing role in promoting its preferred political candidates and parties during the 2009 elections. This demonstration of economic diplomacy is the direct result of the Saudi monarchy's concern about the direct repercussions of an unfavorable electoral outcome and its willingness to employ its resources to affect favorable political outcomes in a region of vital importance. Using its economic power in the region, Gulf Arab governments and private investors may be keen to influence the political development and process of the neighboring Arab states. To illustrate this point, when asked to identify the 'major risks' for the Emirates in the next few years, UAE's Minister of Economy Sheikha Lubna stated that:

> Number one is obviously the political stability of the region. Anything that happens to one of our neighbours has implications for us. We are all investors in and exporters to Lebanon, for example, so when it was brought to the ground [in 2006], the efforts of the past ten years were completely demolished. (Al-Shahrabani and de Boer 2007, 92)

The geopolitical value in upholding the Mashreq is vital to keeping Arab foreign workers from becoming quasi-refugees in the Gulf. Moreover, as noted Gulf Arab citizens vacation in the Mashreq during the intense summer heat of the Gulf. Ensuring the political and economic stability of the Mashreq is a win-win for Gulf Arab interests. Thus, when looking for avenues to diversify their oil-income portfolios, the Mashreq looks to be especially attractive, given the bottom up pressures from Gulf Arab citizens dissatisfied with their governments' investment policies, as well as the complications created by a growing Mashreq expatriate population, which cannot be ignored, let alone alienated by the Gulf Arab monarchies. In this way, interregional investment (and greater intraregional association between the two respective regions) is driven both by state-actors, seeking greater economic and political security, and non-state actors as well, which both directly and indirectly demand greater integration. Local constituencies thus create a greater demand for regionalization, as both the Mashreq and the GCC states diversify and liberalize and diversify their economies.

Conclusion

The GCC states have experienced significant economic growth owing to the rise in oil prices from 2003 to mid-2008. As a result of their limited absorption channels at home, we have seen an outward flow of Gulf Arab capital. During the first oil boom of the 1970s, Gulf Arab investors had recycled their current account surpluses into US securities and investments. After September 11, US-Gulf relations have deteriorated and Gulf Arab investors, government and private, began to worry about the safety of their investments. Coupled with the United States' central role in the 2008 international financial crisis, we may continue to see a shift of Gulf Arab investment away from the American market. This push factor, however, does not explain why we have seen a shift in Gulf Arab investments toward both the Middle East and Asia.

A more nuanced investigation of the intraregional investments in the Middle East suggests the development of a structural shift toward regionalism (as opposed to a strictly global outlook), driven by a coalescence of interests among state actors and their domestic constituencies, who favor closer association with one another for various interlocking political and economic reasons. The structural incentive toward regional integration – structural because it conforms to market pressures to liberalize (albeit very gradually) the domestic industry and financial sector – is defined by economic reforms undertaken both in the Gulf and the Mashreq and driven by the political economy in both regions.

This chapter has argued that there are three political economy rationales prompting Gulf Arab states to increase investments into the Middle East, particularly into Lebanon, Jordan, and Egypt. First, economic reforms in the Mashreq, spurred by years of external pressure, have made the Mashreq more attractive. While global investment continues to shy away from the Mashreq, Gulf Arab investors are at ease with the region and are not as spooked by regional political instability. Second, as the GCC states are undergoing a move toward the diversification of its income streams, fixed assets in the Middle East provide an alternative to the instability of Western liquid assets. Gulf Arab rulers are conscious of their peoples' desires to have efficient and long-lasting investments; something the first oil-boom profits did not provide. Third, through horizontal networks of professional Arab workers in the Gulf, Gulf Arab states are making increased connections with, and prompting investment into, the Mashreq. Preserving the geopolitical stability of the Mashreq, home country of a large number of Arab workers and a summer vacation destination for Gulf Arab citizens, is a key political objective and Gulf Arab investments therefore serve as an important tool for Gulf Arab economic diplomacy in the region.

Chapter 11

The Gulf Arab States and Asia Pacific: Geo-Economics and Interdependency

Christopher M. Davidson

Introduction

An important new relationship is developing between the six monarchies of the Arab states – Saudi Arabia, the United Arab Emirates (UAE), Kuwait, Qatar, Bahrain and Oman – and the three most industrialized states of Asia Pacific – Japan, China and South Korea. With little shared modern economic history, with enormous political and socio-economic disparities, and separated by great geographical distances, the rapidly tightening economic interdependence between the two regions is a recent phenomenon that deserves considerable attention. What began as a simple, mid-twentieth century marriage of convenience based on hydrocarbon exports in exchange for hard currency has now evolved into a multi-dimensional, long-term mutual commitment that will not only continue to capitalize on the Gulf Arab's rich energy resources and Asia Pacific's massive energy needs, but will also seek to develop strong non-hydrocarbon bilateral trade, will facilitate sizeable sovereign wealth investments in both directions, and will provide lucrative opportunities for experienced Asian Pacific construction companies, their technologies and – in China's case – its vast labor force.

Although this increasingly extensive relationship does not encompass the Gulf Arab's military security arrangements – which remains exclusively with the United States, Britain and France – and although few attempts have been made by either side to replace or balance these with new Asia Pacific alliances, there is nonetheless compelling evidence that the two regions have also sought to strengthen their non-economic ties. An abundance of state-level visits, often at much higher levels than with western powers, and a considerable number of cooperative agreements, gifts, loans and other incentives, are undoubtedly binding these great trade partners ever closer. Moreover, with a number of future collaborations including 'hydrocarbon safekeeping', civilian nuclear and solar energy projects and the building of a twenty-first century 'Silk Road'; and with a growing realization that the Pacific-Asian economies, particularly China, may recover more quickly from the global credit crunch than the western economies (*The Guardian*, 7 April 2009; *Deutsche Presse*, 24 June 2009), thus signifying a global shift in economic weight from the West to the East, this chapter argues that the GCC states' eastwards orientation can only intensify and the trajectory of interdependence will continue to accelerate.

Following a brief historical background of relations between the Gulf Arab states and Asia Pacific, an examination of their contemporary hydrocarbon and non-hydrocarbon trade links will then be made, before turning to the sizeable interlinking investments between the nine states involved, and the several examples of major construction and labor contracts in the Gulf Arab states having already been awarded to Pacific-Asian companies. Finally, the efforts to boost diplomatic and other relations will be considered, followed by an analysis of the many recent efforts that have been made to explore innovative future avenues of economic and technical cooperation.

Historical Background

The Gulf Arab's oil trade with the Asian Pacific economies began in the early 1950s, when Japanese oil companies were scouring the globe for resources to fuel Japan's rapid post-war industrialization programme. Most of the Gulf sheikhdoms were off limits to Japan, as they remained part of Britain's 'Trucial System' – a series of nineteenth century peace treaties between London and the various sheikhs that guaranteed British protection in exchange for exclusive political and economic relations (Onley 2007). Saudi Arabia, however, was the key exception, with Britain having formally recognized King Abdul-Aziz bin Saud's independence in 1932, and being unable to prevent the United States' Standard Oil of California from beginning exploration the following year. In 1953, Japan was able to dispatch freely an economic delegation to Saudi Arabia, and the following year formal diplomatic relations began. By 1956, Japan's Arabian Oil Company had secured a 43-year concession to explore and extract Saudi oil and began production as early as 1960, a concession that duly ended in the year 2000.

In parallel, non-hydrocarbon trade between the Gulf Arab states and Japan was also beginning to flourish, although its origins were rather more circuitous. Dubai, as one of the Trucial States, had long been exploring inventive ways of circumventing Britain's tight economic controls (Davidson 2008, 19), and in the 1950s and 1960s the sheikhdom managed to position itself as the primary re-export hub for goods destined for India. Following the latter's independence and the attempts of its first prime minister, Jawaharlal Nehru, to replicate the Soviet miracle by using the state to plan and protect the economy, a number of restrictive practices were introduced that effectively prevented India-based merchants from meeting domestic demand for their products, especially Japanese fabrics. Dubai played the role of an intermediary, with its merchants carefully ordering the necessary materials well in advance so as to overcome the lengthy five month shipping time from Japan. By the late 1970s Dubai's trade with Japan had expanded to include electrical goods, with the re-exporting of millions of Hitachi personal stereos to the subcontinent (Davidson 2008, 313), and by 1982, in time for the Asian games being held in New Delhi that year, thousands of

Japanese television sets were being distributed across India and the Persian Gulf (Buxani 2003, 117–19, 121; Davidson 2008, 71). With Britain's granting of independence to Kuwait in 1961, and with its withdrawal from the Trucial States in 1971, Japan's opportunities for further oil concessions and more formal non-hydrocarbon trade expanded to include all of the Gulf Arab monarchies. Formal diplomatic relations were established with Kuwait in 1961, and in late 1971 Japan was one of the first countries to recognize the newly formed federation of the United Arab Emirates. The following year relations were also established with Qatar, Bahrain and Oman (Ministry for Foreign Affairs (Japan), 2009). The Arabian Oil Company – by this stage 80 percent owned by Japan and 20 percent owned by Saudi Arabia and Kuwait – duly signed concessions in Kuwait in 1961 (CIA World Factbook 2009), and the Japanese Oil Development Company took a stake in an international consortium to exploit UAE offshore oil in late 1972 (Abu Dhabi Marine Operating Company 2006).

Although China was also involved in some of the re-export trade in the Gulf in the 1950s and 1960s, the volume was much lower than with Japan, and most of the activity took place in Qatar and Kuwait, rather than Dubai (Ministry for Foreign Affairs (China) 2009). With sizeable domestic hydrocarbon reserves and less momentum behind its industrialization programme, China's interest in oil trade with the Gulf Arab states was also much lower than Japan's. Moreover, during this period China's open support for anti-imperialist, revolutionary movements stymied most opportunities for closer ties with the Gulf's ruling families (Yetiv and Lu 2007, 201), most of which were beneficiaries of the British Trucial System (Davidson 2005, 29–31). Nonetheless, with an eye on the future, the ruler of Kuwait, Sheikh Abdullah Al-Salim Al-Sabah, visited China in 1965 and diplomatic relations were established in 1971 (Ministry for Foreign Affairds (China) 2009). By 1978, circumstances were already beginning to change, as the initiation of a series of Chinese economic and political reforms – the 'Four Modernizations' – that aimed to stimulate economic growth and support modernization efforts, particularly in the fields of agriculture, industry, technology, and defence (Evans 1995), effectively led to the downgrading of Marxist ideologies in China's external relations (Yetiv and Lu 2007, 201). With the door opened, Oman immediately established diplomatic relations with China, while the UAE followed suit in 1984 (Ministry for Foreign Affairs (China) 2009), and the following year Saudi Arabia held its first official meeting with China on Omani territory. Just days after the 1981 formation of the Gulf Cooperation Council, China had granted it recognition (Yetiv and Lu 2007, 212). Significantly, in 1983 China began to import crude oil from Oman as a temporary measure to alleviate the problem of transporting its own oil from its northern provinces to refineries on the Yangtze River. By 1988, as Chinese demand for oil was accelerating rapidly in tandem with its increasing population and intensifying industrialization, the Omani arrangement was made permanent (Ghafour 2009, 87–89). By 1990, China's presence had extended to all of the

Gulf Arab monarchies, with embassies being set up in Qatar in 1988, in Bahrain in 1989 and in Saudi Arabia in 1990 (Ministry for Foreign Affairs (China) 2009).

Although far less proactive than Japan and China during this period, with its major oil companies not being established until the late 1970s and with most of its other trade links to the Gulf also developing more recently, South Korea was nonetheless also carefully building up the foundations of its present strong relationship during the 1960s and 1970s. For the most part, it established diplomatic relations in the wake of Japan, but ahead of China, with embassies being set up in Saudi Arabia in 1961, in Oman in 1974, in Qatar in 1974, in Bahrain in 1976, in Kuwait in 1979 and finally in the UAE in 1980 (Ministry for Foreign Affairs (South Korea) 2009).

The Hydrocarbon Trade

The hydrocarbon trade undoubtedly remains the central pillar in the relationship between the Gulf Arab states and Asia Pacific, and could be worth as much as $192.2 billion per annum (see Table 11.1). At present, the former region produces a combined total of about 16.6 billion barrels of crude oil per day which is about 19 percent of the global total (CIA World Factbook 2009). The bulk of production takes place in Saudi Arabia, the UAE and Kuwait. The region also produces about 232 billion cubic meters of natural gas per year (CIA World Factbook 2009), which is about 8 percent of the global total. The bulk of production takes place in Qatar, Saudi Arabia and the UAE. But more importantly, perhaps, the Gulf Arab monarchies account for 37 percent of all known crude oil reserves and 25 percent of all known natural gas reserves (CIA World Factbook 2009), with Saudi Arabia alone accounting for 25 percent of global oil reserves (British Petroleum Statistical Review, June 2008) and Qatar accounting for 15 percent of global gas reserves (US Government. Energy Information Administration (EIA) 2009).

At the other extreme, Japan's current hydrocarbon consumption is five million barrels of oil per day, 100 percent of which it has to import, and 100.3 billion cubic meters of gas per year, 95 percent of which it has to import. China's current consumption is 7.9 million barrels of oil per day, 58 percent of which it has to import, and 70.5 billion cubic meters of gas per year, 5 percent of which it has to import. South Korea's current consumption is 2.1 million barrels of oil per day, 100 percent of which it has to import, and 37 billion cubic meters of gas per year, 93 percent of which it has to import. Respectively, Japan and China have the fourth and third greatest oil consumption needs in the world, ahead of Russia, Germany and India, while South Korea has now also entered into the top ten. Japan has the fifth greatest gas consumption needs in the world, ahead of Germany and the United Kingdom, while China and South Korea have now moved into the top 20 and are likely to catch up with Japan in the near future (CIA World Factbook 2009). Certainly, according to the Organization of Petroleum Exporting Countries (OPEC), although Japan's demand for oil is likely to fall by 15 percent

Table 11.1 Persian Gulf and Asian Pacific total value of annual hydrocarbon trade, 2009

	Japan	China	South Korea	Total
Saudi Arabia	$33 billion	$15 billion	$21 billion	$69 billion
UAE	$47 billion	$4.5 billion	$13 billion	$64.5 billion
Kuwait	$15 billion	$0.7 billion	$8.1 billion	$23.8 billion
Qatar	$17 billion	$1 billion	$7 billion	$25 billion
Oman	$2.6 billion	$1.5 billion	$5.1 billion	$9.2 billion
Bahrain	$0.4 billion	–	$0.3 billion	$0.7 billion
Total	$115 billion	$22.7 billion	$54.5 billion	$192.2 billion

Source: CIA World Factbook; British Petroleum Statistical Review.

by 2030, China, South Korea and other Asia Pacific economies are likely to make up 80 percent of net oil demand growth over the same period (*The National*, 5 August 2009).

  Specifically, Japan currently imports about 1.3 million barrels of oil per day from Saudi Arabia, which is over 31 percent of its total oil imports and is worth close to $33 billion per year for Saudi Arabia (Ministry for Foreign Affairs (Japan) 2009). This now makes Saudi Arabia Japan's fifth greatest trading partner, and it makes Japan Saudi Arabia's second greatest trading partner (Saudi Gazette, 22 July 2009). In a close second place, the UAE now exports 800,000 barrels of oil per day to Japan (*The National*, 26 June 2009), with total oil and gas exports from Abu Dhabi – the most resource-rich of the UAE's seven constituent emirates – now worth over $47 billion (Ministry for Foreign Affairs (Japan) 2009). Significantly, over 60 percent of Abu Dhabi's oil exports are now destined for Japan (Ministry for Finance and Industry (UAE) 2009), and in early 2009 the Abu Dhabi National Oil Company (ADNOC) strengthened the connection further by granting a 20 year extension to an existing offshore concession managed by a consortium led by Japan's Cosmo Oil Company (*The National*, 26 June 2009). Similarly, Abu Dhabi's primary gas customer for many years has been Japan, and in particular the Tokyo Electricity Power Company (TEPCO), which purchases over four million tons of liquid natural gas annually from Abu Dhabi Gas Liquefaction (ADGAS), which is a subsidiary of ADNOC (*The National*, 28 July 2009). In 1997 TEPCO even paid ADGAS a one-off fee of $400 million, as Japan sought to stabilize Abu Dhabi's gas revenues during a period of depressed gas prices during the late 1990s (Ministry for Finance and Industry (UAE) 2009).

  China's total hydrocarbon trade with the Gulf Arab monarchies is substantially less than Japan's, mainly due to its domestic gas reserves. Nonetheless, its oil imports have been rising sharply, with $1.5 of imports in 1991, $20 billion in 2004, and nearly $33.8 billion in 2005 (Ghafour 2009, 83–4). Unsurprisingly, during the latter part of this period, China's 10th Five Year Plan (2001–2005) contained its government's first public acknowledgement that overseas oil supplies needed to be secured if China was to enjoy continued economic growth and modernization (Yetiv and Lu 2007, 199). Within the next few years China's imports are likely to double again, with one Chinese official recently stating that 'we need to find oil fast' (*International Herald Tribune*, 2 October 2006) and another commentator explaining that 'if China's demand for oil imports was limited to just two or three million barrels per day, most of this could be sourced from Russia or nearby Central Asian republics, but with the huge oil and gas imports predicted for the next decade and beyond, China is compelled to turn to the Arab Gulf' (Ghafour 2009, 82–3). Certainly, the International Energy Agency (IEA) predicts that China's imports will grow to over 11 million barrels per day by 2030, more than half of which will have to be sourced from the Gulf Arab states (Ghafour 2009, 82). As with Japan, Saudi Arabia is currently China's greatest supplier of oil, with about 500,000 barrels of oil per day – or 30 percent of China's total oil imports (Ghafour 2009, 83) – being shipped by Aramco to the China Petroleum and Chemical Corporation (Sinopec). This compares to 17.5 percent of China's total oil imports in 2005 and just 1.2 percent in 1994 (Yetiv and Lu 2007, 203).

Innovatively, since 2001 30,000 of the imported Saudi barrels have been in part exchange for Aramco being allowed to operate 600 petrol stations in China's Fujian province (Ghafour 2009, 87–8). In 2006, following the signing of five new energy cooperation agreements (Yetiv and Lu 2007, 205), the total Sino-Saudi oil trade reached $15 billion and had witnessed 40 percent growth year-on-year since 1999. By 2010 Saudi imports will increase to 1 million barrels per day in what has been described by Aramco as 'one of the most important energy relationships in the world' (Ghafour 2009, 87–8). This could represent as much as 70 percent of China's total oil imports (Yetiv and Lu 2007, 203). Again in second place with its hydrocarbon exports has been the UAE's Abu Dhabi, with annual oil exports to China having risen from $3.5 billion to $4.5 billion over the past five years (Ministry for Foreign Affairs (China) 2009). For South Korea, the import pattern is much the same as with its larger neighbors, although, much like Japan, it requires both substantial oil and gas imports from the Gulf Arab states, given its lack of domestic gas reserves. Saudi Arabia is its greatest trade partner, supplying about 770,000 barrels of oil per day, as part of an annual hydrocarbon trade worth $21 billion. The UAE is the second greatest trade partner, supplying about 430,000 barrels of oil per day, as part of an annual hydrocarbon trade worth $13 billion (Ministry for Foreign Affairs (South Korea) 2009). This makes South Korea the second greatest importer of Abu Dhabi's oil after Japan (*The National*, 5 August 2009).

The Non-Hydrocarbon Trade

The non-hydrocarbon trade that takes place between the Gulf Arab monarchies and Asia Pacific is on a much smaller scale than the massive oil and gas exports and imports. Nonetheless, as demonstrated there has been an historical precedent for the importing of certain goods from Asia Pacific into the Gulf, especially textiles and electrical goods, and as the latter region's per capita wealth accelerated during the oil era, the demand for such imports has continued to increase, along with new demands for cars, machinery, building materials, and many other products associated with the region's oil and construction booms. In total, such imports from Japan, China and South Korea could be worth as much as $32 billion per year.[1] Importantly, there is no longer a complete imbalance of non-hydrocarbon trade between the two regions, as some of the export-oriented industries that have been established in the GCC states – mostly in an attempt to diversify oil-dependent economies (see Davidson 2008, 99–135 and Davidson 2009, 69–94) – are now among the world's leading producers of metals and plastics. Their export capacity continues to increase, with most of their future surpluses being earmarked for their Asia Pacific customers.

Japan's greatest non-hydrocarbon trade partner in the Persian Gulf is the UAE, as a function of both historic ties to Dubai's entrepôt trade, Abu Dhabi's commitment to building up heavy, non-hydrocarbon related industries (Davidson 2008, 70–71; Davidson 2009, 72–73), and the UAE's high per capita wealth which, as shown, is now in excess of $40,000 (CIA World Factbook 2009). Their total non-hydrocarbon trade is now over $11 billion per year (Ministry for Foreign Affairs (Japan) 2009). Japan's second greatest non-hydrocarbon trade partner in the region is Saudi Arabia, with the two countries having begun to sign economic and technical cooperation agreements as early as 1975 (*Saudi Gazette*, 22 July 2009). Presently, their non-hydrocarbon trade has mushroomed to over $5 billion, most of which is made up of Saudi imports of Japanese cars, machinery and consumer durables, but some of which is also made up of Japanese imports of Saudi metals (Ministry for Foreign Affairs (Japan) 2009). Japan's non-hydrocarbon trade with Kuwait, Qatar and Oman is presently about $2 billion, $1.8 billion and $1.7 billion respectively, again most of which is made up of Japanese exports of cars, machinery and consumer durables. Overall, Japanese non-hydrocarbon trade with the GCC states is set to increase even further as negotiations over a free trade agreement (FTA) between Japan and the six monarchies are currently taking place (*Gulf Daily News*, 29 July 2009), having commenced in 2006 (*Japan Times*, 7 April 2006).

China's greatest non-hydrocarbon trade partner in the GCC states has for many years been Saudi Arabia, with a memorandum of understanding on bilateral trade having been signed in 1988 which, as described, was two years before China even granted diplomatic recognition to Saudi Arabia (Ministry for Foreign Affairs (China) 2009). In 1992, a bilateral trade conference was staged and in 1996, under the auspices of a GCC-China consultative mechanism, annual trade meetings began between the two countries, held alternately in Riyadh and Beijing (Yetiv and Lu 2007, 202). Today, it is estimated that their total non-hydrocarbon trade is worth $1.7 billion, mostly made up of Saudi imports of Chinese textiles

---

1   Author calculations based on subsequently listed country totals.

and machinery (Ministry for Foreign Affairs (China) 2009), making Saudi Arabia China's tenth greatest international export destination (Ghafour 2009, 87). The UAE is presently China's second greatest non-hydrocarbon trade partner amongst GCC states, with their total trade estimated at $500 million, again primarily made up of imports of Chinese textiles and machinery (Ministry for Foreign Affairs (China) 2009). In 1985, China and the UAE signed an agreement on trade and technological cooperation and followed this up by establishing a Joint Commission of Economic, Trade and Technical Cooperation, which has since convened four meetings (Ministry for Foreign Affairs (China) 2009). In the near future it is likely that China's trade with the UAE will increase massively, and perhaps will soon overtake Japan's non-hydrocarbon trade with the UAE. Most of this growth is expected to be as a result of Dubai's strengthening relationship with China, with Dubai Ports World stating in 2008 that China was already Dubai's second greatest trade partner, after Iran, with Chinese non-hydrocarbon trade having increased by nearly 50 percent since 2005 (*Arabian Business*, 31 March 2008).

As with Japan, China intends to increase its non-hydrocarbon trade with the GCC states even further by reaching an FTA with all six of the monarchies in the near future. These FTA negotiations began in 2004 following a GCC delegation's visit to China (Yetiv and Lu 2007, 206), while simultaneously a China-Arab Cooperation Forum was set up between the Chinese Ministry for Commerce and the Arab League. At the meetings of this forum the Chinese Ministry for Commerce predicted that total trade with the GCC states would reach $100 billion by 2010, not all of which would be hydrocarbon trade. Subsequent FTA negotiations were held in 2005 and 2006, by which stage agreements had been reached on tariff reductions. Although the talks have since stalled due to China's unwillingness to lift certain import restrictions on a number of non-hydrocarbon goods from the GCC states, in early 2009 the concept of an FTA was reinvigorated by the President of China, who stated that 'The Gulf FTA is in the fundamental and long-term interests of both sides and will help deepen their mutually beneficial cooperation and achieve common development'. He also pledged that 'China will work actively towards signing the FTA at the earliest date'. In summer 2009 the GCC reciprocated China's sentiments by publishing a white paper entitled 'Economic relations between GCC member states and the People's Republic of China' which similarly urged the FTA negotiations to reach a swift conclusion (*China Daily*, 30 January 2004; *People's Daily*, 12 February 2009; Gulf Cooperation Council Secretariat, June 2009).

South Korea's non-hydrocarbon trade with the GCC states is more modest, although as with Japan and China its relationship is strengthening, with the Gulf Arab monarchies having become collectively South Korea's second greatest export destination after China (Zawya Dow Jones, 8 March 2009), most of the trade being made up of cars, rubber parts and textiles. Individually, South Korea's non-hydrocarbon trade with Saudi Arabia is about $3 billion, with the UAE $2.9 billion, with Qatar $800 million, with Kuwait $700 million, with Oman $300 million and with Bahrain $100 million. South Korea has not yet advanced as far as Japan and

China with a GCC FTA; however negotiations did begin in summer 2008, with a second round being held in spring 2009. Thus far, tariff-related incentives have been discussed and the South Korean Minister for Commerce has predicted that the FTA could be finalized by the end of 2009 (*Kuwait Times*, 8 March 2009).

Investments and Joint Ventures

Alongside the booming hydrocarbon and non-hydrocarbon trades, the relationship between the Gulf Arab monarchies and Asia Pacific has been greatly enhanced by a substantial flow of investments between the two regions. Significantly, these investments are being made in both directions and at all levels, and they include massive sovereign wealth investments. Although the majority are still connected to the oil and gas sectors, there is strong evidence that an increasingly diverse range of non-hydrocarbon joint ventures are also being established. In the short term, these opportunities are providing the Gulf Arab states with a realistic alternative to the mature western economies for their overseas investments. Such an alternative was viewed as being particularly necessary following September 11, 2001, after which many western governments and companies did little to disguise their distrust of Gulf sovereign wealth funds, with many arguing that the funds were not merely commercial and that power politics could be involved (*Arab News*, 7 May 2009; also see Bazoobandi and Niblock in this volume). While in the long term these new opportunities allow both regions to develop even tighter economic dependence, respectively, with their greatest hydrocarbon customers and suppliers (Ghafour 2009, 83).

Japan is presently the largest foreign investor in Saudi Arabia, with over $11 billion of active investments being distributed among 24 different projects, including 16 industrial projects and 8 service sector projects (Saudi Gazette, 22 July 2009). In the other direction, Saudi Arabia's Aramco now holds a 15 percent stake in Japan's fifth largest oil company, Showa Shell Sekiyu (Ministry for Foreign Affairs (Japan) 2009). And in summer 2009, the two countries entered into a $1 billion joint venture when the Saudi Basic Industries Corporation (SABIC) and Japan's Mitsubishi Rayon agreed to build an acrylics factory in Saudi Arabia, with Mitsubishi holding the majority stake (*Reuters*, 11 August 2009; Kuwait Times, 11 August 2009). In the UAE, Abu Dhabi's third largest sovereign wealth fund, the International Petroleum Investment Company (IPIC), has recently sought a $5 billion package from Japan's Mitsubishi UFJ Financial Group and the Sumitomo Mitsui Banking Corporation. This in turn will allow these Japanese banks to have an interest in some of IPIC's overseas investments, including its purchase of Canada's Nova Chemicals Corporation and its stake in Spain's Compania Espanola de Petroleos (CEPSA) (*Associated Press*, 2 August 2009). In the other direction, IPIC has now taken a 20 percent stake in Japan's Cosmo Oil Company which, as described, continues to hold a major Abu Dhabi offshore oil concession (Ministry for Foreign Affairs (Japan) 2009), thus strengthening further the Japanese-UAE interdependence.

In early 2005 the Chinese Ministry for Commerce revealed that Chinese investments in the Gulf Arab monarchies had already reached $5 billion, while Gulf Arab investments in China totaled $700 million (Ghafour 2009, 87). With a flurry of further investments and joint ventures since that announcement, these figures have since mushroomed, and will soon even overtake Japan's interests in the region. In particular, China has sought investments to help build up its oil refining industries, which the Gulf Arab economies have sought to have a dominant presence in a new economic superpower (Yetiv and Lu 2007, 205). At present, China's greatest investment partner from the GCC states is Kuwait, a relationship which strengthened greatly following the establishment of a $9 billion joint venture between the Kuwait Petroleum Corporation and Sinopec in 2005. The two companies will build a 300,000 barrels per day oil refinery and ethylene plant in southern China's Guangdong province. Although the exact location of the facilities has since been changed due to environmental concerns raised by nearby Hong Kong, the project is still expected to come online in 2013 and will become China's largest ever joint project (*Associated Press*, 26 June 2009). In 2006, this deal was followed by the Kuwait Investment Authority (KIA) buying over $700 million in shares of the Industrial and Commercial Bank of China, thereby making Kuwait one of the biggest investors in one of China's first major public offerings. In the other direction, China may soon become heavily involved in Kuwaiti projects, with Sinopec currently having a sizeable stake in an international consortium that is bidding for an $8 billion infrastructural programme (Ghafour 2009, 89). But the most innovative aspect of the investments between the two countries has been the establishment of the Kuwait-China Investment Company (KCIC) in 2005. Set up by the Kuwait government, the KCIC is 15 percent owned by KIA and has a capital base of about $350 million, about half of which is held in cash. It has specialized in investments in Chinese agribusinesses, particularly those producing crops with a high export value such as rice, wheat, corn and sorghum. Significantly, KCIC's investments in China have been defended as being purely commercial and not primarily connected to Kuwaiti or Gulf Arab food security – unlike the recent deals between the Gulf Arab states and Pakistan, which clearly are (see for example *Gulf News*, 7 October 2009). In 2009 the managing director of KCIC stated simply that: 'we think it is an opportune sector that will help Pacific-Asia effectively become the bread basket of the world... we think food security, in the long term, is better served by collaborative investment in Asia as opposed to securing crops exclusively for one country.' Speaking of KCIC's existing collaborations with Chinese agribusinesses, he also stated that: 'our financial skills are paired with agri-sector skills and hopefully both of these skills can help mitigate some of the risks and provide a decent return for the investors' (*Financial Times*, 10 July 2009).

Beyond Kuwait, China is also heavily involved with Saudi Arabia, with Aramco having taken a 25 percent stake in a major joint venture with Sinopec in 2001. Close to completion, this has involved the two companies expanding an existing refinery in China's Fujian Province along with building a new ethylene plant. In the near future another joint venture between the two companies may take place, but this time with Aramco taking the majority stake. This could lead to the building of the largest oil refinery in China and may require as much as $6 billion to complete. Similarly, SABIC has already helped to initiate three petrochemicals projects in China as part of its 'China Plan', which aims to facilitate mutual investments between the two countries, support China's economic development, and satisfy its increasing demand as one of its premier suppliers (Yetiv and Lu 2007, 207–8). In the other direction, Sinopec has recently embarked on yet another joint venture with Aramco, taking an 80 percent, $300 million stake in a new oil and gas exploration company in Saudi Arabia (Ghafour 2009, 87–8).

Construction and Labor Contracts

For some years, construction and labor companies in the Asian Pacific countries have been winning contracts in the GCC states, with the China National Petroleum Company (CNPC) having supplied laborers for projects in Kuwait as early as 1983 (Ghafour 2009, 87–9; Yetiv and Lu 2007, 203), and with a number of other Chinese companies having supplied laborers for tourism and real estate projects in Dubai for about 6 years. However, very recently there have been a large number of major contracts awarded to Japanese, Chinese and South Korean companies to both build and supply labor for multi-billion dollar projects in the GCC states. Significantly, in many cases these companies have competed successfully against Arab and western companies that have had a much longer history of winning contracts in the region and have usually sourced their labor from South Asia. Undoubtedly these new contracts serve to further solidify the economic interdependence between the two regions while also taking advantage of the Asian Pacific companies' experience, technologies and access to abundant labor supply.

Notably, in summer 2006 Japan's Shimizu Corporation won a high profile contract to construct the Dubai Marina Residences real estate project on Dubai's Palm Jumeirah artificial island, defeating several regional competitors (*The National*, 20 July 2009). In summer 2009, the China Railway Construction Company (CRCC) won a similarly fierce contest to be awarded a $500 million contract by the Ministry for Education in Saudi Arabia. This will require the Chinese company to build 200 schools to accommodate 140,000 pupils over a period of one year. Although a total of 3500 schools are now under construction in Saudi Arabia, mostly by Arab companies, this Chinese involvement nonetheless represents a significant departure for the Saudi authorities (*Saudi Gazette*, 26 July 2009). Earlier in 2009 China's Sinopec won a similarly lucrative contract in

Kuwait, worth $400 million, to build five new oil and gas stations. Alone, these new Chinese-built installations will boost Kuwait's oil production by over four million barrels per day by 2020 (*Associated Press*, 26 June 2009). But of the three principal Asian Pacific countries, it has been South Korea that has made the greatest inroads into the Gulf's construction sector. In the UAE, three out of five new gas facilities in Abu Dhabi's Habshan region, to be operated by Abu Dhabi Gas Industries (GASCO), will be constructed by South Korean companies. In 2009 Hyundai Engineering and Construction, GS Engineering and Hyundai Heavy Industries won their contracts, totaling $4.9 billion. Specifically, Hyundai Engineering and Construction's contract is worth $1.7 billion. It will last for four years and will involve building storage and wastewater facilities, in addition to power facilities. Hyundai Heavy Industries' contract is worth $1 billion and GS Engineering's contract is worth $2.2 billion, and both will last for five years. The latter will build similar facilities alongside Hyundai Engineering and Construction and it will be cooperating with Britain's Petrofac as part of a joint venture, but will hold a 55 percent majority stake in the consortium. Remarkably, Hyundai Engineering and Construction is already believed to be working on nine other projects in the UAE and has recently completed the construction of new gas processing facilities in Saudi Arabia's Khurais field. Elsewhere in Saudi Arabia the company won a $1.9 billion contract in late 2008 to build further gas processing facilities in the Karan field, on behalf of Aramco. And three other major South Korean companies – Daelim Industrial, SK Engineering and Construction, and Samsung Engineering – have won a combined $2.8 billion contract to build a new refinery and petrochemicals plant in Saudi Arabia (*Korea Herald*, 17 July 2009).

Diplomacy and Security

Surprisingly for many observers, there is still no obvious security dimension to the increasingly interdependent economic relationship between the Gulf Arab states and Asian Pacific. All of the former are widely considered to be vulnerable given their rich energy resources, small national populations and close proximity to major conflicts and other potential threats. Moreover, their reliance on a western security umbrella is undoubtedly problematic, given the strained relations between the Arab world and the United States, not least over the Arab–Israeli conflict, but also following the 2001 invasion of Afghanistan and the 2003 invasion of Iraq. Equally it would seem to make sense for the Asia Pacific countries to seek a more active role in the security arrangements and defensive shields of their primary energy suppliers.

Part of the explanation is that the Gulf Arab monarchies do not yet see a reliable alternative to the West, as, for all its faults, it was a western-led alliance that liberated Kuwait in 1991 and it is the western presence that has been credited with safeguarding the Gulf from Iraqi or Iranian belligerence. As such, with a few exceptions, notably a modest arms trade with China on the part of both Saudi

Arabia and the UAE (Nuclear Threat Initiative 2007), almost all of the Gulf Arab states' arms imports have been sourced from western manufacturers (further motivated by the need to recycle petrodollars). Moreover, although there has been an appreciable increase in China's naval presence in the region – in part due to anti-pirate operations in the Gulf of Aden – there is little projection of Asian Pacific military power in the Gulf itself. Instead there remain a number of well entrenched US military bases in Kuwait, Bahrain and Qatar, a British base in Oman and even a new French base opened in Abu Dhabi in spring 2009. Some commentators have argued that the same lack of enthusiasm for a security relationship between the two regions applies in reverse: although it is not ideal that the US dominates the Gulf, the Asian Pacific countries nonetheless see little alternative to western-provided security given that the thousands of miles of shipping lanes between themselves and their hydrocarbon suppliers would be so difficult and expensive to protect. Thus far, it has remained more practical and cost effective to rely on experienced western navies, which have already invested in a multi-billion capability for this purpose and enjoy access to a network of maritime bases in allied states (Yetiv and Lu 2007, 200–201).

Another component of the explanation is simply lingering distrust, despite all of the aforementioned economic linkages and converging histories. This is not so much related to Japan or South Korea, which are effectively neutral military powers, but rather to China, which has repeatedly created difficulties for a stronger security relationship. For many of the older generation of Omanis, including their present ruler, Sultan Qaboos bin Said Al-Said, it is still difficult to forget that China helped to sponsor the rebellion in Oman's Dhofar province in the 1960s and 1970s, while Britain played a key role in suppressing the rebels (Calabrese 1990, 867; Ghafour 2009, 89, 91). In the mid-1980s it appeared that China's role in the region would increase, as Saudi Arabia began to buy Chinese CSS-2 East Wind missiles. However, Saudi Arabia was unwilling to go further and purchase Chinese intercontinental ballistic missiles, preferring to keep sourcing its ordinance from the United States. Most seriously, in 1990 China was unwilling to condemn openly Iraq's invasion of Kuwait, and following Kuwait's purchase of nearly $300 million of Chinese howitzers in the mid-1990s a Kuwaiti official later claimed that his government had been pressured into the deal as China was threatening to withdraw its support for future United Nations' sanctions on Iraq (Ghafour 2009, 88–89, 91; Yetiv and Lu 2007, 211). Tellingly, China's Ministry for Foreign Affairs is currently attempting to rewrite this troubled period of history with Kuwait and its neighbours by stating that: 'during the Gulf crisis in 1990, China resolutely opposed Iraq's invasion and occupation of Kuwait and demanded that Iraq should withdraw its troops from Kuwait and restore and respect the independence, sovereignty and territorial integrity of Kuwait… both countries share identical or similar views on many major international and regional issues, constantly rendering sympathy and support to each other' (Ministry for Foreign Affairs (China) 2009).

Regardless of the various explanations, the present reality is that the Gulf Arab states and their Asia Pacific trade and investment partners do not yet have a meaningful security relationship. However, this is in no way jeopardizing their current and future closeness, with both clusters of countries now going to considerable lengths to improve other, non-economic aspects of their interdependency. Indeed, there now appears to be a tacit understanding from both parties that their relationship simply need not contain a military security component, at least for the time being. High level diplomatic visits have, in particular, become central to the strategies of both regions. While economic and trade matters are certainly discussed at these events, they are nonetheless also perceived as valuable opportunities for heads of state and their ministers to meet their counterparts and consider a range of other matters. Often substantial gifts or interest free loans are granted during these meetings, clearly in an effort to build more sturdy political and cultural understandings, and undoubtedly generate further goodwill. In recent years the frequency of these visits has greatly intensified, and the seniority of the visitors – especially from the GCC states travelling to Asia Pacific – is significantly high, and likely to now be higher on average than the seniority of visitors dispatched to western capitals.

Future Initiatives and Collaborations

With the noted exception of military security arrangements, the relationship between the Gulf Arab monarchies and the three principal Asia Pacific economies will continue to strengthen and broaden for the foreseeable future, provided that the former states remain able to balance their existing relationships with the Western powers and Asia Pacific, especially China (Moran and Russell 2008). Thus far, such geopolitical competition would seem to have been avoided given the primary emphasis on bilateral economic linkages, which for the most part have had little direct impact on the Gulf Arab's dealings with the West. Indeed, as this chapter has demonstrated, the hydrocarbon and non-hydrocarbon trade between the two regions has been rapidly rising in volume and value, and is projected to continue doing so. Similarly, it has been shown that the flow of bilateral investments between the two regions continues to rise, and a substantial number of construction and labor contracts are being signed with an ever greater frequency. These trajectories are all being enhanced by improving non-economic ties, especially at the diplomatic level, and, as discussed, it is likely these linkages will grow even tighter in the near future. Furthermore, the relationship will also be enhanced by several new initiatives and collaborations between the two regions, all of which augment existing economic bonds, while some have implications for future non-military security arrangements, and while others are highly symbolic of this twenty-first century partnership.

In spring 2009, the UAE's ADNOC began discussions to establish an Abu Dhabi crude oil reserve on Japanese territory in cooperation with Nippon Oil.

It is intended that ADNOC will begin such storage in late 2009 by using one of Nippon's existing reserve bases in Kagoshima in southern Japan. This agreement will provide the UAE with an alternative outlet for its crude oil sales, not only to Japan and its neighbors, but the entire East Asia region. Such an outlet would prove vital if the Strait of Hormuz – the entrance to the Gulf – was closed in the event of an emergency. From Japan's perspective the agreement is equally beneficial as it would provide Japan with direct access and a pre-emptive right to purchase crude oil in such an emergency. Tellingly, ADNOC's spokesperson stated that the arrangement would 'contribute to enhancing Abu Dhabi's relationship with Asian markets generally and Japan particularly, and guarantee the flow of crude oil supplies to these markets in emergencies' (*The National*, 26 June 2009).

The future energy sector is another likely area of collaboration, with countries from both regions actively seeking to set up solar and nuclear joint ventures. In spring 2009, Japan's Showa Shell Sekiyu announced that it was considering operating solar power plants in Saudi Arabia in cooperation with Aramco, which, as described, is now one of its principal shareholders. Showa intends to build small pilot plants in Saudi Arabia by 2010 to test out its technologies, and should these prove successful then a joint venture with Aramco may be set up (*Associated Press*, 25 June 2009). With the UAE committed to a path of diversifying its energy sources and building up a civilian nuclear programme based on imported technologies from the United States, its government has repeatedly turned to Japan and South Korea for advice and assistance. In early 2009, the UAE signed a nuclear cooperation memorandum of understanding with Japan, and in summer 2009 the UAE signed a similar agreement with South Korea. A 20-strong UAE delegation was then promptly sent to South Korea – at the invitation of the Korea Electric Power Corporation (KEPCO) – to survey its nuclear facilities, and especially its safety procedures and mechanisms. Significantly, should the UAE secure the American technology, the contract for the construction of the UAE's nuclear facilities could be awarded to one of two consortia with a major Asia Pacific involvement: one consortium comprises Japan's Hitachi, while the other is made up of KEPCO, the Korea Hydro and Nuclear Power Corporation and Hyundai Engineering and Construction Company. So lucrative could this contract prove to South Korea that the South Korean President visited the UAE in autumn 2009 in support of the KEPCO bid (*Asia Pulse*, 3 August 2009; Platts, 11 August 2009).

Perhaps most emblematic of the many new developments that will strengthen the link between Asia Pacific and the Gulf Arab states in the near future is China's attempt to reconstruct the old Karakoram Highway. This will effectively connect China to the Gulf by a land route that follows the same path as the ancient Silk Road. To do so, China will build the world's highest altitude motorway in cooperation with the Pakistani government, which will not only involve a massive investment and working with difficult terrain, but will even require the pacifying of local tribes in remote areas beyond the control of the Beijing and Islamabad governments (*The National*, 6 August 2009). Upon completion, this new highway will connect with deep water ports in Pakistan, most notably the port at Gwadar in Baluchistan which has direct access to the Gulf of Oman and lies just 250 miles from the entrance to the Gulf. China has already invested $200 million in Gwadar, with the port having first opened in 2005 with three berths and with China intending for it to soon expand to 10 berths with a new bulk-cargo terminal (Ghafour 2009, 83).

Conclusion

Without a strong security component to their relationship, the Persian Gulf states and the Asia Pacific economies have all gone to considerable lengths to shore up a number of other, non-economic aspects of their interdependency. In particular, there has been a strong focus on aid-giving, grants, and other donations, even if only for symbolic purposes. Moreover, there has been a marked increase in the frequency and seniority of diplomatic visits. While economic and trade matters remain at the heart of these meetings, a broad range of other issues are discussed, and strong efforts are being made to generate the most effective cultural and educational linkages. Furthermore, the increasingly interdependent and multi-dimensional relationship between the two regions is also being enhanced by several new initiatives and collaborations which will take shape over the next few years. These include innovative hydrocarbon storage projects, investments in renewable energies, further improvements to pan-Asian physical trade infrastructure, and the construction and technology transfer of civilian nuclear power from Asia Pacific to the Persian Gulf. All of these developments will augment existing economic bonds, while some may even have an impact on future security arrangements.

The intensifying connection between the two regions also has several broader implications. The lack of significant military collaboration has certainly allowed the US and other Western powers to remain in their role as the ultimate protectors of the Persian Gulf and the guarantors of the international oil industry's most strategic shipping lanes. This has kept to a minimum any tension between the US and China, with the latter regarded by most observers as being the most militaristic of the Asia Pacific states. Given time, however, this will likely change as the Asia Pacific states gradually seek greater influence over their primary energy suppliers. Moreover, the many other linkages between the Persian Gulf and Asia Pacific described in this chapter, including the various economic and diplomatic ties, and perhaps especially the raft of new initiatives and collaborations, will undoubtedly prompt the US and other powers to pay more attention to this new pan-Asian relationship. Such increased attention, if mishandled and too heavy-handed, may in turn reduce trust between the Persian Gulf states and their Western allies and partners, thus providing a fresh wave of opportunities for Asia Pacific governments and companies to win lucrative contracts and thus increase their influence even further.

Chapter 12

Geo-Political Complications of US Free Trade Agreements with Gulf Arab Countries

Fred H. Lawson

Introduction

Existing economic studies of regional and bilateral trading agreements have highlighted the costs and benefits involved, but have not effectively considered the geopolitical rationales behind trade agreements. Sherman Robinson and Karen Thierfelder (1999), for example, claim that preferential trade agreements (PTAs) generate substantial increases in trade among member-states, and that the addition of more countries to any given arrangement can be expected to heighten the welfare of old and new members alike (see also Kemp and Wan 1976). On the other hand, Alan Winters and Won Chang (2000) show that the existence of PTAs compels surrounding states to cut prices for their exports, effectively diminishing global welfare. Jagdish Bhagwati (2008, 69) likewise argues that the proliferation of fundamentally discriminatory PTAs has generated chaos in the international economy, leading to severe 'distortions in trade and investment' in the world as a whole (see also Bhagwati and Panagariya 1996).

I argue that in addition to economic considerations, preferential trading arrangements have strategic and geopolitical rationales that further shape the emergence and trajectory of these agreements. Yet matters related to security and diplomacy remain largely ignored in ongoing debates over the efficacy or deleteriousness of PTAs. Political economists have only recently started to explore the political aspects of such regional arrangements in a systematic fashion. And they have so far limited their investigations to two basic issues: the conflicts of interest among member-states that accompany the formation and consolidation of regional PTAs, and the impact that PTAs have on relations between member-states and outside actors. Much can be learned about each of these matters from a close analysis of the origin and development of preferential trading arrangements in the contemporary Gulf.

Whether or not bilateral free trade agreements in the Gulf are compatible with the multi-lateralist principles that underpin the Unified Economic Agreement of the Gulf Cooperation Council is an ongoing debate. A substantial body of scholarship proposes that regional free trade areas (FTAs) can indeed co-exist with global free trade, and contribute to further multi-lateralism as time goes by (Ethier 1998; Winters 1999; Freund 2000; Baldwin 2006). On the other hand, an alternative line of argument asserts that even the most liberal FTAs interfere with the expansion of global free trade, and thus constitute in Bhagwati's memorable phrase 'stumbling blocks' rather than 'building blocks' to comprehensive commercial liberalization (Bhagwati 1991; Hoekman and Leidy 1992; Levy 1997; Krishna 1998; Riezman 1999; McLaren 2002; Ornelas 2005).

Incompatibilities between regional FTAs and multi-lateral free trade become exacerbated if one or more states in the region concludes a bilateral free trade agreement with an outside party. Prospects for trade deflection heighten as goods from outside gain entry into the region through the local partner in the bilateral free trade agreement (Krueger 1993). At the same time, regional producers of high-cost products – who might well have expected to profit thanks to the implementation of a regional FTA – confront growing competition from suppliers based in the external partner. Producers of finished goods find themselves particularly undercut by the influx of imports from outside the region. Furthermore, the local partner in the bilateral free trade agreement benefits almost immediately from its advantageous position as a regional hub, attracting further investment and commercial activity and thereby augmenting its influence in economic and strategic affairs.

Overlapping Trading Agreements in the Gulf

The primary commercial convenant in the Gulf is the Unified Economic Agreement drawn up in November 1981 (Ramazani 1988, 106–8). The UEA envisages a free trade area (FTA) among the six member-states of the Gulf Cooperation Council (GCC), which started to coalesce in the spring of 1983. The FTA that took shape that March entailed several important exceptions to full liberalization, including a handful of key exemptions involving Saudi Arabia and Oman (Legrenzi 2003). Nevertheless, Article Four of the UEA calls for the steady transformation of the FTA into a customs union. And in January 2003 a proto-customs union did indeed come into existence among the GCC member-states, which fixed the common external tariff for these countries at 5 percent ad valorem (*Arab News*, 16 December 2002; *MEED*, 3 January 2003).

Despite the formal inauguration of the regional customs union, several Gulf Arab governments have continued to impose substantial tariffs on local goods. Divergences of interest among the GCC states regarding trade liberalization are reflected in persistent friction between Saudi Arabia, which has taken a variety of steps to protect its infant industries against foreign competition, and the United Arab Emirates (UAE), which generally favors unrestricted trade with the outside world (Momani 2007; Legrenzi 2008, 117). Stalemate over full implementation of the customs union pushed the GCC in the direction of creating a regional monetary union, as an alternative path toward – and perhaps effective substitute for – a fully-realized regional FTA (Hebous 2006; Rutledge 2009). The regional monetary union, however, has been repeatedly delayed, from 2007 to 2010 to an indefinite date.

Lack of momentum with regard to commercial liberalization along the lines spelled out in the UEA accompanied a pronounced turn toward individual GCC countries opting to negotiate bilateral free trade agreements with the United States. Since 2002, Washington has negotiated bilateral trade investment framework agreements with Kuwait, Saudi Arabia, Qatar, the UAE and Oman, and Bahrain. These frameworks are often seen as precursors toward bilateral free trade agreements and are demanded by the United States to ready states' investment regulations for a liberal environment (see Tobin and Busch 2010). The US made the first step in this direction in September 2004, when Washington signed a bilateral free trade agreement with Bahrain. Two months later, US Trade Representative Robert Zoellick announced plans to pursue bilateral free trade agreements with Oman and the UAE as well (*Daily Star*, 16 February 2005). The US-Oman trade agreement was signed in January 2006, and the one with Bahrain came into force six months thereafter.

Key provisions of the US-Bahrain bilateral free trade agreement included a commitment to eliminate tariffs on 98 percent of US agricultural goods imported into Bahrain, along with all duties on textiles and clothing manufactured from US-supplied yarn (Weiss 2005, 5). The agreement also liberalizes the Bahraini market to US telecommunications, health care, computer, engineering, architectural and package delivery companies. In addition, US insurance companies were accorded immediate access to Bahrain to contract life and health care policies, with other kinds of insurance underwriting to follow no later than six months after the agreement came into force (Weiss 2005, 5). Moreover, in the words of a summary of the pact that was prepared by the US Congressional Research Service, 'the Agreement requires each government to criminalize end-user piracy [of all sorts of intellectual property], providing strong deterrence against piracy and counterfeiting' in the future (Weiss 2005, 6). The bilateral free trade agreement agreed to by Oman and the US contained broadly similar provisions, the most notable difference being that only 87 percent of agricultural products were to receive duty-free treatment at the time the agreement came into force (US Trade Representative 2006).

All finalized and provisional bilateral free trade agreements between the Gulf Arab states and the US include 'cumulation clauses,' whereby goods that are produced jointly with other GCC member-states can enter into the US market on a tariff-free basis by passing through a country that has concluded an agreement with Washington. On the other hand, US officials have insisted on maintaining firm quotas on imports of certain types of manufactured items, most notably textiles. The problem herein is that cloth goods alone account for almost half of all Bahraini exports to the United States, one-quarter of all UAE goods to the United States, and one-fifth of Omani goods. While the bilateral free trade agreements between the US and the Gulf Arab countries have done much to liberalize the investment and finance environment to the delight of US foreign investment, the Gulf Arab countries have not managed to gain concessions on the highly guarded protectionism over textiles.

US Free Trade Agreements with the Gulf Arab States and Saudi Discontent

In the case of the GCC states, bilateral free trade agreements with the United States have opened the door to an influx of US exports to the Gulf, most notably industrial machinery, medical instruments, pharmaceuticals and aircraft. American agricultural products, including poultry, cotton, sugar and vegetable oil, along with a wide range of service activities, have similarly entered the region in unprecedented quantities owing to the new agreements (*Gulf News*, 23 December 2007). Total US trade with the GCC states soared to almost $48 billion during the second quarter of 2008, an increase of more than 60 percent over the same quarter a year earlier (*AME Info*, 3 November 2008).

The influx of American goods into the GCC countries has largely entered through Bahrain, and to a lesser extent through Oman (*MEED*, 6–12 April 2007 and 5–11 June 2009). US exports to Bahrain jumped almost 50 percent in the wake of the ratification of the bilateral free trade agreement (*Gulf Daily News*, 1 August 2007). These goods are then re-exported within the GCC without further restriction, boosting overall levels of intra-GCC trade. In many ways, Bahrain acts as a classic entrepot for US goods into the Gulf.

The influx of US goods has challenged Saudi infant industries. Imports from the US under the auspices of bilateral free trade agreements circumvent the Saudi tariff barriers used to protect its domestic manufacturing, while at the same time pressing Saudi Arabia to compete with the United States on regional markets. It therefore comes as no surprise that officials in Riyadh immediately lambasted Manama for signing a bilateral free trade agreement with the United States. Foreign Minister Sa'ud bin 'Abd al-'Aziz Al Sa'ud publicly charged at a December 2004 security conference in Manama that 'these agreements impede the progressive steps needed to achieve full Gulf integration [and] will ultimately negatively impact the economic sectors in all GCC countries, which in turn will have dire consequences and adversely affect the GCC business community' (*Agence France Presse*, 18 December 2004).

Shortly after the Saudi foreign minister's remarks, Gulf Arab leaders gathered in Manama for the annual GCC summit meeting. Informed observers reported that tensions associated with the Bahrain-US bilateral free trade agreement 'cast a shadow over the meeting' (*Gulf News*, 22 December 2004). Bahrain's Foreign Minister Muhammad bin Mubarak Al Khalifah told reporters that the agreement was 'discussed and analyzed thoroughly' by the six rulers during the course of the summit, but that in the end 'the leaders chose to continue discussing the matter in future meetings' (*Gulf News*, 22 December 2004). Nevertheless, the Omani government continued its negotiations with the United States and signed a bilateral free trade agreement with Washington two months later (*Daily Star*, 16 February 2005). Rather than escalate the regional disagreements in public, GCC finance ministers opted in May 2005 to declare that member-states could sign a bilateral free trade agreement with the United States and this would not contravene the terms of the UEA (*MEED*, 3–9 June 2005; *Agence France Presse*, 6 June 2005).

Despite this somewhat disingenuous compromise, Saudi officials denounced existing and planned bilateral free trade agreements in the Gulf, on the grounds that they were likely 'to jeopardize the future of the GCC' (*Defense News*, 21 March 2005). Criticisms of the pacts were voiced by Saudi economists as well. Anwar Eshki of the Jiddah-based Center for Middle East Strategic and Legal Studies, for example, pointed out that bilateral free trade agreements with the US were unlikely to generate any noticeable economic benefit for the Gulf Arab states, since GCC members 'have nothing much to sell [on] the American market'. Consequently, the most that could be anticipated would be that 'the US can flood [regional] markets with [its] products' (*Defense News*, 21 March 2005).

Heightened Saudi tensions with Bahrain accompanied rising friction between Saudi Arabia and the UAE, which was also engaged in negotiating a bilateral free trade agreement with the US. At the December 2004 GCC summit, the UAE's new ruler announced plans to construct a causeway linking the western end of the country to the neighboring emirate of Qatar (*Gulf States Newsletter*, 15 July 2005). This project could be expected to infringe on waters claimed by Saudi Arabia, which lay immediately off the coastline of a sliver of land that the UAE had ceded to the kingdom as part of the 1974 Jeddah Treaty. A semi-official yearbook issued in early 2006 under the auspices of the public information department of the UAE contained a map in which the Saudi territory that had been included by the Jeddah Treaty was now pictured as lying inside the borders of the UAE (*MEED*, 23 December–5 January 2006). The map also showed the UAE as possessing a larger proportion of the offshore Shaibah oil field than had been allotted to it according to the terms of the 1974 treaty. Shortly thereafter, the UAE ministry of agriculture imposed a ban on the importation of Saudi dates; in response, Saudi border posts began to levy additional fees on goods entering the kingdom by truck from the UAE. In July 2006, officials in Riyadh declared that they had not consented to the construction of a major natural gas pipeline linking Qatar to the UAE, and charged that the project represented an infringement on Saudi sovereignty (*Gulf States Newsletter*, 27 April 2007).

These trade-related disputes soon spilled over into deliberations concerning the GCC monetary union. The governor of the UAE's central bank issued a press release in September 2006 that stated unequivocally that the six 'rulers have agreed that the new GCC Central Bank will be based in Abu Dhabi', and that the Gulf Arab states' long-standing practice of pegging their currencies to the US dollar would 'not make any real sense' after the union came into force in 2010 (*MEED*, 22–28 September 2006). A statement released three days later backed away from the former assertion, but not from the latter. Even more disruptive was Oman's announcement in mid-December 2006 that it intended to remain outside the monetary union until the GCC customs union had been fully implemented (*MEED*, 15–21 December 2006). A month later, the UAE central bank's governor told reporters that there was no need for a regional financial institution after all; instead, the six existing central banks could coordinate monetary policy along the lines of the US Federal Reserve system (*MEED*, 5–11 January 2007). Omani officials confirmed in early February that the sultanate had decided to stay out of the planned monetary union (*MEED*, 9–15 February 2007).

Simmering conflicts of interest between the GCC states most closely connected to the US and those that were doing their best to keep Washington at arm's length in commercial matters led by the fall of 2007 to an unexpected rapprochement between Saudi Arabia and Qatar (*MEED*, 5–11 October 2007). Among the first items on the agenda for the newly-reconciled neighbors were the formal demarcation of land and sea boundaries along the lines spelled out by the 1974 Jeddah Treaty and the creation of a joint commission to oversee joint economic projects (*MEED*, 5–11 December 2008). Whereas Riyadh and Doha adopted broadly similar financial policies in response to the inflationary pressures that began to be felt in the region during the summer and fall of 2008, officials in the UAE carried out sharply divergent measures (*MEED*, 26 September–2 October 2008). Authorities in Bahrain, meanwhile, lobbied Qatar to earmark more natural gas for its GCC partners and cut down on shipments to other parts of the world (*MEED*, 30 May–5 June 2008). When these appeals were ignored, Manama approached Iran to supply natural gas to its expanding industrial sector (*MEED*, 5–11 December 2008). Oman and Kuwait quickly followed Bahrain's lead and initiated discussions with Iran over future energy supplies.

In May 2009, Qatari officials expressed support for locating the proposed GCC central bank in Riyadh. The UAE then announced that it was pulling out of the monetary union (al-Quds al-'Arabi, 21 May 2009). The announcement provoked heightened scrutiny of all trucks entering Saudi Arabia from UAE ports of entry. By mid-June the new measures had backed up vehicles carrying goods across the border into queues that stretched more than 24 kilometers (*Gulf News*, 10 June 2009). Saudi officials also imposed a requirement that any customs duties that might be owed on goods arriving by truck from the UAE must be paid at the border, rather than at the final destination (*Gulf News*, 15 June 2009). Such regulations severely interrupted Saudi-UAE commerce over the course of the following year (al-Quds al-'Arabi, 6 April 2010).

Meanwhile, the US-Bahrain bilateral free trade agreement attracted foreign investment to Bahrain not only from the United States but also from Western Europe and East Asia. In 2007, for example, Kraft Foods inaugurated a $40 million dairy processing facility to turn out cheese products and Tang brand beverage powder 'for distribution throughout the Middle East' (*USINFO*, 17 March 2007). The director of the plant told the Oxford Business Group that Kraft had considered building the factory in Dubai or Saudi Arabia, but 'it was [Bahrain Industrial Investment Park's] duty-free exports to the GCC and the kingdom's lower operating and living costs that tipped the scale toward Bahrain' (Oxford Business Group 2008). Some 70 percent of the Kraft plant output was transported across the causeway to distributors in Saudi Arabia during the first twelve months of operation. Concurrently, a consortium of public agencies and local private interests initiated a massive new industrial zone, Bahrain Investment Wharf (BIW), which was designed to lure Chinese and Indian companies into the country with the promise that goods manufactured in the zone could be exported to the United States 'almost tax-free' (*Bahrain Tribune*, 12 February 2007). The marketing director for the project told reporters that BIW also had the potential to 'be a significant logistic and warehousing hub for distribution and redistribution, specifically targeting the northern side of the Gulf – the Eastern Province of Saudi Arabia, Kuwait, and some parts of Iran'. By the time that BIW was incorporated into Salman Industrial City in early 2010, more than 150 companies employing 15,5000 workers had opened their doors in the enlarged manufacturing zone (*Saudi Gazette*, 28 April 2010).

Furthermore, since Bahrain boasts the most fully developed financial and regulatory infrastructure in the Gulf, US-based services companies have steadily augmented operations there as well. Most notably, Microsoft Corporation upgraded its local presence and in early 2007 'signed a memorandum of understanding with the Bahraini Ministry of Social Development to launch a digital literacy program in the NGO and civil-society sector' (*USINFO*, 17 March 2007). The authorities in Manama had attempted to transform the country into the financial and services center of the Gulf during the early 1980s, but soon lost out to the primary financial hub of the UAE, Dubai. Persistent reports in 2007–08 that Citigroup planned to shift its attention back to Bahrain indicated that the bilateral free trade agreement with Washington had altered the playing field in regional finance in ways that worked to the advantage of US trade partners and to the detriment of surrounding states.

Nevertheless, Saudi Arabia's overtly hostile response to the US-Bahrain trade pact convinced other GCC states to move more slowly and circumspectly in negotiating similar arrangements with Washington. Kuwait ended up putting negotiations over a bilateral free trade agreement with Washington on indefinite hold (*al-Watan*, 22 February 2010), while the UAE and Qatar adopted the more nuanced strategy of encouraging imports and investment from the United States, but at the same time delaying on measures that might lead to the finalization of formal bilateral agreements. Consequently, even as overall US trade with the GCC soared in 2008–09 (Habibi and Woertz 2009, 4), the prospects for additional bilateral free trade agreements with Washington sharply diminished.

Bilateral Free Trade Agreements and Relations with Third Parties

Regional free trade areas confer important strategic advantages on member-states in their relations with third parties. States that form an FTA benefit from significant economies of scale, which enable them to compete more effectively with rival producers located outside the region. More important, regional FTAs provide strong incentives for foreign investment, as external sources of capital find themselves drawn to the larger markets that are created by the agreement. This situation accords local governments considerably greater leverage in their dealings with prospective investors. In addition, the existence of an FTA signals that there exists a putative strategic alignment among the member-states, which increases the likelihood that one or more members will rise to the defense of another if it confronts a serious external threat. Recognizing the predisposition toward collective defense, outside adversaries can be expected to refrain from undertaking foreign policy initiatives that threaten states in the region.

Bilateral free trade agreements undermine all three of the strategic advantages that regional FTAs confer on member-states. A state that concludes a bilateral free trade agreement with an external partner, particularly one that is a well-endowed or highly efficient producer, is likely to take steps to reconfigure its economy to conform more closely to the interests of the new trading partner, rather than continuing to coordinate commercial and industrial policy with other members of the regional FTA. At the same time, foreign investment is likely to gravitate toward the state that signs a bilateral free trade agreement with a powerful outside partner, effectively reducing the leverage that might be exercised by the region as a whole in dealing with foreign investors. Finally, the existence of a bilateral free trade agreement is apt to generate animosity or resentment on the part of other states in the region, leading them to distance themselves from the member-state that aligns itself with an external patron. Such intra-regional fracturing leaves all members of the FTA more vulnerable to threats from surrounding states than they might otherwise have been.

Following the implementation of their respective bilateral free trade agreements with the US, both Bahrain and Oman embarked on industrialization programs that appeared to be tailored either to facilitate the entry of US goods into Gulf markets or advance their own exports to the American market. Oxford Business Group observed in February 2009 that a cluster of new projects in Bahrain was designed to provide foreign 'investors with a competitive cost base while strategically locating them at short distance from Gulf economies, in particular Saudi Arabia's big domestic market.' At the same time, major improvements were made to the smelter operated by Aluminum Bahrain. More than 99 percent of the ingots produced at the plant – along with some 80 percent of cold rolled aluminum products, 60 percent of aluminum wire and 40 percent of other semi-finished aluminum goods – have consistently been shipped to consumers outside the Gulf (*Metalworld*, May 2006).

Similarly, the government of Oman complemented the signing of its bilateral free trade agreement with the inauguration of a massive industrial zone at Sohar on the sultanate's northern coast. The heart of this project was a new large-scale aluminum smelter, whose construction was expected to offset 'a spate of closures in North America and Europe of aging plants' (*MEED*, 5–11 May 2006). Seven other major 'export-oriented manufacturing projects' were carried out at Sohar in the years after 2006, with a further three on the drawing board (*Khaleej Times*, 12 February 2010). Among these is a state-of-the-art pipe-producing facility, whose output has been targeted at foreign buyers (*Oman Daily Observer*, 27 December 2009). Aiming output at customers outside the Gulf left all of these industrial operations vulnerable to periodic slumps in the global economy, a state of affairs that elicited sharp warnings from the Doha-based Gulf Organization for Industrial Consulting for governments in the region to re-examine their investments in manufacturing with an eye toward heightened coordination among GCC countries (*Kuwait News Agency*, 13 July 2009).

In an attempt to offset the region's loss of collective leverage *vis-à-vis* outside investors in the wake of the Bahraini and Omani bilateral free trade agreements, Saudi Arabia spearheaded a campaign to expand commercial relations with several of the United States' major international competitors. In particular, Riyadh took steps to encourage the People's Republic of China (PRC) and India, along with Pakistan, to draw up free trade agreements with the GCC. New Delhi responded first, inviting representatives from Gulf Arab ministries of commerce and industry to Mumbai for discussions about the possibility of setting up a GCC-India trading area (*Gulf News*, 13 February 2004). A year later, officials from the PRC traveled to the Saudi capital to initiate parallel negotiations (*Daily Star*, 9 December 2004). These initiatives reinvigorated talks between the GCC and the European Union, which had stalled over a number of issues at the end of the 1990s (*MEED*, 28 July–3 August 2006). A regional free trade agreement with Singapore was signed in December 2008 (*Straits Times*, 16 December 2008), marking the first time that the GCC had concluded a joint commercial pact with an outside party. At the beginning of 2009, similar pacts were negotiated with Malaysia and South Korea (*Arab News*, 20 January 2009; *Kuwait Times*, 8 March 2009). Subsequent talks took place between GCC representatives and officials from the Association of Southeast Asian Nations (ASEAN) and South America's Common Market of the South or MERCOSUR (*MEED*, 18–24 September 2009).

By late 2009, Saudi Arabia had gone the farthest in developing commercial and financial connections with the People's Republic of China (*MEED*, 18–24 December 2009). Qatar took notable steps to catch up during the late spring of 2010 (*Gulf Times*, 12 May 2010). The leadership of the UAE, meanwhile, assumed a leading role in orchestrating a revival of momentum toward the conclusion of a GCC-EU free trade agreement (*Arab News*, 23 April 2010). Those GCC states that had not bound themselves to Washington in a formal bilateral free trade agreement thus became the most active in trying to improve the region's attractiveness to outside investors by forging arrangements that might offset the deleterious effects of the existing bilateral pacts.

Arguably the most important strategic consequence of the bilateral free trade agreements that link some Gulf Arab states to the US has been the weakening of the presumption that the GCC will rally to the defense of any member-state that confronts a severe external threat. Prior to 2003–04, the six governments harbored a variety of deep-seated antagonisms and divergences of interest (Nonneman 2004), and exerted little effort to construct an integrated defense network (Legrenzi 2008, 109–111). They could nevertheless be expected to put mutual disagreements aside whenever one of them faced a major challenge from outside. Surrounding states recognized the underlying predisposition toward collective defense, and tended to refrain from acting in ways that put the security of the GCC states in jeopardy.

In the aftermath of Bahrain's and Oman's decisions to align themselves with the United States, however, the presumption of unified purpose and action among the GCC states became less compelling. Countries disposed to challenge the regional order have consequently exhibited a greater willingness to carry out policies that threaten one or another of the six member-states. Warnings that Iran had started to exercise more muscle in regional affairs were expressed with greater frequency and vociferousness by Gulf Arab governments beginning in the fall of 2008 (*Gulf News*, 5 September 2008). Members of the Kuwaiti parliament charged that some 25,000 cadres of the Islamic Revolutionary Guards Corps (IRGC) had infiltrated the GCC countries, and were preparing to subvert regimes throughout the Gulf. At the end of the year, a columnist for a leading UAE newspaper lamented that so long as the GCC looked incapable of banding together to meet common threats, Tehran could be expected to take additional steps to augment its 'regional presence and influence' (*al-Ittihad*, 24 December 2008).

More concretely, Iranian naval exercises increased in both scale and frequency after 2003–04. Since the spring of 2006, Iranian commanders have undertaken a succession of large-scale maneuvers, each of which combined naval deployments with test launches of ground-to-ground and anti-ship missiles (Radio Free Europe/ Radio Liberty, 6 April 2006). Subsequent exercises have included submarines and aerial drones, in addition to the fast missile boats favored by the IRGC (*Novosti News Agency*, 28 November 2007; *Fars News Agency*, 4 December 2008). The marked expansion of naval exercises accompanied a sharp rise in the number of armed skirmishes between Iranian warships and unarmed fishing boats up and down the Gulf (*al-Watan* [Riyadh], 4 July 2008).

Meanwhile, Tehran stepped up its long-standing rivalry with the UAE for control of the strategically-situated islands of Abu Musa and the Tunbs. In August 2008, the Iranian authorities constructed an office on Abu Musa to register and monitor near-by shipping, along with a permanent maritime rescue facility. The installations were opened after officials in Tehran reasserted Iran's claim to the three islands and repudiated calls by the GCC's secretary general to take the dispute to the International Court of Justice for adjudication (Stracke 2008). UAE officials complained to the United Nations that the new projects violated the terms of the 1971 memorandum of understanding that regulates Iranian activity on the islands (*Indian News*, 29 August 2008). In response, Tehran replaced Iranian coast guard units operating in the area with IRGC naval forces, which began to indict vessels suspected of conveying contraband from the UAE to ports in southern Iran (www.presstv.ir, 14 October 2008).

More startlingly, trade-related fissures among the GCC states, combined with Bahrain's burgeoning commercial ties to the US, set the stage for an unexpected resuscitation of Iran's claim to sovereignty over the Bahrain archipelago. The editor of an influential Tehran newspaper claimed in July 2007 that a majority of the people of Bahrain, 'one of the provinces of Iran,' quietly harbored the desire to reunite with their 'native land' (*Asia Times*, 19 July 2007). The Islamic Republic's foreign minister hurried to Manama to affirm Tehran's respect for

Bahraini sovereignty and territorial integrity, but a prominent member of the Iranian parliament nevertheless hinted that if Bahrain continued to back the UAE in the simmering dispute over Abu Musa and the Tunbs, it – like other countries in the region that had formerly been integral parts of Iran – would suffer the consequences (*al-Qabas*, 14 July 2007). This same member of parliament in February 2009 proclaimed that if the citizens of Bahrain were ever permitted to express their views in an open referendum, they would choose to merge with the Islamic Republic (*Gulf News*, 8 February 2009). The statement followed reports that a former speaker of the Iranian parliament had told reporters that 'Bahrain was the fourteenth province of Iran until 1970' (*Xinhua News Agency*, 20 February 2009).

Such overt challenges to the security of a GCC state reflect Iran's growing combativeness in regional affairs (Chubin 2009). An IRGC-sponsored cell was reportedly broken up in Kuwait in April 2010 (*al-Hayat*, 18 May 2010). At the same time, Iranian officials pointedly denounced the foreign minister of the UAE for comparing Iran's occupation of Abu Musa and the Tunbs to Israel's occupation of Palestine and southern Lebanon, calling the comparison 'brazen and impudent' (*Times of Oman*, 25 April 2010). Moreover, at the conclusion of the April 2010 Great Prophet military exercises, the commander of the IRGC boasted that 'the waters of the Persian Gulf are now under the total control of the Iranian marine forces' (*al-Nahar* [Kuwait], 28 April 2010). This unprecedented statement appeared especially provocative, due to the fact that Qatar had accepted an invitation from Tehran to dispatch a delegation of high-ranking military officers to observe the maneuvers.

Conclusion

Bilateral free trade agreements with the United States have had harmful strategic consequences for the GCC as a whole, as well as for those GCC states that have refrained from signing such pacts. Friction between Bahrain and the United Arab Emirates on one hand and Saudi Arabia on the other has increased markedly as a result of Washington's campaign to conclude bilateral pacts with governments in the region. Trade-related disputes have disrupted plans to create a GCC monetary union. More important, bilateral agreements with the US have led Bahrain and Oman to embark on industrial ventures that enhance their linkages to external trading partners at the expense of regional economic congruence. Efforts by Saudi Arabia and Qatar to counterbalance these programs by making overtures to China and India have heightened the level of commercial rivalry in the Gulf, while at the same time solidifying the split between the GCC states that have aligned themselves directly with the US and those that have managed to keep Washington at arm's length.

This fracture inside the GCC, combined with the heightened US economic presence in Bahrain and Oman, has convinced Iran that the six member-states are less likely now than they might have been in the past to put aside their differences in the face of external challenges. Tehran has therefore adopted a more confrontational posture toward its southern neighbors: it has stepped up the scale and frequency of military exercises in the Gulf, tightened its grip on Abu Musa and the Tunbs and even revived its long-dormant claim to Bahrain. Such nascent belligerence may well be a concommitant of Iran's ongoing nuclear research program (El-Hokayem and Legrenzi 2006; Kaye and Wehrey 2007). But it also reflects the strategic implications of bilateral free trade agreements in this volatile corner of the world.

Conclusion – Repositioning the Gulf: The GCC in the Twenty-First Century Global Political Economy

Crystal A. Ennis and Paul Doherty

Introduction

The global trend of shifting geo-economic power from industrialized nations to rising powers is mirrored by political economy transformations in the Gulf. These changes have brought the region to the forefront of international economic debates, extending discussion of the Gulf in the global economy from that limited to petroleum supply and price to include financial markets, sovereign wealth funds, foreign direct investment and overseas development assistance. If anything can be concluded from the last decade, it is that there has been a visible transformation in the states of the Gulf Cooperation Council (GCC) – Bahrain, Kuwait, Oman, Saudi Arabia, Qatar and the United Arab Emirates. While scholars may neither agree on the source nor the direction of this change; that transformation has occurred is undeniable. Although rentierism and patrimonialism continues to persist, mounting evidence suggests that even these factors may slowly be evolving. The rapid push to development, which largely began across the region in the 1970s, has continued, with attention now given to diversification away from oil and the strengthening of the private sector. Examining the shifting geo-economic power of the Gulf, this book interrogates the evolving nature of the Gulf rentier state and the new mechanisms it utilizes to persist under conditions of possibly declining oil supplies, unpredictable oil prices, rising national unemployment, globalization and neoliberalism. This chapter explores whether this shift signals greater impending political change or the continuance of pragmatic adaptability to internal and external environments. Do the pressures of globalisation and neoliberalism imply the continued reduction of state power and sovereignty, or do the Gulf states face a future reflecting a past embedded in patrimonialism and authoritarianism? Divided into two sections, this chapter examines this question in light of the insights garnered from the collected essays in this volume. The first section focuses on structural changes in the domestic, regional and international political economy and the second examines the challenges confronting the GCC states in the twenty-first century global political economy. It ultimately suggests that the mechanisms and processes of development utilized throughout the GCC, while growing out of the structures of the past, are gradually shifting to account for the changing structures of the global economy coupled with domestic political and environmental constraints.

Structural Changes in Rentier Political Economy

Development trajectories in the GCC have conventionally centred on the benefits and constraints of resource wealth. While rentierism has been a significant hindrance to other resource-rich states across the world, the Gulf has managed to become a success story. Facing continuing challenges, like how to spend wisely, redistribute wealth, save for the future, educate its population and develop fiscal plans faced with increasingly unstable oil prices, the Gulf states have navigated the course to development relatively well in comparison to their rentier counterparts. Tétreault notes, for example, that GCC states score well on UN human development indices. Indeed, rentierism continues to persist and arguably succeed despite the pressures of globalization, neoliberalism and the imperative to diversify the economy away from oil. Three possible accounts can be employed to explain the resilience of the rentier state in the Gulf which, if taken together, help explain the anomaly that is the Gulf rentier. First, the autonomy granted by oil wealth to states in choosing the methods of development. Second, the economic success achieved through diversification and broadening integration in the global political economy through the expansion of financialization and investment. Finally, the Gulf rentier states' proven flexibility and responsiveness to events and change around them. Combined, these three factors have facilitated regime consolidation as well as the adaptability that allowed for the gradual evolution of the structural underpinnings of Gulf political economy.

Commodity-Driven Development

The first explanation of the resilience of the rentier state in the Gulf relates to its developmental path; that is, the role of oil and state-led development. No discussion of development in the Gulf is complete without the inclusion of oil. Oil has shaped the modern history and political economy of the Gulf, influencing its relations with the rest of the world and constructing power relationships throughout the region. At the global level, the international relations of the Gulf have been characterized by interdependence, or arguably co-dependence, between itself and oil importers (see Tétreault in this volume). At the domestic level, oil has granted the ruling families a high degree of autonomy in development planning and economic decision-making. Oil, controlled by a small group of international companies until the 1960s, began to be nationalized by the 1970s (Tétreault in this volume). During this time, oil prices quadrupled and Gulf states rapidly developed: building infrastructure, social welfare programs and state-led businesses (Tétreault; Hvidt, in this volume). Characterized by resource-driven development, the region still embodies rentierism and authoritarianism.

A state is defined as rentier or 'allocative' when its revenue is generated by resource rent, accrued externally and given directly to the state, which is then distributed throughout society through various circulation mechanisms. Importantly, then, the rentier state is financially independent of society and does not seek legitimacy through democratic representation (see Beblawi and Luciani 1987). Traditionally patrimonial states, such as those in the Gulf, are particularly well-suited to being rentiers. Gulf countries are strongly patrimonial in that networks are created via connections with authorities, and power is exercised through elite networks and relationships of loyalty and dependence on ruling families. Patrimonial states have a strong lineage in modern history, with leaders ruling tribal societies and maintaining reciprocally-beneficial relationships with merchants and the commercial elite (Beblawi and Luciani 1987). Throughout its history, the Gulf Arab region has been characterized by the embeddedness of the merchant class in the global economy, a trend which has remained rather constant *vis-à-vis* the indelible link of oil, investments and trade between the Gulf Arab states and the global economy (see Luciani in this volume).

The most obvious reason for Gulf rentiers to have resisted external and internal pressures for reform is derived from their resource wealth and resultant financial independence. This has allowed them to direct the trajectory of their development according to their interests. Insofar as the Gulf states have been developing competitive private sectors and providing business with increasing levels of autonomy, they have surrendered to some of the tenets of neoliberalism. Indeed, the patrimonial, authoritarian nature of the Gulf states seems to have facilitated their success, allowing them to loosen constraints on the economy while remaining traditional, dynastic political entities. Despite macroeconomic instability in commodity markets in the 1970s, the oil price shock of the mid-1980s and the impact of financial deregulation and futures speculation on oil price stability beginning in the 1990s, the Gulf rentiers have fared much better than their regional neighbours (Tétreault in this volume). Furthermore, rentier states outside the Gulf have generally succumbed to the resource curse, developing oversized bureaucracies, exuding inefficiency in all sectors and rejecting economic reform. This is not entirely the case in the Gulf, where, while resisting most pressures to reform politically, they have managed to develop rather strong economies. The redistribution of rent typically allows rentier states to function well in the absence of an efficient economic foundation for its society. Governments have little incentive to cultivate a productive private sector or employment (Hvidt in this volume). The Gulf puzzle is that, despite such trends, these states have emerged as relatively stable and even economically prosperous. In the second oil boom, GCC economies have attained the capacity to absorb and circulate oil revenue through their domestic economies. They have increased their investment and spending and reduced their debt (Abboud in this volume). GCC state financial resources, while encountering some difficulty during the 1980s, are strong, private sectors are sturdy and growing, public-private partnerships abound, and Gulf businesses are generally quite profitable (Tétreault; Hertog; Hvidt; Abboud in this volume). Significantly, oil seems to have forged the consolidation and facilitated the longevity of regimes that, without oil, may not have endured to the present.

Prosperity, Progress and Regime Consolidation

As much as oil has reinforced regimes in the Gulf, contemporary success and progress in economic and business endeavours has served to further support existing governing systems. As long as Gulf leaders are seen as facilitating national success, the population is likely to remain quiescent. Increasing privatization, economic liberalization and greater integration into financial markets leads scholars to question how the Gulf rentier is transforming. Structural change is apparent on several fronts. Hvidt sees a shift from Luciani's traditional conception of the 'allocation state' to a more production-oriented model. Abboud similarly perceives a shift in rentier structures facilitating a greater role for finance in economic growth and diversification. In much the same way, Hertog notes greater autonomy for the private business sector, which has meant declining state authority over how rents are recycled and an increasing role for business in economic policy-making. Successful attempts at diversification away from oil and expanding integration into the global economy away from petroleum-related activities to finance and investment has arguably contributed to the consolidation of the Gulf Arab states. Simultaneously, it has meant that traditional power structures and rent-recycling mechanisms are being altered.

The initial shift toward greater economic reforms began in the 1990s, with neoliberalism being diffused throughout the world by the Washington Consensus. This provided the motivation for increased privatization, the marketization and regulation of economic activity and financial investment and expansion in the GCC (Hvidt; Abboud in this volume). Hvidt suggests that these changes mark the beginning of the shift in the reform process away from the rentier status quo toward a production-oriented model. Abboud notes another structural shift whereby oil revenues have been utilized for the generation of finance-led growth, allowing increasing financialization to be a tool through which states move away from oil dependence. Indicative of this change is the shift in the Gulf from users to providers of financial services. Finance is therefore being employed as a device for growth and diversification (Abboud in this volume). The increases in financial activity and services as well as the increase of construction and service provision projects are illustrative of the shift in rentier structures toward production and finance-driven development. Added to this, structural shifts in the conventional means of conducting business in the Gulf has occurred, with much of private business further removed from the rent distribution decisions of the state than in the past. An increasingly liberalized economy has had clear consumption and demand implications, allowing business to cater to private demand that has been generated by public salaries being recycled in the increasingly private economy.

Business has also been given a more prominent role in economic policy-making, with business representatives part of the debate during the law-drafting process (Hertog, this volume). The fact that the Gulf states routinely perform well in competitiveness, macroeconomic stability, and development indicators like literacy and life expectancy seems to support this notion that structures in the Gulf are changing (Hvidt; Tétreault in this volume).

Despite critique of 'mock compliance' in regulatory, liberalization and privatization matters, the Gulf states have fared well, with all six placed among the 50 most competitive nations in the world and Saudi Arabia and Bahrain ranked among the 25 most business-friendly nations (Hvidt in this volume). Notwithstanding this, as many chapters in this volume point out, the Gulf states face numerous challenges in this shift toward a production and/or finance-driven economy: educational reform, investment in research and development, labour market reform, reducing vulnerability to global macroeconomic deficiencies, attaining regulatory parity in investments and financialization, transparency and accountability in investments, and deciding on the future of their monetary affairs and currency. If Gulf Arab states are not able to deal with these impending challenges and ensure employment and national prosperity, popular political acquiescence may be challenged.

One could argue that globalization and perhaps even neoliberalism has facilitated the consolidation of patrimonialism and rentierism in the Gulf. With domestic unrest either nonexistent or successfully subordinated through wealth conferral or cooption into business elite or governmental networks (though some exceptions exist, notably in Bahrain), a pro-capitalist economy has engendered prosperity thereby helping sustain political order. Unless oil scarcity seems more imminent and economic diversification away from oil desists, rentier patterns are likely to persevere. It seems it is rentierism combined with economic developmental progress that has served to further consolidate Gulf regimes, at least for the time being.

Flexibility and Responsiveness

A final explanation, which can be employed to expound the reasons the rentier state has persisted in the GCC states, includes its flexibility and responsiveness to change in the global order. History and experience has taught the region to choose pragmatism and cooperation instead of antagonism with the West. Integration into the global economy, with its incipient oil wealth, carried it through the initial stages of development. The experiences of its regional neighbours have illustrated the failures of socialism, religious fundamentalism and antipathy to the West. Some authors note awareness of good business practices, a willingness to grant greater autonomy to the business sector and moves toward privatization as facilitating private sector efficiency and economic growth (Tétreault; Hertog; Luciani in this volume). Pragmatism, a characteristic lending to Luciani's explanation of the continued currency peg to the dollar, has also helped facilitate and sustain economic and security cooperation with the West for decades. Arguably then, given this tradition of responsiveness, greater integration into international institutions and increased proximity with global norms on transparency and accountability, may positively affect Gulf business and investment practices (see Finnemore and Sikkink 1998 and Barnett and Finnemore 2004 for more on international norm socialization). However, the likelihood of this process is still unclear, with shifting power structures and possibly normative pressures from West to East. The item of most relevance remains the Gulf's demonstrable ability to be responsive to its environment.

This flexibility has been facilitated mostly by the nondemocratic nature of the Gulf states. It seems, in fact, that by virtue of their authoritarianism Gulf monarchies have been rendered agile, autonomous economic actors. Indeed, the Gulf states that experiment most with democratization struggle most economically and face the most policy choice constraints. This is especially evident by the obstacles democratization has placed in the path of Kuwait's economic development (Hertog 2010, 294). Authoritarianism and rentierism have afforded Gulf states the flexibility which lends to their increased durability. Commodity-driven development, continued economic progress and responsiveness to domestic and global changes have smoothed the way for measured modifications in the structural underpinnings of Gulf political economy.

Novel Challenges in the Global Political Economy

Beyond the pressures of diminishing oil reserves and the concomitant imperative to diversify the economic base away from oil, several novel challenges to the Gulf in the global political economy exist and are arguably mounting. These challenges stretch beyond, but are inextricably connected to, the question of oil and gas. They include international standards and regulatory compliance regarding accountability and transparency, especially concerning SWFs, lagging innovation, the broader implications of labour nationalization, attaining and/or maintaining international authority and achieving sustainable development. Indeed, despite many economic successes, the Gulf states remain either factor-driven or efficiency-driven and have failed considerably to achieve any laudable progress on innovation. Furthermore, most states are weak in education, investment transparency and regulatory mechanisms (Hvidt; Tétreault; Bazoobandi and Niblock in this volume).

Regulatory Compliance, Accountability and Transparency

This trichotomy of challenges, while impacting several arenas, is most potent in discourse around Sovereign Wealth Funds (SWF). As several of our authors mention, SWFs are viewed as 'sinister' and deemed a 'threat' to the international financial system. This largely stems from the perception that Gulf Arab SWFs lack transparency and accountability, and is particularly salient since the estimated value of Gulf SWFs approaches one trillion dollars in total assets (Malkin and Ziemba in this volume). Accountability can only exist if transparency mechanisms are in place which would allow some actors to hold others to a set of standards or regulations. Accountability therefore suggests that actors are held accountable to certain accepted standards of behavior and face the possibility of sanction should they fail to comply with these standards (see Grant and Keohane 2005). Behrendt identifies a fairly low commitment level among the Gulf Arab states to the 'Santiago Principles' – standardizing governance, transparency and accountability for SWFs. He argues that SWFs held by nondemocratic regimes exhibit a lower degree of compliance with governance standards, and are altogether less transparent and accountable. Despite these observations, Bazoobandi and Niblock suggest that enhanced transparency may not result in outcomes desired by Western states. Instead, the flow of investment from Gulf SWFs to the Western world would likely decrease, shifting toward Asia.

From Consensus to Labour Market Reform

Several regional and domestic problems challenge the GCC states economic prowess and international effectiveness. Regional consensus remains exigent. Lawson (in this volume) implies that a core predicament may be the unwillingness of GCC states to achieve consensus when confronting external challenges. He uses the Iranian threat as a case in point, pointing to the overt heightening of Iran's confrontational positions *vis-à-vis* the GCC states. GCC consensual reluctance has been exacerbated, in Lawson's view, by bilateral free trade agreements between the US and governments in the region, inciting Gulf governments to pursue bilateral agreements rather than, or even at the expense of, regional ones. Indeed, consensus remains a core challenge at the GCC level, where plans to further an economic union and achieve a monetary union continues to face obstacles (see Legrenzi 2008; Luciani in this volume).

Domestic challenges also affect the international relations of the GCC states. Hvidt notes, despite their status as competitive economies, the Gulf states score poorly on innovation and most also perform poorly on education indicators. Increased investment in research and development along with a focus on educational reform is imperative and likely to help assuage national employment problems as well. Education and innovation shortcomings necessarily affect the competitiveness and situation of the economy as a whole, as well as exacerbate the problem of rising regional unemployment. Indeed, as Hertog notes, the most formidable challenge in Gulf societies may be labour nationalization. Labour nationalization refers to government policies across the region to reduce reliance on expatriate labour and, through job quotas and education and training programs, increase local employment opportunities. This system unavoidably shifts some of the employment burden from the public to private sectors, increasing private sector labour costs and reducing the advantages achieved through the availability of low-cost migrant labour. Hertog's chapter in this volume suggests that in addition to clashing with business interests, transferring the employment burden to the private sector could potentially change the nature of demand and consumption, effecting the domestic economy and state-business and state-population relationships. Beyond the local political implications, these challenges affect international competitiveness as well as expatriate remittances to their country of origin.

Financial Power to International Authority

The financial power held by the GCC states, given their hydrocarbon reserves, has been a geo-economic reality for years. This power has been evolving and gaining greater potency in recent years, with massive oil profits invested in SWFs and other public investment agents. Further diversification in financial products, with growth in financial regionalization and Islamic banking, is an important component of economic diversification as well as a means of acquiring greater global economic power (Abboud; Momani in this volume). The Gulf states have indeed shifted from passive accumulators of securities to aggressive investors, and large portfolio investors in a wide array of assets (Tétreault, this volume). There is also much regional shifting transpiring, with a geographical contest in Islamic finance between Malaysia and the GCC states seeming likely to favour the GCC, and shifting interdependence from that between the US and the GCC states to between the GCC states and China, Japan and South Korea (Baker; Davidson in this volume). Yet does the amassing of financial strength equate international authority?

Power, in conventional IR/IPE, and particularly realist, scholarship, refers to the ability of states to get others to do what they would not otherwise want to do. Susan Strange calls this relational power, which she distinguishes from structural power in that structural power encompasses the ability of states to shape structures in the global political economy and global institutions which thereby determines outcomes in the international system (1996, 17–27). The Gulf's ability to shape structures in the global political economy and its institutions is difficult to ascertain definitively. Nevertheless, change is definitely apparent as several Gulf states have been asserting themselves in international economic affairs, attaining media attention, for example, with the Dubai ports controversy. The 'real' power of the Gulf states however remains to be determined. Moreover, to be considered an authority, an actor must have legitimacy. Although often convoluted, a distinction between power and authority exists. An actor only has authority if its power is combined with legitimacy, implying the consent and social unity of the regulated or governed (Hall and Biersteker, 2–5; Cutler 1999, 63). The maintenance of legitimacy, in the Gulf context, is predicated on the Gulf governments' ability to continue delivering public goods. This applies both internally and externally.

The shifting geo-economic role of the Gulf in the global economy, while interlinked to the trajectory of oil politics, is now imbued with the implications of the increasing financialization of the Gulf, and particularly the growth of SWFs. Despite concerns to the contrary, Gulf SWFs, along with the Chinese, injected key capital into western financial institutions following the recent financial crisis. These capital infusions contributed to the political economy shift which rendered the financial sector dominant in Gulf investment (see Malkin and Ziemba and Abboud in this volume). Though the future of the power and authority the Gulf may emit in the international system is yet unclear, what is clear are the shifting structures of the global economy, which necessarily affect the geo-economic repositioning of the Gulf.

Conclusion

This book makes an important contribution to the fields of global political economy and Gulf studies. It is particularly relevant to academics and policy-makers interested in the contemporary redistribution of power in the global economy away from the West and to the East and the South. Altogether, this book examined the evolving nature of the Gulf rentiers and the new mechanisms they have employed to persevere in the face of the many challenges of the twenty-first-century global political economy. While the pressures of globalization and neoliberalism have definitely changed aspects of the international, regional and domestic affairs of the Gulf states, their patrimonial and authoritarian nature has served to consolidate their power and, contingent on continued economic success, seems likely to facilitate their survival for some time to come. In the short run, the future of the Gulf rentiers seems likely to mirror their past. Their ability to remain pragmatic and responsive to the international environment is a key factor in their durability. Increased international interconnectedness of course renders their economic vitality inseparably linked with various international financial systems. Global macroeconomic instability, compounding debt pressures and growing financialization combined with the direction of the SWF debate and the Eastward shift encouraged by continued investment difficulties in the West will all affect Gulf economic outcomes. Indeed, the mechanisms of development in the Gulf states from the oil and gas to the finance sector, while growing out of past rentier structures, are steadily shifting to account for global economic, political and environmental changes. Whether the GCC member states will be considered new power brokers alongside other recent arrivals to global economic significance like Brazil, China and India, remains to be seen. The Gulf Arab states' continued control over vast hydrocarbon resources combined with their more recent prominence in international finance makes this seem possible despite their continued security vulnerability.

References

Abdelal, R., Khan and A., Khanna, T. 2008. Where Oil-Rich Nations are Placing their Bets. *Harvard Business Review*, 86(9), 119–28.

Abed, G.T. 1983. Arab Financial Resources: An Analysis and Critique of Present Deployment Policies, in *Arab Resources: The Transformation of a Society*, edited by A. Ibrahim. London: Croom Helm, 43–70.

Abed, G.T and Davoodi, H.R. 2003. *Challenges of Growth and Globalization in the Middle East and North Africa*. Washington, DC: International Monetary Fund.

Abed, G.T., Erbas, N.S. and Guerami, B. 2003. *The GCC Monetary Union: Some Considerations for the Exchange Rate Regime*. IMF Working Paper No. WP/-3/66, pp. 1.13. Washington, DC: International Monetary Fund.

Abu Dhabi Marine Operating Company. 2006. *History: Four Decades in the Petroleum Industry*. [Online: Abu Dhabi – Abu Dhabi Marine Operating Company (ADMA-OPCO)]. Available at: http://www.adma-opco.com/Default. aspx?TabId=65 [accessed: 14 April 2010].

AFP. 2008. *Gulf States Look to Harvest Food from Investment in Asia*. [Online: Inquirer.net]. Available at: http://services.inquirer.net/print/print.php?article_id=20080720-149605 [accessed: 21 July 2008].

Agénor, P.R. 1992. *Parallel Currency Markets in Developing Countries: Theory, Evidence and Policy Implications*, Princeton Essay in *International Finance*, No. 188. Princeton, NJ: Princeton University, International Finance Section.

Ahmed, T. 2002. Accounting Issues for Islamic Banks, in *Islamic Finance: Innovation and Growth*, edited by S. Archer and R. Karim. London: Euromoney and AAOIFI.

Aissaoui, A. 2009. The Shrinking MENA Energy Investment Outlook, *Oxford Energy Forum* (77), 7–9.

Al-Awwad, A. 2007. *IFC Smart Lessons: Eliminating Minimum Capital Requirement and Facilitating Business Start-Up in Saudi Arabia*. Washington, DC: International Finance Corporation/World Bank.

al Otaiba, Y. 2008. *Abu Dhabi's Investment Guidelines: Letter from Abu Dhabi to Western Financial Officials*. [Online: The Wall Street Journal]. Available at: http://online.wsj.com/article/SB120578495444542861.html?mod=European-Business-News [accessed: 1 September 2010].

Al-Shahrabani, A. and de Boer, K. 2007. *Modernizing the United Arab Emirates: An Interview with Minister of Economy Lubna Al Qasimi*. [Online: The Mckinsey Quarterly]. Available at: http://www.docin.com/p-6515337.html [accessed: 1 September 2007].

Al-Suwaidi, N. 2008. *Statement to the International Monetary Fund, International Monetary and Financial Committee, by His Excellency Sultan N. Al-Suwaidi, Governor of the United Arab Emirates Central Bank, on behalf of Bahrain, Egypt, Iraq, Jordan, Kuwait, Lebanon, Libya, Maldives, Oman, Qatar, Syria, United Arab Emirates, and Yemen*. Washington, DC: International Monetary Fund.

Anderson, E.C. 2009. *Take the Money and Run: Sovereign Wealth Funds and the Demise of American Prosperity*. Westport, Connecticut: Praeger Security International.

ANIMA Investment Network. 2009. *Country Profile – Jordan: A Business Friendly Economy Open to Foreign Investors*. [Online: ANIMA Investment Network]. Available at: www.invest-in-med.eu/../20090716170320ain_jordan_eng_14-11-08.pdf [accessed: 2 June 2009].

ANIMA Investment Network. 2009. *Foreign Direct Investment in the Med Countries in 2008: Facing the Crisis. Invest in Med. Survey No. 3*. [Online: ANIMA Investment Network]. Available at: www.animaweb.org/../Inv_Et3_ Med-FDI-Survey-2008_VE_29-5-09_ locked.pdf [accessed: 1 March 2009].

Antkiewicz, A. and Momani, B. 2009. Pursuing Geopolitical Stability through Interregional Trade: The EU's Motives for Negotiating with the Gulf Cooperation Council (GCC). *Journal of European Integration*, 31(2), 217–35.

Arab Investment and Export Credit Guarantee Corporation, The. 2007. *Investment Climate in the Arab Countries 2007 – Executive Summary*. Kuwait: The Arab Investment and Export Credit Guarantee Corporation.

Archer, S. and Ahmed, T. 2003. *Emerging Standards for Islamic Financial Institutions: The Case of Accounting and Auditing Organization for Islamic Financial Institutions*. Washington, DC: Mimeo, World Bank.

Aysan, A.F., Nabli, M.K. and Veganzones-Varoudakis, M.A. 2006. *Governance and Private Investment in the Middle East and North Africa*. Washington, DC: World Bank Policy Research Working Paper 3934.

Bahgat, G. 2008. Sovereign Wealth Funds: Dangers and Opportunities. *International Affairs*, 84(6), 1189–204.

Bakar, D.M. 2002. The Shariah Supervisory Board and Issues of Shariah Rulings and their Harmonization in Islamic Banking and Finance, in *Islamic Finance: Innovation and Growth*, edited by S. Archer and R. Karim. London: Euromoney and AAOIFI.

Baker, A. 2006. *Participation in the Deliberative Spaces of the Global Financial Architecture: A Transgovernmental Analysis*. [Online: Garnet Working Paper, 21/07]. Available at: http://www.garnet-eu.org/index.php?id=27 [accessed: 18 April 2010].

Baker, A. 2008. The Group of Seven. *New Political Economy*, 13(1), 103–16.

Baker, A. 2009. Deliberative Equality and the Transgovernmental Politics of the Global Financial Architecture. *Global Governance*, 15, 195–218.

Baker, A. 2010. International Deliberative Financial Governance and Apex Policy Forums: Where we are and where we should be headed, in *From Reform to*

Crisis: Financial Integration and the 'New Architecture' of International Financial Governance, edited by G. Underhill, J. Blom and D. Mügge. Cambridge: Cambridge University Press.

Baldwin, R.E. 2006. Multilaterising Regionalism: Spaghetti Bowls as Building Blocs on the Path to Global Free Trade. *The World Economy*, 29(11), 1451–1518.

Baliño, T., Bennet, A. and Borensztein, E. 1999. *Monetary Policy in Dollarized Economies*. Washington, DC: IMF Occasional Paper 171.

Barsky, R.B. and Lutz, K. 2004. Oil and the Macroeconomy Since the 1970s. *Journal of Economic Perspectives*, 18(4), 115–34.

Barnett, M. and Finnemore, M. 1999. The Politics, Power and Pathologies of International Organizations. *International Organizations*, 54(3), 669–732.

Barnett, M. and Finnemore, M. 2004. *Rules for the World: International Organizations in Global Politics*. Ithaca and London: Cornell University Press.

Barysch, K., Tilford, S. and Whyte, P. 2008. *State, Money and Rules: An EU Policy for Sovereign Investments*. London: Centre for European Studies Reforms.

Beblawi, H. 1990. The Rentier State in the Arab World, in *The Arab State*, edited by G. Luciani. London: Routledge, 65–84.

Beblawi, H. and Luciani, G. 1987. *The Rentier State*. London: Croon Helem.

Beck, R. and Fidora, M. 2008. The Impact of Sovereign Wealth Funds on Global Financial Markets. *Intereconomics*, 43(6), 349–58.

Beck, R. and Kamps, A. 2009. *Petrodollars and Imports of Oil Exporting Countries*. Frankfurt: European Central Bank.

Behrendt, S. 2009. New Perspectives on Managing Political Risk, in *Sovereign Risk Management*, edited by Malan Rietveld. London: Central Banking Publications, 143–51.

Bergsten, F. 2009. The Dollar and the Deficits. *Foreign Affairs*, 55(5).

Bhagwati, J. 1991. *The World Trading System at Risk*. Princeton: Princeton University Press.

Bhagwati, J. 2008. *Termites in the Trading System*. Oxford: Oxford University Press.

Bhagwati, J. and Panagariya, A. 1996. Preferential Trading Areas and Multilateralism – Strangers, Friends, or Foes? in *The Economics of Preferential Trade Agreements*, edited by J. Bhagwati and A. Panagariya. Washington, DC: AEI Press.

Biberovic, N. 2008. *A Common European Approach to Sovereign Wealth Funds – Continuity of the Status Quo?* [Online]. Available at: ww2.grc.to/data/contents/uploads/GCC-EU_no_10_7945.pdf [accessed: 1 May 2008].

Blair, J.M. 1976/1978. *The Control of Oil*. New York: Vintage.

Bloomberg. 2009. *China's Yu Tells U.S. Not to be Complacent About Debt* (Update 1). [Online]. Available at: http://www.bloomberg.com/apps/news?pid=newsarchive&sid=aatNgaPM2wQM&refer=home [accessed: 3 April 2010].

British Petroleum Statistical Review. 2008. London: British Petroleum Statistical Review of World Energy.

Buxani, R. 2003. *Taking the High Road*. Dubai: Motivate.

Calabrese, J. 1990. From Flyswatters to Silkworms: The Evolution of China's Role in West Asia. *Asian Survey*, 30(9), 862–76.

Cerny, P. 1993. The De-Regulation and Re-Regulation of Financial Markets in a More Open World, in *Finance and World Politics: Markets, Regimes and States in the Post-Hegemonic Era*, edited by P. Cerny. Aldershot: Edward Elgar.

CIA World Factbook. 2009. *People and Economics Overviews of Japan, China, South Korea, Saudi Arabia, the UAE, Kuwait, Qatar, Oman, and Bahrain*. [Online]. Available at: https://www.cia.gov/library/publications/the-world-factbook/ [accessed: 14 April 2010].

Chakrabarti, A. 2001. The Determinants of Foreign Direct Investment: Sensitivity Analyses of Cross-Country Regressions. *Kyklos*, 54, 89–114.

Chapra, M. 2005. Challenges Facing the Islamic Financial Industry, in *Handbook on Islamic Financing and Banking*, edited by K. Hassan and M. Lewis. Aldershot: Edward Elgar.

Chatham House. 2008. *The Gulf as a Global Financial Centre: Growing Opportunities and International Influence*. London: Chatham House.

Chaudhry, K.A. 1997. *The Price of Wealth: Economics and Institutions in the Middle East*. Ithaca, NY: Cornell University Press.

Cho, D. 2008. A Few Speculators Dominate Vast Market for Oil Trading. *Washington Post*, 21 August, A01.

Chubin, S. 2009. Iran's Power in Context. *Survival*, 51(1), 165–90.

Clark, W. 2005. *Petrodollar Warfare: Dollars, Euros and the Upcoming Iranian Oil Bourse*. [Online: Post Carbon Institute]. Available at: http://www.energybulletin.net/node/7707 [accessed: 2 August 2005].

Cleveland, H.V.B. and Brittain, B.W.H. 1975. A World Depression? *Foreign Affairs*, 53(2), 223–41.

Clinton, H. 2008. Interview with Jim Cramer. *CNBC*, 2 April.

Cohen, B.J. 1998. *The Geography of Money*. Ithaca, NY: Cornell University Press.

Cohen, B.J. 2009. Sovereign Wealth Funds and National Security: The Great Tradeoff. *International Affairs*, 85(4), 713–31.

Committee on Foreign Affairs House of Representatives. 2008. *The Rise of Sovereign Wealth Fund: Impacts on U.S. Foreign Policy and Economic Interest*. [Online]. Available at: www.internationalrelations.house.gov/110/42480.pdf [accessed: 21 May 2008].

Congressional Research Service. 2006. *Saudi Arabia: Current Issues and US Relations*. [Online]. Available at: www.fas.org/sgp/crs/mideast/IB93113.pdf [accessed: 24 February 2006].

Cooper, A. and Momani, B. 2009. The Challenge of Re-branding Countries in the Middle East: Opportunities through New Networked Engagements versus Constraints of Embedded Negtaive Images. *Place Branding and Public Diplomacy*, 5(2), 103–17.

Crystal, J. 1995. *Oil and Politics in the Gulf: Rulers and Merchants in Kuwait and Qatar*. Cambridge: Cambridge University Press.

Cutler, C.A. 1999. Locating 'Authority' in the Global Political Economy. *International Studies Quarterly*, 43(1), 59–81.

Das, U., Lu, Y., Mulder, C. and Amadou, S. 2009. *Setting up a Sovereign Wealth Fund: Some Policy and Operational Considerations*, IMF Working Paper, WP/09/179. Washington, DC: International Monetary Fund.

Davidson, C.M. 2005. *The United Arab Emirates: A Study in Survival*. Boulder, CO: Lynne Rienner Press.

Davidson, C.M. 2008. *Dubai: The Vulnerability of Success*. New York: Columbia University Press.

Davidson, C.M. 2009. *Abu Dhabi: Oil and Beyond*. New York: Columbia University Press.

Demarolle, A. 2008. *Report to the Government of France on Sovereign Wealth Funds*. [Online: Paris Europlace]. Available at: http://www.paris-europlace. net/links/doc063922.htm [accessed: 11 July 2008].

Deutsche Bank Research. 2008. *How They Spend it: Commodity and Non-Commodity Sovereign Wealth Funds*. Frankfurt aM: Deutsche Bank Research.

Dinmore, G. 2008. Italy set to curb sovereign wealth funds. *Financial Times*, 21 October.

Dore, R. 2008. Financialization of the global economy. *Industrial and Corporate Change*, 17(6), 1097–112.

Drezner, D.W. 2008. Sovereign Wealth Funds and the (In)security of Global Finance. *Journal of International Affairs*, 62(1), 115–30.

Economist, The. 2007. The Dollar: Time to break free. *The Economist*, 22 November.

Economist, The. 2009. *The Scramble for Land in Africa and Asia*. [Online: The Economist]. Available at: http://www.economist.com/world/international/ displayStory.cfm?story_id=13692889 [accessed: 1 September 2010].

Economist Intelligence Unit (EIU). 2008. *Labour Rations in the Gulf*. [Online]. Available at: http://www.economist.com/research/articlesBySubject/displaystory. cfm?subjectid=9499922&story_id=E1_TNDPJSSS [accessed: 3 September 2010].

Economist Intelligence Unit (EIU). 2009. *The GCC in 2020: Outlook for the Gulf and the Global Economy*. [Online: Economist Intelligence Unit]. Available at: http://viewswire.eiu.com/report_dl.asp?mode=fi&fi=174383002.PDF&rf=0 [accessed: 1 September 2010].

Economist Intelligence Unit (EIU). 2009. Lebanon: Back to Beirut. *Business Middle East*. 16 January.

Eid, F. 2008. The New Face of Arab Investment, in *The Gulf Region: A New Hub of Global Financial Power*, edited by J. Nugée and P. Subacchi. London: Chatham House, 69–80.

El Gamal, M. 2006. *Overview of Islamic Finance*, Occasional Paper, No. 4. Washington, DC: Department of the Treasury, International Affairs.

El Gamal, M. 2008. *Comments on Prof Andrew Baker's 'International Financial Apex Policy Forums: Why they Exist? How they Work?'*, on file with the author.

El-Hokayem, E. and Legrenzi, M. 2006. *The Arab Gulf States in the Shadow of the Iranian Nuclear Challenge.* Washington, DC: The Henry L. Stimson Center.

Engelen, E. 2008. The Case for Financialization. *Competition & Change*, 12(2), 111–19.

Epstein, G.A. 2005. Introduction: Financialization and the World Economy, in *Financialization and the World Economy*, edited by G.A. Epstein. Northhampton: Edward Elgar, 3–16.

Essayad, M. and Algahtani, I. 2005. Policy Issues Related to Substitution of the US Dollar in Oil Pricing. *International Journal of Global Energy Issues* 23(1), 71–92.

Essayad, M. and Marx, D. 2001. OPEC and optimal currency portfolios. *Oil, Gas, and Energy Quarterly*, 49(2), 363–84.

Ethier, W. 1998. The New Regionalism. *Economic Journal*, 108(449), 1149–61.

Ethier, W. 1999. Multilateral Roads to Regionalism, in *International Trade Policy and the Pacific Rim*, edited by J. Piggott and A. Woodland. London: Macmillan, 153–6.

Europa Publications. 2007. *The Middle East and North Africa Handbook 2008.* London: Europa Publications.

Evans, P.B. 1989. Predatory, Developmental and Other Apparatuses: A Comparative Political Economy Perspective on the Third World State. *Sociological Forum*, 4(4), 561–87.

Evans, P. 2008. Is an Alternative Globalization Possible? *Politics and Society* 36(2), 271–305.

Evans, R. 1995. *Deng Xiaoping and the Making of Modern China.* London: Penguin.

Farrell, D. and Lund, S. 2008. Windfall in the Gulf. *The Miliken Institute Review*, 10(2), 24–35.

Fasano, U. and Iqbal, Z. 2002. Common Currency. *Finance and Development*, 39(4), 42–6.

Fattah, H. 1997. *The Politics of Regional Trade in Iraq, Arabia and the Gulf, 1745–1900.* Albany: State University of New York Press.

Fattouh, B. 2008. OPEC's dance with the market. *Oxford Energy Forum*, 75, 13–16.

Ferguson, N. 2009. An Empire at Risk. *Newsweek*, 7 December.

Financial Times. 2008. Sovereign Funds Cool on Rescue Finance. *Financial Times*, 9 November.

Finnemore, M. and Sikkink, K. 1998. International Norm Dynamics and Political Change. *International Organization*, 52(4), 887–917.

Foran, J. 1993. *Fragile Resistance: Social Transformation in Iran from 1500 to the Revolution.* Boulder, CO: Westview.

Foreign Investment by States Owned Entities 2009. Canberra: Parliament of Australia Senate.

Frankel, J. 2003. A Proposed Monetary Regime for Small Commodity Exporters: Peg to the Export Price (PEP). *International Finance*, 6(1), 61–88.

Freund, C. 2000. Different Paths to Free Trade: The Gains from Regionalism. *Quarterly Journal of Economics*, 115(November), 1317–41.

Gasiorowski M.J. 1987. The 1953 *Coup d'Etat* in Iran. *International Journal of Middle Eastern Studies*, 19(3), 261–6.

Ghafour, M. 2009. China's Policy in the Persian Gulf. *Middle East Policy*, 16(2), 80–92.

Girgis, M. 2002. *Would Nationals and Asians Replace Arab Workers in the GCC?* [Online: Egyptian Centre for Economic Studies]. Available at: http://www.eces.org.eg/Uploaded_Files/%7B3D6C8AB9-D53E-4D52-B195-1AA1FC8CA91F%7D_ECESWP74.pdf [accessed: 3 September 2010].

Global Investment House. 2008. *Oman Economic and Strategic Outlook: Witnessing a Period of Accumulative Growth.* Kuwait: Global Investment House.

Global Investment House. 2009. *GCC Macroeconomics – Changing Paradigms.* Kuwait: Global Investment House.

Government Accounting Office (GAO). 1979. *Are OPEC Financial Holdings a Danger to the US Banks or the Economy? ID 7–45.* Washington, DC: US GAO.

Grant, R.W. and Keohane, R.O. 2005. Accountability and Abuses of Power in World Politics. *American Political Science Review*, 99(1), 29–42.

GSDP. 2008. *Qatar National Vision 2030.* Doha: General Secretariat for Development Planning.

Gulf Cooperation Council. 2007. *International Institute for Finance, Regional Briefing.* [Online]. Available at: http://iif.com/emr/emr-af [accessed: 31 May 2007].

Gulf Cooperation Council Secretariat. 2009. *Economic Relations between GCC Member States and the People's Republic of China.* Riyadh: Studies and Research Department.

Gulf News. 2007. *Dubai Issues List of Freehold Locations.* [Online]. Available at: http://gulfnews.com/business/property/dubai-issues-list-of-freehold-locations-1.28554 [accessed: 30 April 2007].

Gulf News. 2009. *Bahrain Plans to Buy Air-to-Air Missiles.* [Online]. Available at: http://www.gulfinthemedia.com/index.php?id=483131&news_type=Top&lang=en [accessed: 9 August 2009].

Gulf Research Center. 2007. *Security and Terrorism – Energy Security.* [Online]. Available at: http://www.grc.ae/data/contents/uploads/Issue_No_6_3564.pdf [accessed: 18 October 2010].

Habibi, N. and Woertz, E. 2009. *US-Arab Economic Relations and the Obama Administration.* Middle East Brief No. 34. Brandeis University: Crown Center for Middle East Studies.

Hall, B. 2008. Sarkozy plans fund to fend off 'predators'. *Financial Times*, 24 October.

Hall, R.B. and Biersteker, T.J. (eds). 2002. *The Emergence of Private Authority in Global Governance*. Cambridge: Cambridge University Press.

Hallwood, P. and Sinclair, S. 1981. *Oil, Debt and Development: OPEC in the Third World*. London: Allen & Unwin.

Hancock, M. 2008. Special report Oman: Planning drives economic growth. *Middle East Economic Digest*, 52, 30–1.

Handelsblatt. 2010. Deutschland verfügt über Weltklasse-Unternehmen. *Handelsblatt*, 11 January.

Hanna, D. 2006. *A New Fiscal Framework for GCC Countries Ahead of Monetary Union*. [Online: International Economics Programme]. Available at: se2.isn. ch/serviceengine/Files/ESDP/25144/../Open_Brief_May06.pdf [accessed: May 2006].

Hanna, D. 2008. The Gulf's Changing Financial Landscape: From Capital Source to Destination and Emerging Hub, in *The Gulf Region: A New Hub of Global Financial Power*, edited by J. Nugée and P. Subacchi. London: Chatham House, 105–17.

Hebous, S. 2006. *On the Monetary Union of the Gulf States*. Working Paper No. 4331. Kiel: Kiel Institute for the World Economy.

Helleiner, E. 2009. Enduring Top Currency, Fragile Negotiated Currency: Politics and the Dollar's International Role, in *The Future of the Dollar*, edited by E. Helleiner and J. Kirshner. Ithica: Cornel University Press, 70–87.

Helleiner, E. and Kirshner, J. 2009. The Future of the Dollar: Whither the Key Currency? in *The Future of the Dollar*, edited by E. Helleiner and J. Kirshner. Ithica: Cornel University Press, 1–23.

Hertog, S. 2007. The GCC and Arab Economic Integration: A New Paradigm. *Middle East Policy*, 14(1), 52–68.

Hertog, S. 2010a. *Princes, Brokers and Bureaucrats: Oil and the State in Saudi Arabia*. Ithaca, New York: Cornell University Press.

Hertog, S. 2010b. Defying the Resource Curse: Explaining Successful State-Owned Enterprises in Rentier States. *World Politics*, 62(2), 261–301.

Hettne, B. and Soderbaum, F. 1998. The New Regionalism Approach. *Politeia*, 17(3), 106–12.

Hettne, B. and Soderbaum, F. 2008. The Future of Regionalism: Old Divides, New Frontiers, in *Regionalization and Global Governance, the Taming of Globalization?* edited by A. Cooper et al. New York: Routledge, 61–79.

Hill, C.W.L. 1999. *International Business. Competing in the Global Marketplace*. Boston: Irwin/McGraw-Hill.

Hirschman, A. 1979. *Exit, Voice, and Loyalty: Responses to Decline in Firms, Organizations, and States*. Cambridge, MA: Harvard University Press, Cambridge.

Hoarders, C. and Legrenzi, M. 2008. *Beyond Regionalism? Regional Cooperation, Regionalism and Regionalization in the Middle East*. Burlington: Ashgate Publishing Company.

Hoekman, B.M. and Leidy, M.P. 1992. Cascading Contingent Protection. *European Economic Review*, 36(4), 883–92.

Hurrell, A. 2005. The Regional Dimension in International Relations Theory, in *The Global Politics of Regionalism: Theory and Practice*, edited by M. Farrell et al. London: Pluto Press, 38–53.

Hvidt, M. 2002. The role of oil in the process of modernization in the Middle East (in Danish), in *The Middle East Handbook*, edited by M. Hvidt and I.H. Sørensen. Odense: Odense University Press, 37–44.

Hvidt, M. 2003. The Middle East: Globalization out of spite (in Danish), in *A New Middle East?* edited by L.E. Andersen and P. Seeberg. Odense: Odense University Press, 201–22.

Hvidt, M. 2004. Limited Success of the IMF and the World Bank in Middle Eastern Reforms. *Journal of Social Affairs*, 21(81), 77–103.

Hvidt, M. 2007. Public–Private Ties and their Contribution to Development: The case of Dubai. *Middle Eastern Studies*, 43(4), 557–77.

Hvidt, M. 2009. The Dubai Model: An outline of key development-process elements in Dubai. *International Journal of Middle East Studies*, 41(3), 397–418.

Ilahi, N. and Shendy, R. 2008. *Do the Gulf Oil-Producing Countries Influence Regional Growth? The Impact of Financial and Remittance Flows.* IMF Working Paper 08, No. 167. Washington, DC: International Monetary Fund.

Institute of International Finance (IIF). 2007. *Tracking GCC Petrodollars: How and Where They are Being Invested Around the World.* Washington, DC: The Institute of International Finance, Inc.

Institute of International Finance (IIF). 2008a. *Record Oil Prices Fuel Major Expansion of Gulf Economies and Large Gains in Surplus Funds – Foreign Assets Reach $1.8 trillion.* Washington, DC: Institute of International Finance, Inc.

Institute of International Finance (IIF). 2008b. *Summary Appraisal: Gulf Cooperation Council Countries.* Washington, DC: Institute of International Finance, Inc.

Institute of International Finance (IIF). 2008c. *Economic Report: Gulf Cooperation Council Countries*, Washington: Institute of International Finance.

International Forum of Sovereign Wealth Funds (IFSWF). 2009. *Sovereign Wealth Funds Issue 'Baku Statement' Reaffirming the Need for Maintaining Open Investment Environment.* Baku: International Forum of Sovereign Wealth Funds.

International Monetary Fund (IMF) (Fiscal Affairs Department). 1995. *Unproductive Public Expenditures: A Pragmatic Approach to Policy Analysis*, IMF Pamphlet No. 48. Washington, DC: International Monetary Fund.

International Monetary Fund (IMF). 2006. *Regional Economic Outlook: Middle East and Central Asia.* IMF Working Paper. Washington, DC: International Monetary Fund.

International Monetary Fund (IMF). 2006. *World Economic Outlook 2006.* Washington, DC: International Monetary Fund.

International Monetary Fund (IMF). 2007. *Bilateral Surveillance over Members' Policies: Executive Board Decision.* Washington, DC: International Monetary Fund.

International Monetary Fund (IMF). 2008. *Sovereign Wealth Funds: A Work Agenda,* Washington, DC: International Monetary Fund.

International Monetary Fund (IMF). 2008b. *Regional Economic Outlook: Middle East and Central Asia.* [Online: International Monetary Fund]. Available at: http://www.imf.org/external/pubs/ft/reo/2008/MCD/eng/mreo0508.pdf [accessed: 1 May 2008].

International Monetary Fund (IMF). 2009a. *IMF Sees Spending by Middle Eastern Oil Exporters Softening Global Financial Crisis Impact,* Press Release No. 09/28. Washington, DC: International Monetary Fund.

International Monetary Fund (IMF). 2009b. *Regional Economic Outlook: Middle East and Central Asia.* Washington, DC: International Monetary Fund.

International Working Group of Sovereign Wealth Funds (IWGSWF). 2008. *Sovereign Wealth Funds Generally Accepted Principles and Practices.* Kuwait: International Working Group of Sovereign Wealth Funds.

International Working Group of Sovereign Wealth Funds (IWGSWF). 2009. *'Kuwait Declaration', Establishment of the International Forum of Sovereign Wealth Funds.* Kuwait: International Working Group of Sovereign Wealth Funds.

Iqbal, Z. and Mirakhor, A. 2002. The Development of Islamic Financial Institutions and Future Challenges, in *Islamic Finance: Innovation and Growth,* edited by S. Archer and R. Karim. London: Euromoney and AAOIFI.

Janardhan, M. 2009. *Development: Gulf Eyes 'Oil-For-Food' Deal With Neighbours.* [Online: Inter Press Service]. Available at: http://ipsnews.net/news.asp?idnews=42877 [accessed: 19 June 2009].

Jen, S. 2007. *Currencies: How Big Could Sovereign Wealth Funds be in 2015?* New York: Morgan Stanley Research.

Jen, S. 2008. The GCC: Transforming Oil Wealth into Financial Portfolios, in *The Gulf Region: A New Hub of Global Financial Power,* edited by J. Nugée and P. Subacchi. London: Chatham House, 164–75.

Kapiszewski, A. 2006. *Arab Versus Asian Migrant Workers in the GCC Countries.* [Online: United Nations Expert Group Meeting On International Migration And Development In The Arab Region]. Available at: http://www.un.org/esa/population/meetings/EGM_Ittmig_Arab/P02_Kapiszewski.pdf [accessed: 22 May 2006].

Katada, S.N. 2008. From Supporter to Challenger? Japan's Currency Leadership in Dollar Dominated East Asia. *Review of International Political Economy,* 15(3), 399–417.

Katzman, K. 2009. *Kuwait: Security, Reform, and U.S. Policy*. [Online: Congressional Research Service]. Available at: http://www.fas.org/sgp/crs/mideast/RS21513.pdf [accessed: 20 May 2009].

Kaye, D.D. and Wehrey, F.M. 2007. A Nuclear Iran: The Reactions of Neighbours. *Survey*, 49(2), 111–28.

Kemp, M.C. and Wan, H. 1976. An Elementary Proposition Concerning the Formation of Customs Unions. *Journal of International Economics*, 6, 95–7.

Kimmitt, R.M. 2008. Public Footprints in Private Markets: Sovereign Wealth Funds and the Global Economy. *Foreign Affairs*, 87(1), 119–30.

Kissinger, H.A. and Feldstein, M. 2008. The Rising Danger of High Oil Prices. *International Herald Tribune*, 15 September.

Khalaf, R. and England, A. 2008. Gulf oil boom spreads to poorer lands. *Financial Times*, 19 January.

Kireyev, A. 1998. Key issues Concerning Non-Oil Sector Growth, in *Saudi Arabia's Recent Economic Developments and Selected Issues*, edited by International Monetary Fund. Washington, DC: International Monetary Fund, 29–33.

Knaup, H. and von Mittelstaedt, J. 2009. *Foreign Investors Snap Up African Farmland*. [Online: Salon.com]. Available at: http://www.salon.com/news/feature/2009/07/31/african_farmland/ [accessed: 31 July 2009].

Krishna, P. 1998. Regionalism and Multilateralism: A Political Economy Approach. *Quarterly Journal of Economics*, 113(1), 22751.

Krueger, A.O. 1993. Free Trade Agreements as Protectionist Devices: Rules of Origin, in *Trade, Theory and Econometrics*, edited by J.R. Melvin, J.C. Moore and R. Riezman. London: Routledge, 91–102.

Kuwait Times. 2009. *Dollar to Remain Key Reserve Currency: Geithner*. [Online]. Available at: http://www.gulfinthemedia.com/index.php?lang=en&m=&id=479752 [accessed: 16 July 2009].

Kubursi, A.A. 1999. Prospects for Regional Economic Integration after Oslo, in *Middle East Dilemma. The Politics and Economics of Arab Integration*, edited by M.C. Hudson. London: I.B. Tauris, 299–319.

Laabas, B. and Abdmoulah, W. 2009. *Determinants of Arab Intraregional Foreign Direct Investments, API/WPS 0905*. Kuwait City: The Arab Planning Institute.

Legrenzi, M. 2011. Defense Cooperation: Beyond Symbolism? in *Political Change in the Arab Gulf States: Stuck in Transition*, edited by Mary Ann Tétreault, Gwenn Okruhlik and Andrzej Kapiszewski. Boulder: Lynne Rienner Publishers, 271–287.

Legrenzi, M. 2003. *The Long Road Ahead: Economic Integration in the Gulf States*. [Online]. Available at: http://ssc.undp.org/uploads/media/CoopSouth_E-37-49.pdf [accessed: 5 April 2010].

Legrenzi M. 2008. Did the GCC Make a Difference? Institutional Realities and (Un)Intended Consequences, in *Beyond Regionalism? Regional Cooperation, Regionalism and Regionalization in the Middle East*, edited by C. Harders and M. Legrenzi. Farnham: Ashgate, 104–24.

Levy, W.J. 1978/79. The Years that the Locust Hath Eaten: Oil Policy and OPEC Development Prospects. *Foreign Affairs*, 57(2), 287–305.

Levy, P.I. 1997. A Political-Economic Analysis of Free Trade Agreements. *American Economic Review*, 87(4), 506–19.

Luciani, G. 1990. Allocation vs. Production States: A Theoretical Framework, in *The Arab State*, edited by G. Luciani. London: Routledge, 65–84.

Luciani, G. 2005. Saudi Arabian business: From private sector to national bourgeoisie, in *Saudi Arabia in the Balance*, edited by P. Aarts and G. Nonneman. London: Hurst, 144–81.

Luciani, G. 2007. *The GCC Refining and Petrochemical Sectors in Global Perspective in Gulf Geoeconomics*. Dubai: Gulf Research Centre.

Lund, S. and Roxburgh, C. 2009. *The Financial Power Brokers: Crisis Update*. [Online: McKinsey Quarterly]. Available at: http://www.mckinseyquarterly. com/The_new_financial_power_brokers_Crisis_update_2439 [accessed: 14 April 2010].

Mabro, R. 1987. *Netback Pricing and the Oil Price Collapse of 1986*. Oxford, UK: Oxford Institute for Energy Studies.

Mabro, R. 2000. *Oil Markets and Prices*. [Online: Oxford Energy Comment]. Available at: http://www.oxfordenergy.org/comment_prn.php?0008 [accessed: August 2000].

Magnus, G. 2006. Petrodollars: Where are they and do they matter? *UBS Investment Research*, 19 July.

Maloney, S. 2009. The Gulf's Renewed Oil Wealth: Getting it Right this Time? *Survival*, 50(6), 129–50.

Marcel, V. 2006. *Oil Titans: National Oil Companies in the Middle East*. London: Royal Institute for International Affairs.

Marchik, D.M. and Slaughter, M.J. 2008. *Global FDI Policy: Correcting a Protectionist Drift*, Council Special Report, No. 34. New York, NY: Council on Foreign Relations.

Martin, M. 2009. *Delivering Manama's Economic Vision*. [Online: Middle East Economic Digest]. Available at: http://www.meed.com/supplements/delivering-manamas-economic-vision/3001749.article?sm=3001749 [accessed: 29 October 2009].

McKinsey & Company. 2007. *The New Power Brokers: How Oil, Asia, Hedge Funds, and Private Equity are Shaping Global Capital Markets*. [Online: The McKinsey Quarterly]. Available at: http://www.mckinsey.com/mgi/publications/The_New_Power_Brokers/ [accessed: 1 October 2007].

McKinsey & Company. 2008. *The New Role of Oil Wealth in the World Economy*. [Online: The McKinsey Quarterly]. Available at: http://www.mckinseyquarterly. com/Middle_East/The_new_role_of_oil_wealth_in_the_world_economy_ 2093 [accessed: 1 January 2008].

McKinsey Global Institute. 2007. *The New Power Brokers: How Oil, Asia, Hedge Funds, and Private Equity Are Shaping Global Capital Markets*. San Francisco: McKinsey & Company.

McKinsey Global Institute. 2009. *The New Power Brokers: How Oil, Asia, Hedge Funds, and Private Equity are Faring in the Financial Crisis.* San Francisco: McKinsey Global Institute.

McLaren, J. 2002. A Theory of Insidious Regionalism. *Quarterly Journal of Economics*, 117, 571–608.

Menegatti, C. and Setser, B. 2006. *Are GCC Dollar Pegs and Impediment to Global Adjustment? And does Pegging to the Dollar Make Domestic Sense?* [Online: Roubini Global Economic Service]. Available at: http://www.rgemonitor.com/ [accessed: 1 September 2006].

Mikdashi, Z. 1972. *The Community of Oil Exporting Countries: A Study in Governmental Cooperation.* Ithaca, New York: Cornell University Press.

Ministry for Foreign Affairs (China). 2009. Overview files on the GCC states.

Ministry for Foreign Affairs (Japan). 2009. Overview files on the GCC states.

Ministry for Foreign Affairs (South Korea). 2009. Overview files on the GCC states.

Ministry for Finance and Industry (United Arab Emirates). 2009. Overview file on trade with Japan.

Mirza, A. 2009. Construction prices offer window of opportunity in oil and gas sector. *Middle East Economic Digest*, 44(30), 5.

Molavi, A. 2007. The CEO Sheik. *Newsweek*, 6 August, 26–9.

Momani, B. 2004. American Politicization of the International Monetary Fund. *Review of International Political Economy*, 11(5), 880–904.

Momani, B. 2007. A Middle East Free Trade Area: Interdependence and Peace Reconsidered. *World Economy*, 30(11), 1682–700.

Momani, B. 2008a. Reacting to Global Forces: Economic and Political Integration of the Gulf Cooperation Council. *Journal of the Gulf and Arabian Peninsula Studies*, 34(128), 47–66.

Momani, B. 2008b. Gulf Cooperation Council Oil Exporters and the Future of the Dollar. *New Political Economy*, 13(3), 293–314.

Moosa, I. 2008. The Determinants of Foreign Direct Investment in MENA Countries: An Extreme Bounds Analysis. *Applied Economics Letters*, 16(15), 1466–4291.

Moran, D. and Russell, J. 2009. *Energy Security and Global Politics: The Militarization of Resource Management.* London: Routledge.

Morse, E.L. 2009. The Impact of Low Oil Prices on Investments. *Oxford Energy Forum*, 77, 3–5.

Mundell, R.A. 1961. A Theory of Optimum Currency Areas. *American Economic Review*, 51(4), 657–65.

Naibari, A. 1990. *Interviews in Kuwait with Mary Ann Tétreault.* Spring.

National Bank of Kuwait. 2007. *GCC Economic Outlook 2010: The Boom Goes On.* Kuwait City: NBK Economic Research.

Newman, P. 2005. What Role Derivatives? *Oxford Energy Forum*, 12(13).

Niblock, T. and Malik, M. 2007. *The Political Economy of Saudi Arabia.* London: Routledge.

Nield, R. 2009. *Saudi Arabia Embraces Reform*. [Online: Middle East Economic Digest]. Available at: http://www.meed.com/sectors/economy/saudi-arabia-embraces-reform/2013620.article [accessed: 10 November 2009].

Nielson, D. and Tierney, M. 2003. Delegation to International Organizations: Agency Theory and World Bank Environmental Reform. *International Organization*, 57, 241–76.

Nonneman, G. 1996. Linkages between Political and Economic Liberalization, in *Political and Economic Liberalization: Dynamics and Linkages in Comparative Perspective*, edited by G. Nonneman. Boulder, CO: Lynne Rienner, 307–13.

Nonneman, G. 2004. The Gulf States and the Iran-Iraq War, in *Iran, Iraq and the Legacies of War*, edited by L.G. Potter. Gordonsville, VA: Palgrave Macmillan, 167–92.

Noreng, O. 2004. Oil, the Euro, and the Dollar. *Journal of Energy and Development*, 30(1), 53–80.

Norges Bank. *Norges Bank*. [Online]. Available at: http://www.norges-bank.no/ [accessed: 1 September 2010].

Noland, M. and Pack, H. 2007. *The Arab Economies in a Changing World*. Washington, DC: Peterson Institute for International Economics.

Norway Ministry of Finance. 2005. *Ethical Guidelines for Government Pension Fund-Global of Norway*. Oslo: Norway Ministry of Finance.

Nsouli, S.M. 2006. *Petrodollar Recycling and Global Imbalances*. [Online: International Monetary Fund]. Available at: http://www.imf.org/external/np/speeches/2006/032306a.htm [accessed: 24 March 2006].

Nuclear Threat Initiative. 2007. *China's Missile Exports and Assistance to the Middle East*. Monterey: James Martin Center for Non-proliferation Studies.

Nugée, J. and Subacchi, P. 2008. Introduction, in *The Gulf Region: A New Hub of Global Financial Power*, edited by J. Nugée and P. Subacchi. London: Chatham House, 1–8.

Ocampo, J.A. 2009. Special Drawing Rights and the Reform of the Global Reserve System, in *Reforming the International Financial System for Development*, edited by J.K. Sundaram. Washington, DC: International Group of Twenty-Four (G24).

Official Journal of the European Communities. 2008. *The Treaty Establishing the European Community*. [Online]. Available at: http://eur-lex.europa.eu/LexUriserv/LexUriserv.do?uri=OJ:C:2008:115:0047:0199:EN:PDF [accessed: 9 May 2008].

Onley, J. 2005. Transnational Merchants in the Nineteenth Century Gulf: The Case of the Safar Family, in *Transnational Connections and the Arab Gulf*, edited by M. Al-Rasheed. London: Routledge, 59–89.

Onley, J. 2007. *The Arabian Frontier of the British Raj: Merchants, Rulers, and the British in the Nineteenth-Century Gulf*. Oxford: Oxford University Press.

Onley, J. 2007. Transnational Merchants in the Nineteenth and Twentieth Century Gulf, in *The Gulf Family: Modernity and Kinship Policies*. A. Alshareskh. London: Saqi Books, 37–56.

Onyeiwu, S. 2008. *Does Investment in Knowledge and Technology Spur Optimal FDI in the MENA Region: Evidence from Logit and Cross-Country Regressions.* Paper to the African Economic Development Conference Organized by ADB and ECA, Tunis, 12–14 November 2008, available at: http://www.afdb.org/ fr/2009-african-economic-conference/past-aecs/aec-2008/sessions-papers/13-november-2008/ [accessed: 14 November 2008].

Ornelas, E. 2005. Trade Creating Free Trade Areas and the Undermining of Multilateralism. *European Economic Review*, 49, 1717–35.

Organisation for Economic Cooperation and Development. 2008. *Opening Remarks by Angel Gurría at the Global Forum on International Investment.* [Online: Organisation for Economic Cooperation and Development]. Available at: http://www.oecd.org/document/13/0,3343,en_2649_34863_40336589_1_ 1_1_1,00.html [accessed: 27 March 2008].

Organisation for Economic Cooperation and Development. 2008. *OECD Declaration on SWFs and Recipient Country Policies.* Washington, DC: OECD.

Organisation for Economic Cooperation and Development. 2008. *Sovereign Wealth Funds and Recipient Country Policies.* Washington, DC: OECD.

Organisation for Economic Co-operation and Development. 2009. *OECD Code of Liberalisation of Capital Movements.* Paris: Organisation for Economic Co-operation and Development.

Owen, R. and Pamuk, S. 1998. *A History of Middle East Economies in the Twentieth Century.* Cambridge: Harvard University Press.

Oxford Analytica. 2009. *Sovereign Wealth Funds Focus on the Home Front.* [Online: Gulfnews.com]. Available at: http://gulfnews.com/business/opinion/ sovereign-wealth-funds-focus-on-the-home-front-1.68665 [accessed: 14 May 2009].

Palley, T.I. 2007. *Financialization: What it is and Why it Matters.* Working Paper Series Number 153. Amherst: Political Economy Research Institute.

Paulson, H. 2008. *Paulson Remarks on Open Investment Before the US-UAE Business Council.* [Online: US Department of Treasury]. Available at: http:// www.ustreas.gov/press/releases/hp1001.htm [accessed: 2 June 2008].

Pearce, J. 1983. *The Third Oil Shock: The Effects of Lower Oil Prices.* London: Royal Institute of International Affairs, Chatham House Special Paper.

Truman, E.M. 2008. *A Blueprint for Sovereign Wealth Funds Best Practices.* [Online: Peterson Institute]. Available at: http://www.petersoninstitute.org/ publications/pb/pb08-3.pdf [accessed: 3 April 2008].

Ramazani, R.K. 1988. *The Gulf Cooperation Council: Record and Analysis.* Charlottesville: University of Virginia Press.

Redfern, B. 2008a. *Abu Dhabi: Reshaping the economy.* [Online: *MEED*]. Available at: http://www.meed.com/story.aspx?storyCode=1505057 [accessed: 3 December 2009].

Redfern, B. 2008b. *Special Report: Abu Dhabi – Reforms Deliver Strong Growth.* [Online: *MEED*]. Available at: http://www.meed.com/sectors/

economy/special-report-abu-dhabi-reforms-deliver-strong-growth/1505041. article [accessed: 3 December 2009].

Riezman, R. 1999. Can Bilateral Trade Agreements Help to Induce Free Trade? *Canadian Journal of Economics*, 32, 751–66.

Richards, A. and Waterbury, J. 2008. *A Political Economy of the Middle East.* Boulder, CO: Westview Press.

Risso, P. 1989. Muslim Identity in Maritime Trade: General Observations and Some Evidence from the Eighteenth-Century Persian Gulf/Indian Ocean Region. *International Journal of Middle Eastern Studies*, 21(3), 381–92.

Robinson, S. and Thierfelder, K. 1999. *Trade Liberalization and Regional Integration: The Search for Large Numbers.* Washington, DC: International Food Policy Research Institute.

Rozanov, A. 2005. Who Holds the Wealth of Nations? *Central Banking*, 15(4), 52–7.

Rubinoff, E.L. and Savio, T.R. 2008. *Global Issues: International Law & Trade – Law Firms CFIUS Implements FINSA Amendments to Exon-Florio Foreign Investment Law.* [Online: The Metropolitan Corporate Counsel]. Available at: http://www.metrocorpcounsel.com/current.php?artType=view&artMonth=May&artYear=2008&EntryNo=8232 [accessed: at: 17 July 2010].

Rutledge, E.J. 2009. *Monetary Union in the Gulf.* London: Routledge.

SAGIA. 2003. *Izalat mu'wiqat al-bi'a al-Istithmariyya fi l-mamlaka al-'arabiyya as-sa'udiyya [Removing obstacles in the investment environment in the Kingdom of Saudi Arabia].* Riyadh: Saudi Arabian General Investment Authority.

Saidi, N. 2009. *The Global Financial Crisis and the Role of Financial Investors in the Gulf*, in *Sovereign Risk Management*, edited by Malan Rietveld. London: Central Banking Publications, 43–51.

Samba Chief Economist Office. 2008. *Tracking GCC Foreign Investments: How the Strategies are Changing with Markets in Turmoil.* [Online: Samba Financial Group]. Available at: http://www.gulfinthemedia.com/files/article_en/452506. pdf [accessed: 1 December 2008].

Sampson, A. 1974. *The Seven Sisters: The Great Oil Companies and the World They Shaped.* New York: Viking.

Sankari, F. 1976. The Character and Impact of Arab Oil Embargo, in *Arab Oil: Impact on the Arab Countries and Global Implications*, edited by N.A. Sherbiny and M.A. Tessler. New York: Prager, 279–94.

Setser, B. 2007. *The Case for Exchange Rate Flexibility in Oil-Exporting Economies. Peterson Institute for International Economics, Policy Brief Number PB07-8.* Washington, DC: Peterson Institute for International Economics.

Setser, B. 2008. A Neo-Westpalian International Fiancial System? *Journal of International Affairs*, 62(1), 17–34.

Setser, B. and Ziemba, R. 2007. *Understanding the New Financial Superpower – the Management of GCC Official Foreign Assets.* [Online: Roubini Global

Economics Monitor]. Available at: www.cfr.org/content/publications/../
SetserZiembaGCCfinal.pdf [accessed: 1 December 2007].

Setser, B. and Ziemba, R. 2009. *GCC Sovereign Funds: Reversal of Fortune,* Center for Geoeconomic Studies Working Paper. New York: Council on Foreign Relations.

Seznec, J.F. 2008. The gulf sovereign wealth funds: Myths and reality. *Middle East Policy*, 15(2).

Sfakianiakis, J. 2008. *Giving a Boost.* Riyadh: Saudi-British Bank (SABB) Notes.

Sfakianiakis, J. 2010. *Saudi Arabia's 2010 Budget: 'Open for Business'*, Banque Saudi Fransi Report. Riyadh: Banque Saudi Fransi.

Sfakianakis, J. and Woertz, E. 2007. *Strategic Foreign Investments of GCC Countries in Gulf Geoeconomics.* Dubai: Gulf Research Centre.

Sharabi, H. 1988. *Neo-Patriarchy: A Theory of Distorted Change in the Arab World.* Oxford: Oxford University Press.

Shihata, I. and Mabro R. 1982. The OPEC Aid Record, in *The Other Face of OPEC: Financial Assistance to the Third World*, edited by I.F.I. Shihata. London: Longman, 55–74.

Siddiqi, M. 2005. Banking Report Strong Regional Economy Sees Banking Profits Soar. *The Middle East*, 34–43.

Siddiqi, M. 2006. *Gulf Cooperation Council Goes for Growth.* [Online: The Middle East Magazine]. Available at: http://www.africasia.co.uk/themiddleeast/me. php?ID=1102 [accessed: 1 December 2006].

Siddiqi, M. 2009. *Global Crunch Presents Stiff Challenges to FDI Despite New Incentives.* [Online: Middle East Magazine]. Available at: http://www.africasia. com/themiddleeast/me.php?ID=2113 [accessed: 1 September 2009].

Slackman, M. 2009. The Possibility of a Nuclear-Armed Iran Alarms Arabs. *New York Times*, 1 October, A16.

Slaughter, A.M. 2005. *A New World Order.* Princeton, NJ: Princeton University Press.

Smaller, C. and Mann, H. 2009. *A Thirst for Distant Lands: Foreign Investment in Agricultural Land and Water.* Manitoba: International Institute for Sustainable Development.

Smith, P. 2007. Gulf Investors Focus on Arab and African Neighbours. *The Middle East*, 1 August, 38–43.

Smith-Diwan, K. 2009. Sovereign Dilemmas: Saudi Arabia and Sovereign Wealth Funds. *Geopolitics*, 14(2), 345–59.

Soros, G. 2008. *The Perilous Price of Oil.* [Online: New York Review of Books]. Available at: http://www.nybooks.com/articles/21792 [accessed: 25 September 2008].

Sovereign Wealth Fund Institute. 2009. *Sovereign Wealth Fund Rankings: Largest Sovereign Wealth Funds by Assets Under Management.* [Online]. Available at: http://www.swfinstitute.org/fund-rankings/ [accessed: 14 July 2009].

State Street. 2008. *Sovereign Wealth Funds: Assessing the Impact,* Boston, MA: State Street Corporation.

Story, J. and Walter, I. 1997. *The Political Economy of Financial Integration in Europe: The Battle of the Systems.* Cambridge: MIT Press.

Stracke, N. 2008. *Where is the UAE Islands Dispute Heading?* Dubai: Gulf Research Center.

Strange, S. 1996. *The Retreat of the State: The Diffusion of Power in the World Economy.* Cambridge: Cambridge University Press.

Sturm, M., Strasky, J., Adolf, P. and Peschel, D. 2008. *The Gulf Cooperation Council countries: Economic Structures, Recent Developments and Role in the Global Economy, Occasional Paper Series 92.* Frankfurt: European Central Bank.

Summers, L. 2007. *Funds that Shake Capitalist Logic.* [Online: *Financial Times*]. Available at: http://www.ft.com/cms/s/2/bb8f50b8-3dcc-11dc-8f6a-0000779fd2ac.html [accessed: 14 April 2010].

Sundarajan, V. 2005. *Development of the Islamic Financial Architecture and Infrastructure: Challenges and Strategies – Paper prepared for The Islamic Research and Training Institute.* Jeddah: Islamic Development Bank.

Symes, Peter. (n.d.). *Gulf Rupees – A History.* [Online: Reference Site for Islamic Banknotes]. Available at: http://www.islamicbanknotes.com/gulfrupees%20 28article%29.htm [accessed: 23 September 2010].

Tétreault, M.A. 1980. Measuring Interdependence. *International Organization,* 34(3), 429–43.

Tétreault, M.A. 1985. *Revolution in the World Petroleum Market.* Westport, CT: Quorum Books.

Tétreault, M.A. 1995. *The Kuwait Petroleum Corporation and the Economics of the New World Order.* Westport, CO: Quorum Books

Tétreault, M.A. 2000. *Stories of Democracy: Politics and Society in Contemporary Kuwait.* New York: Columbia University Press.

Timmons, H. 2006 Asia finding rich partners in Mideast. *New York Times,* 1 December 2006.

Tobin, J. and Busch, M.L. 2010. A BIT is Better than a Lot: Bilateral Investment Treaties and Preferential Trade Agreements. *World Politics,* 62(1), 1–42.

Todaro, M.P., Smith, S.C. 2009. *Economic Development.* Harlow, England: Pearson/Addison Wesley.

Toksov, M. 2008. The GCC: prospects and risks in the new oil boom, in *The Gulf Region: A New Hub of Global Financial Power,* edited by J. Nugée and P. Subacchi. London: Chatham House, 81–98.

Treichel, V. 1999. Stance of Fiscal Policy and Non-Oil Economic Growth, in *Oman Beyond the Oil Horizon,* edited by A. Mansur and V. Treichel. IMF Occasional Paper No. 185, Washington, DC.

Truman, E.M. 2007a. *A Scoreboard for Sovereign Wealth Funds.* [Online: Peterson Institute for International Economics]. Available at:http://nzsuper.co.nz/files/ A%20scoreboard%20for%20Sovereign%20Wealth%20Funds%20paper%

20Edwin%20M%20Truman%20Peterson%20Institute%20Oct%2007.pdf [accessed: 19 October 2007].

Truman, E.M. 2007b. *Sovereign Wealth Funds: The Need for Greater Transparency and Accountability*, Policy Brief No. PB07-6. Washington, DC: Peterson Institute for International Economics.

Truman, E.M. 2008. *A Blueprint for Sovereign Wealth Fund Best Practices*, Policy Brief, s.l., Washington, DC: Peterson Institute for International Economics.

Truman, E.M. 2008. *Making the World Safe for Sovereign Wealth Funds*. [Online: Web Peterson Institute for International Economics]. Avaialble at: http://www. petersoninstitute.org/realtime/?p=105 [accessed: 14 April 2010].

Truman, E.M. 2010. *Sovereign Wealth Funds: Threat or Salvation?* Washington, DC: Peterson Institute for International Economics.

Tschoegl A.E. 2001. Maria Theresa's Thaler: A Case of International Money. *Eastern Economic Journal*, 27(4), 445–64.

Tsingou, E. 2008. Transnational private governance and the Basel process: Banking regulation, private interests and Basel II, in *Transnational Private Governance and its Limits*, edited by A. Nölke and J.C. Graz. London: Routledge, ECPR/ Routledge Series.

UN Development Programme. 2009. *Overcoming Barriers: Human Mobility and Development: Human Development Report 2009*. [Online: United Nations Development Programme]. Available at: http://hdr.undp.org/en/reports/global/ hdr2009/ [accessed: 18 October 2010].

UN Population Division. 2009. *Source: Population Division of the Department of Economic and Social Affairs of the United Nations Secretariat, World Population Prospects: The 2008 Revision*. [Online: United Nations Population Division]. Available at: http://esa.un.org/unpp/index.asp?panel=2 [accessed: 25 November 2009].

UNCTAD. 2009. *FDIStat Database: UNCTAD*. [Online: United Nations Conference on Trade and Development]. Available at: http://stats.unctad.org/ fdi/ReportFolders/reportFolders.aspx?sCS_referer=&sCS_ChosenLang=en [accessed: 20 November 2009].

US Department of State. 2009. *Middle East Partnership Initiative*. [Online: MEPI Regional Office: Abu Dhabi]. Available at: http://www.abudhabi.mepi.state. gov/ [accessed: 1 September 2009].

US Department of the Treasury. 2008. *Treasury Reaches Agreement on Principles for Sovereign Wealth Fund Investment with Singapore and Abu Dhabi*, Washington, DC: US Department of the Treasury.

US Government Accountability Office. 2008. *Sovereign Wealth Funds: Publicly Available Data on Sizes and Investments for Some Funds Are Limited – Report to the Committee on Banking, Housing, and Urban Affairs, U.S. Senate*. Washington, DC: GAO.

US Government Energy Information Administration. 2009. *Qatar Energy Profile*. [Online]. Available at: http://www.eia.doe.gov/country/country_energy_data. cfm?fips=QA [accessed: 2 July 2010].

US Trade Representative. 2006. *United States and Oman Sign Free Trade Agreement*. Washington, DC: US Trade Representative.

Verleger, P.K. Jr. 2007. How Wall Street Controls Oil: And How OPEC Will be the Fall Guy for $90 Oil. *The International Economy*, 14–17, 60.

von Braun, J. and Meinzen-Dick, R. 2009. *'Land Grabbing' by Foreign Investors in Developing Countries: Risks and Opportunities*. [Online: IFPRI Policy Brief]. Available at: www.landcoalition.org/pdf/ifpri_land_grabbing_apr_09.pdf [accessed: 13 April 2009].

Walter, A. 2008. *Governing Finance: East Asia's Adoption of International Standards*. Ithaca and London: Cornell University Press.

Watson, M. 2009. Investigating the potentially contradictory microfoundations of financialization. *Economy and Society*, 38(2), 255–77.

Weiss, M.A. 2005. *Proposed U.S. – Bahrain Free Trade Agreement. Congressional Research Service Report for Congress*, No. RS21846. Washington, DC: Congressional Research Service/The Library of Congress.

Wilson, R. 2009. *The Development of Islamic Finance in the GCC*. London: Kuwait Programme on Development, Governance and Globalization in the Gulf States.

Winters, A.L. 1999. Regionalism versus Multilateralism, in *Regional Integration*, edited by R. Baldwin, D. Cole, A. Sapir and A. Venables. Cambridge: Cambridge University Press, 7–49.

Winters, A.L. and Chang, W. 2000. Regional Integration and Import Prices: An Empirical Investigation. *Journal of International Economics*, 51, 363–3.

Woertz, E. 2009. *Revisit Investment Strategy*. [Online: *Financial Times*]. Available at: http://www.ft.com/cms/s/0/bf3e8d46-76cd-11de-b23c00144feabdc0.html?nclick_check=1 [accessed: 22 July 2009].

World Bank. 2008. *Doing Business in the Arab World: Comparing regulation in 20 economies*. Washington, DC: The International Bank for Reconstruction and Development/The World Bank.

World Bank. 2009a. *Doing Business 2010: Reforming through Difficult Times*. Washington, DC: The International Bank for Reconstruction and Development/ The World Bank.

World Bank. 2009b. *Governance Matters 2009: Worldwide Governance Indicators, 1996–2008*. [Online: The World Bank]. Available at: http://info.worldbank.org/governance/wgi/index.asp [accessed: 14 April 2010].

World Economic Forum. 2007. *The Arab World Competitiveness Report 2007*. Geneva, Switzerland: World Economic Forum.

World Economic Forum. 2008. *The Global Competitiveness Report 2008–2009* (Geneva, Switzerland: World Economic Forum.

World Economic Forum. 2009. *The Global Competitiveness Report 2009–2010*. Geneva, Switzerland: World Economic Forum.

Yetiv, S.A. and Lu, C. 2007. China, Global Energy, and the Middle East. *Middle East Journal*, 61(2), 263–80.

Ziemba, R. 2008. *Raiding the Sovereign Rainy Day Fund*. [Online: Roubini Global Economics]. Available at: http://www.roubini.com/globalmacro-monitor254790/raiding_the_sovereign_rainy_day_fund [accessed: December 16 2010].

Index

THE INTERNATIONAL POLITICAL ECONOMY OF NEW REGIONALISMS SERIES

Other titles in the series

For Product Safety Concerns and Information please contact our
EU representative GPSR@taylorandfrancis.com Taylor & Francis
Verlag GmbH, Kaufingerstraße 24, 80331 München, Germany